VENICE

AN ILLUSTRATED ANTHOLOGY

VENICE

AN ILLUSTRATED ANTHOLOGY

Compiled by Michael Marqusee

Introduction by
Anthony Burgess

CONRAN OCTOPUS

VENETIA
CITTA NOBILISS.ᵐᵃ E SINGOLARE
DESCRITTA DAL SANSOVINO CON NOVE É COPIOSE
AGGIVNTE DI D. GIVSTINIAN MARTINIONI.

First published in 1988 by
Conran Octopus Limited
37 Shelton Street
London WC2H 9HN

Copyright preface and commentary
© Conran Octopus Limited 1988
Copyright introduction
© Anthony Burgess 1988

ISBN 1 85029 138 1

Catalogue in Publication Data
Venice: an illustrated anthology.
    1. English literature. American writers.
    Special subjects. Italy. Venice.
    Anthologies
    I. Marqusee, Michael
    810.8′324531

Project editor: Emma Callery
Text editor: Mary Davies
Picture research: Nadine Bazar
Art director: Mary Evans
Art editor: Trevor Vincent
Editorial assistant: Simon Willis
Production: Michel Blake
Jacket photograph: Tony Stone Photo Library
Typeset by MS Filmsetting Limited
Printed and bound in Hong Kong

CONTENTS

VENICE: A WORD

BY ANTHONY BURGESS

In this book you will learn a great number of facts about Venice. All I need offer briefly here are my personal impressions. I never really knew Venice until my wife firmly embarked me on to *vaporetti, gondole* and *motoscafi* and forcibly educated me in the beauty of the city, the water it rests on, the wide sky over it which boils in winter and is pellucid in summer. I had previously resisted Venice as I had resisted Florence: there were too many people burbling about how wonderful it was. It is wonderful enough, but I do not like to be told. My wife merely said: 'Look.' She is not merely Italian, whatever Italian means; she is a daughter of the Adriatic, and of the Adriatic Venice is the queen, or was.

Of course, the queenly power is long gone, and it is reasonable, for those who commit the error of importing reason into human affairs, to ask why it should ever have existed in the first place. For that matter, why perch a city on water? The answer there is to be found in the predations of Attila the Hun, who ravaged Adriatic cities and forced some of the Italic tribes of the fifth century AD to dwell on the hosts of offshore islands that were eventually linked up into an urban unity. With the formation of artificial islands on wooden piles and the artificial waterways which joined them, you got a prototypical Venice which looked east and found trade there. 'Once did she hold the gorgeous East in fee,' Wordsworth wrote, and so she did. It was from mediaeval Venice that Marco Polo and his father and uncle set off to meet Kublai Khan and establish the mythical bond which long held the water-city and the whole of China in an amiable net of commerce. Venice is now merely part of Italy; before Napoleon extinguished its independence it was a great independent republic.

It had to decay, as its sister-port Trieste had to decay. The Turks took Constantinople, the Cape route was discovered, the European powers arose and squabbled in Italy itself. Bonaparte entered in 1796, and it was in that year that Wordsworth wrote his elegy on the extinction of the Venetian republic. For two centuries Venice has lived in the past.

There is nothing wrong with living in the past, especially when the past is more attractive than the present. There has never been anything quite like the Venetian school of painters – Antonio Veneziano, the Vivarini, Jacopo Bellini and his sons and pupils, Carpaccio, Giorgione, Titian – I need not go on. I am not writing a guide book and I yawn even at mentioning the glassware of Murano. I promised or threatened personal impressions, and here they are.

I like the sound of Venetian speech. The Florentines say '*Ho finito*' for 'I've finished', but the Venetians '*Go fini'o*'. There is a Slavonic touch about that g replacing the classical aspirate. Some Venetian girls are Titian-haired, as they should be. The poles of the gondoliers stir up ancient muck from the depths of the side-canals. The Venetian light, especially in winter, is unique. Wintry Venice is shrewdly rheumatic. It seems to have been my peculiar destiny to be in Venice more in winter than in summer, bitterly blown by gales across the lagoon in coming from the airport, my feet drenched in the puddles of Piazza San Marco. The opera-lovers at La Fenice are sadly provincial in their tastes. There is nothing exceptional about either the cuisine or the wine: the best meals are in Mestre, on dry land. Having said this, and forborne to say more, I have to admit that Venice is the best examplar of human wit and ingenuity.

6

Despair of man and go to Venice: you will cease to despair. If human beings can build a city like this, their souls deserve to be saved.

In Benjamin Britten's opera based on Thomas Mann's *Death in Venice*, the chorus makes far too much of the reverential cry '*Serenissima!*' There is too much Venice-worship in that work, and Venice does not take kindly to postures of self-abasement, which make the knees wet anyway, or else foul with pigeon-droppings. Venice was a very richly adorned whore, ravishing but venal. The venality is still there and, through the miracle of all ancient Italic urbifactions, the beauty is perhaps greater than ever it was. But to love Venice is to face one's own mortality, and Mann was right to kill off Aschenbach there. In this book you can wonder at the incredible achievement of a long-dead past and question if the term 'progress' has any meaning. Not all the town planners of the world could ever dream up another Venice.

COMPILER'S NOTE

The subject of Venice is the oldest cliché in travel writing, but it has nonetheless elicited some of the best prose and poetry from those bold or innocent souls who took up its challenge.

If Venice itself produced few writers of note, for outsiders it has been the source of a continuous stream of praise, ponderings, and perplexity.

'Nothing can be said here (including this statement),' Mary McCarthy wrote, 'that has not been said before.' Henry James lamented, 'there is notoriously nothing more to be said on the subject.' Even as early as 1494, Canon Pietro Casola, stopping in Venice on his way to Palestine, declared, 'so much has been said . . . there appears nothing more to be said.'

Having offered their caveats, these writers proceeded to write at length of Venice and it wonders, unperturbed, often exhilarated by the paradox.

Venice has always been a city of strangers. Coryat called it '*Orbis Forum*', the marketplace of the world. For centuries, foreigners were awed by its prosperity and power. But as the Republic gradually transformed itself from the world's marketplace to its playground, the music, the theatres, the Carnival, the *gondole*, the prostitutes, became legendary. For generations of visiting writers, this enigmatic abandonment to pleasure in the face of palpable economic and political decline exerted a powerful spell.

Many of these visitors are as integral to the Venetian mystique as green water and worn Istrian marble. Byron's exploits rapidly became part of the poetry of the place, alongside the heroic doges and the Renaissance painters. For Ruskin, every detail of the city's fabric was a springboard for speculation, and the sheer gravitas (and volume) of his studies helped save much of that fabric from ruin and 'restoration'. What Pasternak called 'the barnacle-like incrustation of centuries of travellers' enthusiasm' has become inseparable from the brick and stone.

'For the true Venice lover,' James declared, the subject 'is always in order.' That so many have written so much and so well of it, is in itself sufficient warrant for this anthology. For what is left out (and the choices were all impossible) I can only apologise.

MICHAEL MARQUSEE

ORIGINS

*The Venetian diplomat
and scholar* BERNARDO
GIUSTINIANI
*described the lagoon and its
maintenance by the first settlers
in his* History of the Origin
of Venice *(1498).*

The narrow coast bends around the furthest gulf of the Adriatic Sea, at whose back lie vast swamps, partly due to the discharging of the rivers, and partly due to the tides of the sea. Nature, the master artisan of things, protects the swamps from the waves of the sea by a shore produced by accumulated heaps of sand. For the sea would wash away whatever is piled among them if the shores, almost like rampart walls, did not hinder it, and if the labour of mortals did not aid nature by placing huge obstacles of stones and palisades against the storms of the sea and the force of winds.

*The first recorded mention of
the Venetian people is in a
letter from* CASSIODORUS,
*minister to the Ostrogothic
King Theodoric, to the tribunes
of the Venetii in c. AD 500.
He hoped to persuade them to
loan ships to transport goods
from Istria (in what is now
called Yugoslavia) to
Theodoric's capital, Ravenna,
and in praising their industry,
he paints a vivid portrait of the
life led by the early inhabitants
in the lagoon.*

You own many and many a ship; your vessels fear not the stormy winds. They come home safely to port, nor do they ever founder, they who time after time set sail from shore. The famous Venetia, already rich in nobility, touches, to the south, Ravenna and the Po; to the east it enjoys the smiling shores of the Ionian Sea, where the alternate ebb and flow cover and uncover the face of the land. There lie your houses, like water-fowl, now on land, now on islands; and when the change comes, they are seen scattered like the Cyclades over the face of the waters – habitations not made by nature, but founded by the industry of man. For the land is made solid by wattled piles, nor do you dread to offer so fragile a bulwark to the waves of the sea when the low-lying islands fail to beat back the weight of water because they are not high enough. Fish alone is abundant; rich and poor live there on equal terms. A single food nourishes all alike; the same sort of house shelters you all; you envy not the lot of others, and living thus you flee the vice that rules the world. All your rivalry is expended in your salt-works; in place of ploughs and sickles you turn your drying-pans, and hence comes all your gain, and what you have made is your very own. All products are dependent on your industry; for it may well be that some seek not gold, but there lives not a man who does not need salt, which seasons all our food.

*All peoples create myths
to explain their origins –
how and why they came to live
in their 'native land'.*

Let us consider for a moment the pregnant legend of St Mark who, journeying from Aquileia to Ravenna, touched at the island mud flats of Rialto. As he slept upon the forlorn and empty lagoon marked by low island desolation, by a few boats, by an occasional net or salt-pan, an angel

'You own many a ship and your vessels fear not the stormy winds' – Venice, from a manuscript of 1338.

appeared and greeted him with the words '*Pax tibi, Marce, hic requiescet corpus tuum*' [Peace to you, Mark; here will your body rest]: a sad enough prophecy except that it was coupled with promise of the birth of a great city on those barren islets, no mirage city but one which would sit as lightly on the mud. This dream glimmer was ever present in the Venetian mind, this mirage image, product of hard days upon sedgy wastes where distant low islands seem to maintain a slight suspension above the thin water and trickling reeds.

For the Venetians this function was performed by the story of St Mark, discussed here by the art critic ADRIAN STOKES *in his* Venice: An Aspect of Art *(1945).*

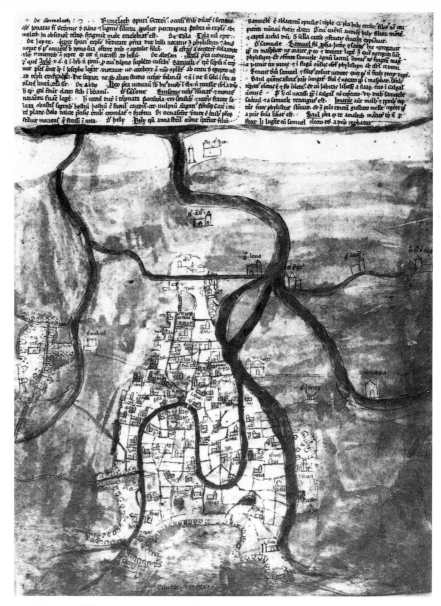

Earliest map of Venice, from a manuscript of 1346.

In the Discourses *(1519),*
a political treatise,
NICCOLO MACHIAVELLI
ascribed Venice's rise to power
to its unique geographical
situation.

Numerous peoples who had sought refuge in certain islets at the top of the Adriatic Sea that they might escape the wars which daily arose in Italy after the decline of the Roman empire owing to the arrival of a new lot of barbarians. There, without any particular person or prince to give them a constitution, they began to live as a community under laws which seemed to them appropriate for their maintenance. And in this they were happily successful owing to the long repose the situation afforded them in that the sea at their end had no exit and the peoples who were ravaging Italy had no ships in which to infest them. This being so, a beginning, however small, sufficed to bring them to their present greatness.

The Henetians of Paphlagonia, their King Palemon being dead at the siege of Troy, joyned themselves to Antenor, and possessing these parts, after they had driven out the Euganeans, called the countrey Venice, and through their great vertue were made Citizens of Rome, and their chiefe men Senators thereof. But when Attila King of the Huns invaded Italy, and the Empire of the West being weakned, did destroy the same, the said Henetians came out of Histria, now called Frioli, and from the Territory of Paduoa, and other Italians came from adjoyning parts, into certaine Ilands compassed with marshes, that they might be safe from those Barbarians; and about the yeere of our Lord, 421, began to build a City, which proving a safe retreate from the tyranny then continually oppressing Italy, in process of time by civill Arts grew incredibly.

How they came to be founded in the midst of the waters I could never meet with any clear memorial. The best and most of their authors ascribe their best beginnings rather to chance or necessity, than counsel: which yet in my opinion will amount to no more than a pretty conjecture intenebrated by antiquity, for thus they deliver it: they saw that among the tumults of the middle age, when nations went about swarming like bees, Atylas, that great captain of the Hunnes, and scourge of the world (as he was styled) lying along with a numerous army at the siege of Aquileia, it struck a mighty affrightment and confusion into all the nearer parts. Whereupon the best sort of the bordering people out of divers towns, agreed either suddenly, or by little and little (as fear will sometimes collect, as well as distract) to convey themselves and their substance into the uttermost bosom of the Adriatick Gulf and there possessed certain desolate islets, by tradition about seventy in number, which afterwards (necessity being the mother of art) were tacked together with bridges, and so the city took a rude form, which grew civilized with time, and became a great example of what the smallest things well fomented may prove.

The English traveller FYNES MORYSON *recorded this account of the origins of Venice – part myth, part history – in 1596, first published in his* Itinerary *(1617). At the time it was fashionable to trace Britain's own origins back to the siege of Troy, and Moryson was undoubtedly attracted by the similar tales told of Venice.*

HENRY WOTTON, *as English ambassador to the Republic, spent many years in Venice and dreamed of writing its history. This letter, written to a friend in 1622, contains what was intended to be its first chapter.*

Stone carving from San Marco.

Woodcut of the Piazetta, 1484.

'Figures on the Piazzetta', by Edward Pritchett (flourished 1828–64).

ARRIVALS

First impressions of Venice are rarely forgotten. The essayist and art critic JOHN ADDINGTON SYMONDS *was a frequent visitor in the latter part of the nineteenth century, and in* A Venetian Medley *(1898) compared his original response with subsequent and more sober reactions.*

Venice inspires at first an almost Corybantic rapture. From our earliest visits, if these have been measured by days rather than weeks, we carry away with us the memory of sunsets emblazoned in gold and crimson upon cloud and water; of violet domes and bell-towers etched against the orange of a western sky; of moonlight silvering breeze-rippled breadths of liquid blue; of distant islands shimmering in sun-litten haze; of music and black gliding boats; of labyrinthine darkness made for mysteries of love and crime; of statue-fretted palace fronts; of brazen clangour and a moving crowd; of pictures by earth's proudest painters, cased in gold on walls of council chambers where Venice sat enthroned a queen, where nobles swept the floors with robes of Tyrian brocade. These reminiscences will be attended by an ever-present sense of loneliness and silence in the world around; the sadness of a limitless horizon, the solemnity of an unbroken arch of heaven, the calm and greyness of evening on the lagoons, the pathos of a marble city crumbling to its grave in mud and brine.

These first impressions of Venice are true. Indeed they are inevitable. They abide, and form a glowing background for all subsequent pictures, toned more austerely, and painted in more lasting hues of truth upon the brain. Those have never felt Venice at all who have not known this primal rapture, or who perhaps expected more of colour, more of melodrama, from a scene which nature and the art of man have made the richest in these qualities. Yet the mood engendered by this first experience is not destined to be permanent. It contains an element of unrest and unreality which vanishes upon familiarity. From the blare of that triumphal bourdon of brass instruments emerge the delicate voices of violin and clarinette. To the contrasted passions of our earliest love succeed a multitude of sweet and fanciful emotions.

John Addington Symonds.

The day that I made my entry into Venice they sent to meet me as far as Fusina, which is five miles from Venice; there you leave the boats which bring you down the river from Padua, and get into little boats covered with tapestry and very neat, with fair carpets within, and velvet cushions to sit upon. To this place you come from Venice by sea, as it is the next place to Venice upon *terra firma*; but the sea (unless agitated by some storm) is very calm, which is the reason of the great abundance of all sorts of fish. I was extremely surprised at the situation of this city, to see so many churches, monasteries, and houses, and all in the water; and the people have no other passage up and down the streets but in boats, of which, I believe, they have near thirty thousand, but they are very small. About the city, within less than the compass of half a French league, there are seventy religious houses both of men and women, all situated in little islands, very beautiful and magnificent both in building and furniture, with fair gardens belonging to them; without reckoning those in the city, where there are the four orders of mendicants, and seventy-two parishes, besides several fraternities; and, indeed, it is most strange to behold so many stately churches in the sea.

...I was conducted through the principal street, which they call the Grand Canal, and it is so wide that galleys frequently cross one another; indeed I have seen vessels of four hundred tons or more ride at anchor just by the houses. It is the fairest and best-built street, I think, in the world, and goes quite through the city; the houses are very large and lofty, and built of stone; the old ones are all painted; those of about a hundred years

The French ambassador PHILIPPE DE COMMYNES *was received by the* signorie *in 1495. An experienced diplomat, familiar with the great courts of Europe, Commynes was nonetheless deeply impressed by his official reception and by his first sight of the famous city in the sea, recorded in his* Memoirs *(1598).*

standing are faced with white marble from Istria (which is about a hundred miles from Venice), and inlaid with porphyry and serpentine. Within they have, most of them, two chambers at least adorned with gilt ceilings, rich marble chimney-pieces, bedsteads of gold colour, their portals of the same, and most gloriously furnished. In short, it is the most triumphant city that I have ever seen . . .

Venice reaped vast profits from its strategic position on the pilgrimage route from Europe to the Holy Land. In 1517, SIR RICHARD TORKINGTON *passed through Venice on his way to Jerusalem, and noted his impressions in his journal.*

The same Day we sayled toward Venys, and a bowt iii of the cloke at aftyr none we com to the goodly and ffamose cite of Venys.

Ther I was well at ese, ffor ther was no thyng that I Desyred to have but I had it shortly.

At Venyse, at the fyrst howse that I cam to except oon, the good man of the howse seyd he knew me by my face that I was an englysshman. And he spake to me good englyssh, thane I was Jous and glade, ffor I saw never englyssh man ffrom the tyme I Departed owt of Parys to the tyme I cam to Venys, which is vii or viii C myles.

'That landing place that takes the breath away' – etching, *c.*1770.

It was written, then, on my page in the Book of Fate that at five in the afternoon of the twenty-eighth day of September in the year 1786, I should see Venice for the first time as I entered this beautiful island-city, this beaver-republic. So now, thank God, Venice is no longer a mere word to me, an empty name, a state of mind which has so often alarmed me who am the mortal enemy of mere words.

When the first gondola came alongside our boat – this they do to bring passengers who are in a hurry to Venice more quickly – I remembered from early childhood a toy to which I had not given a thought for perhaps twenty years. My father had brought back from his journey to Italy a beautiful model of a gondola; he was very fond of it and, as a special treat, he sometimes allowed me to play with it. When the gondolas appeared their shining steel-sheeted prows and black cages greeted me like old friends.

As soon as we had doubled the cape of this diminutive island, an expanse of sea opened to our view, the domes and towers of Venice rising from its bosom. Now we began to distinguish Murano, St Michele, St Giorgio in Alga, and several other islands, detached from the grand cluster, which I hailed as old acquaintances; innumerable prints and drawings having long since made their shapes familiar. Still gliding forward we every moment distinguished some new church or palace in the city, suffused with the rays of the setting sun, and reflected with all their glow of colouring from the surface of the waters...

We were now drawing very near the city, and a confused hum began to interrupt the evening stillness; gondolas were continually passing and repassing, and the entrance of the Canal Reggio, with all its stir and bustle, lay before us. Our gondoliers turned with much address through a crowd of boats and barges that blocked up the way, and rowed smoothly by the side of a broad pavement, covered with people in all dresses and of all nations.

Arrived at Mestre the place of embarcation for Venice 5 miles off. Here we took a boat & sailed for the famous city. It looked for some time like nothing but New York. We entered the Grand Canal & passed under the Rialto & [were] presently stepped out of the boat into the front entry of the Grande Bretagna. The front entry of the Grande Bretagna opens also upon a little bridge which connects by a narrow alley with the Piazza of St Mark so out we went under the full moon to see the same. It was all glorious to behold. In moonlight this arabesque square is all enchantment – so rich & strange & visionary.

JOHANN WOLFGANG
VON GOETHE
was thirty-seven, and famous throughout Europe as the author of Werther *and* Faust, *when he made his first trip to Italy in 1786. He had already studied the country in books and was familiar at second-hand with its legendary sights. His first entry into Venice thus struck him as the fulfilment of a life-long destiny, as he noted in his* Italian Journey *(1816–17).*

A stop in Venice was mandatory for young English aristocrats making the Grand Tour of Europe, which was regarded, in the eighteenth century, as an essential part of their education. The Gothic fantasist WILLIAM BECKFORD *arrived in Venice in 1780, having already spent several years tramping across the continent in quest of exotic sights and sensations. He later recorded his arrival in* Dreams, Waking Thoughts and Incidents *(1783).*

The American essayist and poet RALPH WALDO EMERSON *was less than overwhelmed by his first sight of Venice in June of 1833, but later he warmed to the city, as he noted in this entry in his* Journal.

HANS CHRISTIAN
ANDERSEN'S *early novel*
The Improvisatore *(1835) tells
the story of a wandering Italian
composer and singer of popular
ballads, and was based on the
author's own lonely,
impoverished years wandering
through Italy.*

I stepped down into the black gondola, and sailed up into the dead street, where every thing was water, not a foot-breadth upon which to walk. Large buildings stood with open doors, and with steps down to the water; the water ran into the great door-ways, like a canal; and the palace-court itself seemed only a four-cornered well, into which people could sail, but scarcely turn the gondola. The water had left its greenish slime upon the walls: the great marble palace seemed as if sinking together: in the broad windows, rough boards were nailed up to the gilded, half-decayed beams. The proud giant-body seemed to be falling away piecemeal; the whole had an air of depression about it. The ringing of the bells ceased, not a sound, excepting the splash of the oars in the water, was to be heard, and I still saw not a human being. The magnificent Venice lay like a dead swan upon the waves.

JOHN RUSKIN,
*whose voluminous writings on
Venice permanently
transformed the English vision
of the city, began Volume II of
The Stones of Venice (1852)
with this imaginary re-creation
of the old grand sea-borne entry
into Venice, replaced in his
own day by the more mundane,
back-door arrival by train.*

Not but that the aspect of the city itself was generally the source of some slight disappointment, for, seen in this direction, its buildings are far less characteristic than those of the other great towns of Italy; but this inferiority was partly disguised by distance, and more than atoned for by the strange rising of its walls and towers out of the midst, as it seemed, of the deep sea, for it was impossible that the mind or the eye could at once comprehend the shallowness of the vast sheet of water which stretched away in leagues of rippling lustre to the north and south, or trace the narrow line of islets bounding it to the east. The salt breeze, the white moaning sea-birds, the masses of black weed separating and disappearing gradually, in knots of heaving shoal, under the advance of the steady tide, all proclaimed it to be indeed the ocean on whose bosom the great city rested so calmly; not such blue, soft, lake-like ocean as bathes the Neapolitan promontories, or sleeps beneath the marble rocks of Genoa, but a sea with the bleak power of our own northern waves, yet subdued into a strange spacious rest, and changed from its angry pallor into a field of burnished gold . . . And at last, when [the city's] walls were reached, and the outmost of its untrodden streets was entered, not through towered gate or guarded rampart, but as a deep inlet between two rocks of coral in the Indian Sea; when first upon the traveller's sight opened the long ranges of columned places, – each with its black boat moored at the portal, – each with its image cast down, beneath its feet, upon that green pavement which every breeze broke into new fantasies of rich tessellation; when first, at the extremity of the bright vista, the shadowy Rialto threw its colossal curve slowly forth from behind the palace of the Camerlenghi; that strange curve, so delicate, so adamantine, strong as a mountain cavern, graceful as a bow just bent; when first, before its moon-like circumference was all risen, the gondolier's cry, '*Ah! Stalì,*' struck sharp

'That strange curve . . . graceful as a bow just bent' – from a drawing by John Ruskin.

upon the ear, and the prow turned aside under the mighty cornices that half met over the narrow canal, where the splash of the water followed close and loud, ringing along the marble by the boat's side; and when at last that boat darted forth upon the breadth of silver sea, across which the front of the Ducal palace, flushed with its sanguine veins, looks to the snowy dome of Our Lady of Salvation, it was no marvel that the mind should be so deeply entranced by the visionary charm of a scene so beautiful and so strange, as to forget the darker truths of its history and its being. Well might it seem that such a city had owed her existence rather to the rod of the enchanter, than the fear of the fugitive; that the waters which encircled her had been chosen for the mirror of her state, rather than the shelter of her nakedness; and that all which in nature was wild or merciless, – Time and Decay, as well as the waves and tempests, – had been won to adorn her instead of to destroy, and might still spare, for ages to come, that beauty which seemed to have fixed for its throne the sands of the hour-glass as well as of the sea.

The English novelist
GEORGE ELIOT *first visited
Venice in 1860. She recorded
her impressions in her journals,
published twenty years later,
after her death.*

It was about ten o'clock on a moonlight night – the 4th of June – that we found ourselves apparently on a railway in the midst of the sea: we were on the bridge across the Lagoon. Soon we were in a gondola on the Grand Canal, looking out at the moonlit buildings and water. What stillness! What beauty! Looking out from the high window of our hotel on the Grand Canal, I felt that it was a pity to go to bed. Venice was more beautiful than romances had feigned.

And that was the impression that remained, and even deepened, during our stay of eight days. That quiet which seemed the deeper because one hears the delicious dip of the oar (when not disturbed by clamorous church bells), leaves the eye in full liberty and strength to take in the exhaustless loveliness of colour and form.

*Venice was to inspire some of
HENRY JAMES's greatest prose.
However, on his first visit, in
1869, he still felt very much a
Yankee provincial. In this letter
to his brother he compared
Venice to the sedate New
England resort of Newport.*

I was more than ever struck with the resemblance of Venice ... to Newport. The same atmosphere, the same luminosity. Standing looking out at the Adriatic with the low-lying linked islands on the horizon was just like looking out to sea from one of the Newport beaches, with Narragansett afar. I have seen the Atlantic as blue and smooth and musical – almost! If words were not so stupid and colorless, *fratello mio*, and sentences so interminable and chirography so difficult, I should like to treat you to a dozen pages more about this watery paradise.

BORIS PASTERNAK
*arrived in Venice, like many
before and after, an aspiring
poet and penniless student, in
desperate need of cheap
lodgings. He recalled the
moment in his memoir,* Safe
Conduct *(1932).*

When I emerged from the station building, with its provincial façade in a customs and excise style, a sort of fluency softly slipped up to me somewhere below my feet. Something ominously dingy, like water from a kitchen sink, yet touched with the glitter of two or three stars. Almost imperceptibly ebbing and rising again, it was like an age-blackened painting in a fluctuating frame. It was not immediately that I grasped that this depiction of Venice was Venice itself. That I really was in Venice, it was no dream.

In the novella
Death in Venice *(1912),*
THOMAS MANN's
*doomed hero Von Aschenbach
entered Venice in the grand
style, approaching the Piazza
San Marco from the sea.*

He saw it once more, that landing-place that takes the breath away, that amazing group of incredible structures the Republic set up to meet the awe-struck eye of the approaching seafarer: the airy splendour of the palace and Bridge of Sighs, the columns of lion and saint on the shore, the glory of the projecting flank of the fairy temple, the vista of gateway and clock. Looking, he thought that to come to Venice by the station is like entering a palace by the back door. No one should approach, save by the high seas as he was doing now, this most improbable of cities.

Somewhere about Ravenna the Adriatic appears far below like a blur of smoke. Beyond the swampy lagoons of Comacchio, where Garibaldi hid from his hunters, and his wife Anita died, we pass over the meandering mouths of the Po; and then over the mouth of the Adige; and then the headland of Chioggia crops out into the sea. The man at my side said, 'Ecco Venezia!' We were thrumming in over the long razor-shell of the island of Palestrina towards the lean breakwater of the Lido – the whole string of sandy breakwaters are a *lido*, or bank – and my heart thumped on all six cylinders as I recognized the Venetian lagoons. There were the islets, small as boats, which I was soon to know as Poveglia and Santo Spirito and La Grazia and San Clemente, rowing among which, at night, I was so often to feel alone in the world under that deep behind deep of tinted air which men so weakly call the blue Venetian night. There were the larger islands flattening out to the north, Murano and Burano and Mazzorbo and Torcello. In between lay the great island of Venezia herself; although, anatomically, Venice consists of about a hundred islets sewn together by threads of bridges into one patchwork mass. I saw no canals. They were buried deep between the houses.

Before landing on the Lido airfield the plane circled. I saw a cluster of opals set in a crescent lagoon backed by the Euganean Hills, and the heights of Vicenza and the valleys of Cadore that rose to tiers of haze that must have been the foothills of the Julian Alps. Then the world whirled its mirror and the landing-strip came sloping up to meet us in gushes of bumping heat. After that, the final approach across the warm yet balmy lagoon was as gentle as a folding wing, as drugged as a falling eyelid, more quiet than a floating leaf. It was a slow fading into a Castle of Indolence.

For the beginning and the end of Venice is that immediately you step into your first gondola the amiable pirate in browning straw hat with red ribbons, rowing behind your back, who lives in three rooms of Number 1576, Torreselle, two twists off the Grand Canal, with his wife, mother-in-law, sister and six water-rats, is not a gondolier, but the child of Circe and Silence; that he will hush you in his arms away from this mortal world as softly as the boat glides from the pier; that it will be well with you if you can ever return to it; or if you do, ever bear to live in it again. People say that anybody who travels in Japan is never the same person after. I once knew of a man who had made love to an Indian priestess and after that Western women meant nothing to him. Browning's fish went from cool to warm water and was never after happy in either. One's first visit to Venice is a climb to a Mount of Revelation. It unseats the reason.

My reason told me that men and women in Venice have to pay the grocer's bills, go to the movies, suffer toothaches, have trouble with the kid's school reports, the maid, the stove and the choked drains, but though

In 1948, the Irish writer SEAN O'FAOLAIN *approached the city from the air. He described the splendours of the ancient lagoon as seen from on high in* A Summer in Italy *(1949).*

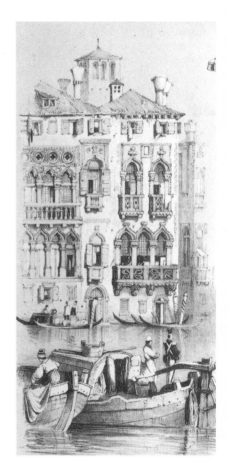

Canal traffic, 19th century.

my reason told me all this, it did so over a flying shoulder. When next I met the poor thing it had a shivering hand and bloodshot eye. It never quite recovered from the hunted life it had been leading in the meantime.

Introducing A History of Venice *(1977), the British historian* JOHN JULIUS NORWICH *recalled his own first brush with the Venetian mystique.*

First experiences should be short and intense. When my parents took me to Venice in the summer of 1946, we stayed only a few hours; but I can still feel – not remember, *feel* – the impact it made on my sixteen-year-old brain. With his usual blend of firmness and commonsense, my father limited to two the buildings we actually entered: the Basilica of St Mark and Harry's Bar. For the rest of the time, wandering on foot or drifting gently in a gondola, I subconsciously absorbed the first essential Venetian lesson – a lesson, incidentally, that poor Ruskin, beavering away at his crockets and cusps round the Doge's Palace, never learnt: that in Venice, more than anywhere else, the whole is greater than the sum of the parts. However majestic the churches, however magnificent the *palazzi*, however dazzling the pictures, the ultimate masterpiece remains Venice itself. Interiors, even the great golden mystery of St Mark's, are but details. The relation of Piazza and Piazzetta, the sublime setting of S. Giorgio Maggiore at precisely the right angle to the Molo, the play of light at a canal's curve, the slap of water against the hull of a gondola, the all-pervading smell of the sea – for let there by no mistake about it, except when the wind is blowing across from Mestre and Marghera, Venice is the sweetest-smelling city in Europe – these are the first things to be experienced and understood. There will be time for Titian and Tintoretto later. Even Carpaccio must wait his turn.

In Gemini *(1975), a story of twins finding and losing each other in modern Venice, the French novelist* MICHEL TOURNIER *described the trip from the mainland airport across the lagoon to the city with which even the stranger is already familiar.*

When I landed at Marco Polo Airport this morning, it was pouring rain. I refused to shelter in the cabin of the *vaporetto*, which was packed with a crowd of all nationalities. I stayed on deck and all through the forty-five minute journey I watched the passing posts, each capped with a sulky sea gull, that lined the channel. To know Venice, there is no need to have been there, it is so much a part of the mental landscape of every European. At most, one goes there in order to *recognize* it. That lane of piles driven into the mud of the Lagoon is the trail of white pebbles dropped by Tom Thumb to find his way home. For any moderately educated Westerner, there can be no city with more preconceived ideas about it than Venice.

'Still sea-wraithed, still sea-veiled' – painting by Francesco Guardi (1712–93).

SEA-BRIDE

Although one may read the greater part of everything that has even been written about Venice since its hey-day, from Goldoni to Corvo, one will never get any other feeling but that this exquisite and magnificent, this solid and squalid city conjured out of the wraiths of the sea is, for them all, still sea-wraithed, still sea-veiled as with the iridescent spray and the spume of the goddess-mouth that blew it from her conch. None of us who write of it can stop ourselves from so glorifying this creation of the past that its dawns, its days and its nights become intimations of immortality. It is a confession, whether we know it or not, that Venice is an inviolate work of art, a projection of the Schopen-hauerian will, a timeless essence, one of the greatest achievements of the whole cosmic movement of human desire for its insatiable satisfaction.

The Irish writer SEAN O'FAOLAIN, *in his* A Summer in Italy *(1949), considered the essence of the Venetian magic, and ascribed it, in the end, to water.*

Reason, by this time flying distraught from me, perhaps to the island of San Lazzaro to study Armenian with the Mechitarists, or to study lunacy in the islet of San Servolo where the mad are housed, snarls at me over its shoulder: 'I suppose you know, dotty, what all this comes from? Water! Merely water!' And Reason is quite right and, as it so often is, it is also very silly. Merely water? One might as well say merely history. Everything Venetian has been dictated by the sea: her origin, her power, her architecture, the temper of her people, her ruin and her final transfiguration into an object of delight.

The English poet
SAMUEL ROGERS's
extensive Italian travels inspired his long poem Italy *(1816), immensely popular in its day, but little read now.*

There is a glorious City in the Sea.
The Sea is in the broad, the narrow streets,
Ebbing and flowing; and the salt sea-weed
Clings to the marble of her palaces.
No track of men, no footsteps to and fro,
Lead to her gates. The path lies o'er the Sea,
Invisible; and from the land we went,
As to a floating City

On Ascension Day the head of the Venetian Republic, the Doge, celebrated a symbolic marriage to the Adriatic by dropping a wedding ring into the water of the lagoon, and declaring his 'perpetual dominion' over the sea. La Sensa, *as the Venetians called it, was the premier festival in the Venetian calendar, marking the beginning of the pilgrimage season to Jerusalem, and attracting hordes of foreign visitors, one of whom, the English traveller* SIR RICHARD TORKINGTON, *recorded the details of the lavish ceremony in his journal (1517).*

The Duke with grett Triumphe and solemnyte with all the Senyorye went in ther Archa triumphali, which ys in maner of a sayle of a straange facion and wonder stately, etc...

And so they rowed in to the see, with the assistens of ther Patriarche, And ther Spoused the see with a ryng. The spousall words be *In signum*

'In signum veri perpetuique Domini' – the Doge weds the Adriatic.

veri perpetuique Domini. And therwith the Duke lete fall the ryng in to the see, the processe and the cerymonyes whereof war to long to wryte.

Thanne thaye Rode to the Abbey of Seynt Nicholas of blake Monkys that stond by juste be them, And all thaye brake ther fastes, And so retornyd a geyne to Venys, To the Dukys palace, Wher they had provyd for them a mervelows Dyner, wher at we Pilgrymes war present and see them servyd. At which Dyner her was viii Corse of soundery metys, And att every Corse the Trunpettes and the mynystrellys com inne a for them.

Apparatus for hauling *gondole* from one water level to another.

To describe the Bucentaur in one word, I shall call it a show-galley. The old Bucentaur, of which pictures still exist, justifies the epithet still more than the present one which, by its splendour, makes one forget the original. I always return to my old contention that any artist can create something genuine if he is given a genuine task. In this case, he was commissioned to construct a galley worthy of carrying the heads of the Republic on their most solemn day to the sacrament of their traditional sea power, and this task was admirably performed. One should not say that it is overladen with ornaments, for the whole ship is one single ornament. All the wood carving is gilded and serves no purpose except to be a true monstrance showing the people their masters in a splendid pageant. As we know, people who like to decorate their own hats like to see their superiors elegantly dressed as well. This state barge is a real family heirloom, which reminds us of what the Venetians once believed themselves to be, and were.

The Bucentaur was the ceremonial barge, used by the Doge for La Sensa *and other public occasions. When* JOHANN WOLFGANG VON GOETHE *described it in his* Italian Journey *(1816–17), it was already a mere memory, a relic of past grandeur.*

On his visit to Venice in 1494, the Milanese cleric CANON PIETRO CASOLA *tried to count the city's boats – not an easy exercise, as he recorded in his travel journals, first published in the nineteenth century.*

I fatigued myself very much by trying to find out of possible – and with the aid of people very familiar with Venice and the surrounding places – the number of all the ships, both large and small, to be found in Venice, beginning with the boats otherwise called gondolas, up to the largest nave and galley in the Grand Canal. I commenced the work; but although the days were long, because it was the month of May, I found it was no task for me any more than for Saint Augustine – as they recount – to write about the Trinity, for the number is infinite.

The English traveller FYNES MORYSON, *visiting the city in 1596, was fascinated by Venice's waterways, and described them in his* Itinerary, *first published in 1617.*

Channels of water passe through this City (consisting of many Ilands joyned with Bridges) as the bloud passeth through the veines of mans body; so that a man may passe to what place he will both by land and water. The great channell is in length about one thousand three hundred paces, and in breadth forty paces, and hath onely one bridge called Rialto, and the passage is very pleasant by this channell; being adorned on both sides with stately Pallaces . . . And if a stranger know not the way, hee shall not need to aske it, for if hee will follow the presse of people, hee shall be sure to bee brought to the market place of Saint Marke, or that of Rialto; the streets being very narrow (which they pave with bricke,) and besides if hee onely know his Hosts name, taking a boat, he shall be safely brought thither at any time of the night. Almost all the houses have two gates, one towards the street, the other towards the water; or at least the bankes of the channels are so neere, as the passage by water is as easie as by land.

The origins of the gondola, that uniquely Venetian mode of transport, are shrouded in history. As a symbol of Venice, and all that makes it fascinatingly singular, the gondola has enticed generations of writers. For the sixteenth-century Tuscan scholar and wit PIETRO ARETINO, *it was one of the many delights of what became his adopted country.*

What a heartfelt pleasure it is to get right away from everyone in a gondola! Carriages for those that like them! Litters too! Away with horseback! The first are likely to break down, the second bury you

'Didst ever see a Gondola?' – woodcut, 1597.

alive and the third bounce your bones, flesh and guts all over the place. But the dear little gondola rests, soothes and consoles the mind, the limbs and the whole body. Truth, wisdom and certainty are its gifts. Charon had good reason to take it as a model for his bark. He knew very well what he was doing when he copied it and needed its comfort for his task!

Didst ever see a Gondola? For fear
   You should not, I'll describe it you exactly:
'Tis a long cover'd boat that's common here
   Carved at the prow, built lightly, but compactly,
Row'd by two rowers, each call'd 'Gondolier,'
   It glides along the water looking blackly.
Just like a coffin clapt in a canoe,
Where none can make out what you say or do.

And up and down the long canals they go,
   And under the Rialto shoot along,
By night and day, all paces, swift or slow,
   And round the theatres, a sable throng,
They wait in their dusk livery of woe, –
   But not to them do woeful things belong,
For sometimes they contain a deal of fun,
Like mourning coaches when the funeral's done.

In his long poem Beppo *(1818), a satirical meditation on Venice and its mores, the poet* LORD BYRON *introduced his English audience to the charm of the gondola.*

The silent streets are paved with water, and you hear nothing but the dashing of the oars, and the occasional cries of the gondolieri. I heard nothing of Tasso. The gondolas themselves are things of a most romantic and picturesque appearance; I can only compare them to moths of which a coffin might have been the chrysalis. They are hung with black, and painted black, and carpeted with grey; they curl at the prow and stern, and at the former there is a nondescript beak of shining steel, which glitters at the end of its long black mass.

PERCY BYSSHE SHELLEY *visited Byron in Venice in 1818, and noted his impressions of the famous gondola – and the gondolier, reputed to sing the songs of the Italian poet Tasso – in this letter to Thomas Love Peacock.*

I am however also looking well just now and don't want admirers either, and as my acquaintances are of a lower rank they only express their sentiments to John and opinion of me before my face. The other day when I was rowing the Gondola in the Grand Canal the Valet de Place started from his reverie and said to John in French, '*Ah! Monsieur, comme votre femme est belle,*' continuing that he had seen a great many English but never any like me, and he supposed there were not ten more beautiful in England. John said that I was well enough and would do if I was as good as I was pretty.

John Ruskin's unfortunate wife, EFFIE GRAY, *must have been a strange sight to the Venetians as she rowed a gondola down the Grand Canal. She described the scene in a letter to her family in November 1849.*

The German composer
RICHARD WAGNER
*was stricken by fear on his first
encounter with the gondola in
1857, as he recalled years later
in his autobiography,* My Life
(1870–81).

The weather had suddenly turned somewhat unpleasant, and the sight of the gondola itself had shocked me a bit; for despite all I had heard of these conveyances, painted black on black, the actual sight of one was still a rude surprise: when I had to go under the black awning, my first thought was a revival of a fear of cholera that I had previously mastered; it decidedly seemed to me as if I were taking part in a funeral procession during an epidemic.

ARTHUR HUGH CLOUGH's
*paradoxical paean to the
gondola appeared in his long
dialogue poem* Dipsychus
*(1852). Here, the principal
character, Dipsychus, speaks.*

Per ora. To the Grand Canal.
Afterwards e'en as fancy shall.

Afloat; we move. Delicious! Ah,
What else is like the gondola?
This level floor of liquid glass
Begins beneath it swift to pass.
It goes as though it went alone
By some impulsion of its own.
How light it moves, how softly! Ah,
Were all things like the gondola!

How light it moves, how softly! Ah,
Could life, as does our gondola,
Unvexed with quarrels, aims, and cares,
And moral duties and affairs,
Unswaying, noiseless, swift, and strong,
For ever thus – thus glide along!
How light we move, how softly! Ah,
Were all things like the gondola!

With no more motion than should bear
A freshness to the languid air;
With no more effort than exprest
The need and naturalness of rest,
Which we beneath a grateful shade
Should take on peaceful pillows laid –
How light we move, how softly! Ah,
Were all things like the gondola!

In one unbroken passage borne
To closing night from opening morn,
Uplift at whiles slow eyes to mark
Some palace front, some passing bark;
Through windows catch the varying shore,
And hear the soft turns of the oar –

Traghetto and *vaporetto*, crossing paths.

How light we move, how softly! Ah,
Were all things like the gondola!

So live, nor need to call to mind
Our slaving brother set behind!

The little closed cabin of this perfect vehicle, the movement, the darkness and the plash, the indistinguishable swerves and twists, all the things you don't see and all the things you do feel – each dim recognition and obscure arrest is a possible throb of your sense of being floated to your doom, even when the truth is simply and sociably that you are going out to tea. Nowhere else is anything as innocent so mysterious, nor anything as mysterious so pleasantly deterrent to protest.

In his essay 'Two Old Houses and Three Young Women' (1899), republished in Italian Hours, HENRY JAMES *contemplated the enigma of the gondola.*

Is there anyone but must repress a secret thrill, on arriving in Venice for the first time – or returning thither after long absence – and stepping into a Venetian gondola? That singular conveyance, come down unchanged from ballad times, black as nothing else on earth except a coffin – what pictures it calls up of lawless, silent adventures in the plashing night; or even more, what visions of death itself, the bier and solemn rites and last soundless voyage! And has anyone remarked that the seat in such a bark, the arm-chair lacquered in coffin-black, and dully black-upholstered, is the softest, most luxurious, most relaxing seat in the world? Aschenbach realized it when he had let himself down at the gondolier's feet, opposite his luggage, which lay neatly composed on the vessel's beak. The rowers still gestured fiercely; he heard their harsh, incoherent tones. But the strange stillness of the water-city seemed to take up their voices gently, to disembody and scatter them over the sea. It was warm here in the harbour. The lukewarm air of the sirocco breathed upon him, he leaned back among his cushions and gave himself to the yielding element, closing his eyes for very pleasure in an indolence as unaccustomed as sweet. 'The trip will be short,' he thought, and wished it might last forever.

Von Aschenbach, the doomed author-hero of THOMAS MANN's *novella* Death in Venice *(1912), surrendered himself to the morbid pleasure of the gondola.*

I painted the Venetian gondoliers from nature in a very entertaining manner to those who are acquainted with the language and manners of my country.

I wished to be reconciled to this class of domestics who were deserving of some attention, and who were discontented with me.

The gondoliers at Venice are allowed a place in the theatre, when the pit is not full; but as they could not enter at my comedies, they were forced to wait for their masters in the streets, or in their gondolas. I had heard them myself distinguish me with very droll and comical epithets; and having

As fascinating and uniquely Venetian as the gondola is its master, the gondolier. CARLO GOLDONI *(1707–93) was the first Venetian dramatist to put gondoliers on stage, speaking their own dialect, as he recalled in his* Memoirs, *(1787).*

procured them a few places in the corners of the house, they were quite delighted to see themselves brought on the stage, and I became their friend.

In his travel book
The Innocents Abroad *(1869),*
MARK TWAIN, *as an old Mississippi riverboat man, paid tribute to the remarkable skills of the gondolier.*

He uses a single oar – a long blade, of course, for he stands nearly erect. A wooden peg, a foot and a half high, with two slight crooks or curves in one side of it and one in the other, projects above the starboard gunwale. Against that peg the gondolier takes a purchase with his oar, changing it at intervals to the other side of the peg or dropping it into another of the crooks, as the steering of the craft may demand – and how in the world he can back and fill, shoot straight ahead, or flirt suddenly around a corner, and make the oar stay in those insignificant notches, is a problem to me and a never diminishing matter of interest. I am afraid I study the gondolier's marvellous skill more than I do the sculptured palaces we glide among. He cuts a corner so closely, now and then, or misses another gondola by such an imperceptible hair-breadth that I feel

Gondoliers' protest, 1961.

myself 'scrooching', as the children say, just as one does when a buggy wheel grazes his elbow. But he makes all his calculations with the nicest precision, and goes darting in and out among a Broadway confusion of busy craft with the easy confidence of the educated hackman. He never makes a mistake.

Così di ponte in ponte, altro parlando
che la mia comedìa cantar non cura,
   venimmo, e tenavamo il colmo, quando
restammo per veder l'altra fessura
   di Malebolge e li altri pianti vani;
   e vidila mirabilmente oscura.
Quale nell'arzanà de' Viniziani
   bolle l' inverno la tenace pece
   a rimpalmare i legni lor non sani,
– chè navicar non ponno, e in quella vece

The Venetian Arsenal was for centuries the envy of the world, a state-controlled centre of ship-building and armament manufacture at the hub of a Mediterranean empire.
DANTE ALIGHIERI *must have seen it sometime c. 1300, and refers to it in the* Inferno, *Canto XXI.*

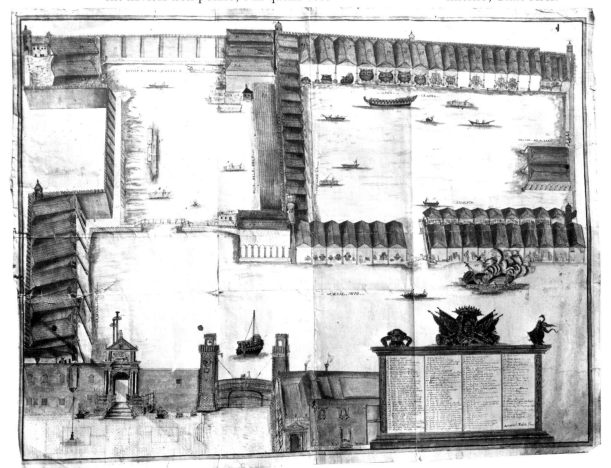

Plan of the Arsenal, 16th century.

chi fa suo legno novo e chi ristoppa
le coste a quel che più vïaggi fece;
chi ribatta da proda e chi da poppa;
altri fa remi e altri volge sarte;
chi terzeruolo e artimon rintoppa –
tal, non per foco, ma per divin' arte,
bollìa là giuso una pegola spessa,
che 'nviscava la ripa d'ogni parte.
I' vedea lei, ma non vedea in essa
mai che le bolle che 'l bollor levava,
e gonfiar tutta, e riseder compressa.

Thus from bridge to bridge, talking of other things of which my Comedy is not concerned to sing, we came on and reached the summit, when we stopped to see the next fissure of Malebolge and the next vain tears; and I saw it strangely dark. As in the Arsenal of the Venetians they boil the viscous pitch in winter to caulk their unsound ships – for they cannot sail then, and instead one builds himself a new ship and another plugs the ribs of his that has made many voyages, one hammers at the prow and another at the stern, this one makes oars, that one twists ropes, another patches jib and mainsail; so, not by fire but by divine art, a thick tar was boiling below there which stuck to the bank on every side. I saw it, but saw in it nothing but the bubbles raised by the boiling and the whole swelling up and settling together again.

In the last decades of the nineteenth century the vaporetto, *or steam-boat, began carrying passengers the length of the Grand Canal. The gondoliers, whose livelihood was threatened, went on strike. Their trade union is one of the oldest in Europe, and at times one of the most militant, as* HORATIO BROWN, *recorded in his* Life on the Lagoons *(1884).*

When the city woke on Tuesday morning, it found all the *traghetti* [jetties] deserted, and the Italian flag flying from a post at each, placed there by the gondoliers in sign that, though rebellious, they were still good sons of Italy. The Grand Canal looked strange and unfamiliar; the bright and keen November sunlight fell upon the palace fronts, but not a boat moved across the spacious waterway; each ferry stood forlorn, and empty of its crowd of chattering gondoliers; only the hated steamers plied backwards and forwards with their numerous passengers ... The gondoliers behaved with order and sobriety; there was no rioting; only the wine-shops were a little fuller than usual, and you met tall, grave fellows, in slouched hats, with coat over one shoulder, talking quietly on the bridges, and at the corners of the narrow streets. The little canals were full of gondolas lying idle; packed so tight that you might walk across them without seeing the water.

'The most joyous view in all the world' – the Rialto, etching by Frank Duveneck, 1883.

VEDUTE

Generations of travellers have returned from Venice with
vedute (views) in oil or watercolour, daguerreotype or picture postcard.
Writers, too, have tried to capture in words those fleeting visions or impressions
of the city which are one of its chief attractions, and which linger in the
memory when historical dates and old doges have been long forgotten.

It seems to me, Honoured Sir, that I would commit the sin of ingratitude if I did not repay with praise some part of the debt which I owe to the heavenly situation of your house ... Certainly its builder chose the finest position on the Canal. And since that Canal is the patriarch of all others and since Venice is a female pope among cities, I can truthfully say that I enjoy both the fairest highway and the most joyous view in all the world.

Whenever I look out of my windows at that time when the merchants foregather I see a thousand persons in as many gondolas. The squares to my right are those of the butchers' and fishmongers' markets. To my left I

In 1529, the Tuscan exile
PIETRO ARETINO was
given a long lease on a palazzo
near the Rialto, a token of
Venice's appreciation of the
writer whose satirical talents
had made him unwelcome
elsewhere. He wrote this letter
of thanks to his new landlord.

behold the much frequented Bridge and the warehouses of the German traders. There are grapes in the barges below, game of all kinds in the shops and vegetables laid out on the pavements. There is no need for me to long for meadows watered by streams when I can marvel at dawn over waters covered with an endless variety of merchandise, each article in its due season.

What sport it is to watch those who bring in great quantities of fruit and vegetables handing them out to others who carry them to their appointed places! All is tumult and bustle, except where about a score of sailing-boats laden with melons are moored together, making a sort of island to which crowds hurry off to count, sniff and weigh, so as to test the quality of the goods. Of the ladies, gleaming in gold and silk and jewels, though they are mere housewives, I will not speak, lest I grow tedious with the description of such pomp and circumstance. But what makes me roar with laughter are the whistles, catcalls and jeers directed by the boatmen at those whose rowers are not equipped with scarlet hose.

And who would not laugh till he cried at the sight of a boatload of Germans who had just reeled out of a tavern being capsized into the chilly waters of the Canal? . . .

Next, so that nothing should be lacking to please my eye, I can gaze in one direction upon the orange trees that gild the base of the Palazzo de' Camerlinghi and in another on the rio San Giovanni Crisostomo and its bridge. Even the burning winter sun never rises without first sending word of its arrival to my bedroom, my study, my other private apartments and my great hall . . .

And what of the lights, which after nightfall resemble stars scattered over the places where all that is necessary for our feasts and banquets is sold? Or the music which in the dark reaches my ears with soothing harmonies?

Nor must I forget the great foreign lords of the world who often pass me at the entrance to my palace nor the pride that lifts me to heaven when I see the Bucentaur plying hither and thither, nor the triumphant festivities continually in progress over that part of the Canal dominated by my windows.

The view from the top of the Campanile in the Piazza San Marco has been much prized by tourists, including Goethe, Elizabeth Barrett Browning, Henry James and the indefatigable English traveller

From every side . . . you have the fairest and goodliest prospect that is (I thinke) in all the world. For therehence may you see the whole model and forme of the citie *sub uno intuito*, a sight that doth in my opinion farre surpasse all the shewes under the cope of heaven. There you may have a Synopsis, that is, a general view of little Christendome (for so doe many intitle this citie of Venice) or rather of the Jerusalem of Christendome . . . There you may behold all their sumptuous Palaces adorned with admir-

'Night is nowhere else so wonderful' – Venice, by Mortimer Menpes.

able variety of beautiful pillars: the Church of S. Marke which is but a little way therehence distant, with the Dukes stately Palace adjoyning unto it, being one of the principall wonders of the Christian world; the lofty Rialto, the Piazza of Saint Stephen which is the most spacious and goodly place of the Citie except St Markes; all the six parts of the citie. For into so many it is divided, as I have before said; their streetes, their Churches, their Monasteries, their market places, and all their other publike buildings of rare magnificence. Also many faire gardens replenished with diversity of delicate fruites, as Oranges, Citrons, Lemmons, Apricocks, muske melons, anguriaes, and what not; together with their little Islands bordering about the citie wonderfully frequented and inhabited with people, being in number fifty or there about. Also the Alpes that lead into Germany two waies, by the Citie of Trent, and the

THOMAS CORYAT, *who published this account in his* Crudities *(1611).*

Grisons country; and those that leade into France through Savoy, the Appennines, the pleasant Euganean hils, with a little world of other most delectable objects . . .

In Dreams, Waking Thoughts and Incidents *(1783),*
the Gothic fantasist
WILLIAM BECKFORD
described the view from the balcony of his hotel near the Rialto.

I established myself to enjoy the cool, and observe, as well as the dusk would permit, the variety of figures shooting by in their gondolas.

As night approached, innumerable tapers glimmered through the awnings before the windows. Every boat had its lantern, and the gondolas moving rapidly along were followed by tracks of light, which gleamed and played upon the waters. I was gazing at these dancing fires when the sounds of music were wafted along the canals, and as they grew louder and louder, an illuminated barge, filled with musicians, issued from the Rialto, and stopping under one of the palaces, began a serenade, which stilled every clamour and suspended all conversation in the galleries and porticos; till, rowing slowly away, it was heard no more. The gondoliers catching the air, imitated its cadences, and were answered by others at a distance, whose voices, echoed by the arch of the bridge, acquired a plaintive and interesting tone. I retired to rest, full of the sound; and long after I was asleep, the melody seemed to vibrate in my ear.

HENRY JAMES
captured the essence of Venetian memories in his essay, entitled simply 'Venice' and published in 1882.

Certain little mental pictures rise before the collector of memories at the simple mention, written or spoken, of the places he has loved. When I hear, when I see, the magical name I have written above these pages [Venice], it is not of the great Square that I think, with its strange basilica and its high arcades, nor of the wide mouth of the Grand Canal, with the stately steps and the well-poised dome of the Salute; it is not of the low lagoon, nor the sweet Piazzetta, nor the dark chambers of St Mark's. I simply see a narrow canal in the heart of the city – a patch of green water and a surface of pink wall. The gondola moves slowly; it gives a great smooth swerve, passes under a bridge, and the gondolier's cry, carried over the quiet water, makes a kind of splash in the stillness. A girl crosses the little bridge, which has an arch like a camel's back, with an old shawl on her head, which makes her characteristic and charming; you see her against the sky as you float beneath. The pink of the old wall seems to fill the whole place; it sinks even into the opaque water. Behind the wall is a garden, out of which the long arm of a white June rose – the roses of Venice are splendid – has flung itself by way of spontaneous ornament. On the other side of this small water-way is a great shabby façade of Gothic windows and balconies – balconies on which dirty clothes are hung and under which a cavernous-looking doorway opens from a low flight of slimy water-steps. It is very hot and still, the canal has a queer smell, and the whole place is enchanting.

Night in Venice! Night is nowhere else so wonderful, unless it be in winter among the high Alps. But the nights of Venice and the nights of the mountains are too different in kind to be compared.

There is the ever-recurring miracle of the full moon rising, before day is dead, behind San Giorgio, spreading a path of gold on the lagoon which black boats traverse with a glow-worm lamp upon their prow; ascending the cloudless sky and silvering the domes of the Salute; pouring vitreous sheen upon the red lights of the Piazzetta; flooding the Grand Canal, and lifting the Rialto higher in ethereal whiteness; piercing but penetrating not the murky labyrinth of *rio* linked with *rio*, through which we wind in light and shadow, to reach once more the level glories and the luminous expanse of heaven beyond the Misericordia.

This is the melodrama of Venetian moonlight; and if a single impression of the night has to be retained from one visit to Venice, those are fortunate who chance upon a full moon of fair weather. Yet I know not whether some quieter and soberer effects are not more thrilling. To-night, for example, the waning moon will rise late through veils of *scirocco*. Over the bridges of San Cristoforo and San Gregorio, through the deserted Calle di Mezzo, my friend and I walk in darkness, pass the marble basements of the Salute, and push our way along its Riva to the point of the Dogana. We are out at sea alone, between the Canalozzo and the Giudecca. A moist wind ruffles the water and cools our forehead. It is so dark that we can only see San Giorgio by the light reflected on it from the Piazzetta. The same light climbs the Campanile of S. Mark, and shows the golden angel in a mystery of gloom. The only noise that reaches us is a confused hum from the Piazza. Sitting and musing there, the blackness of the water whispers in our ears a tale of death. And now we hear a plash of oars, and gliding through the darkness comes a single boat. One man leaps upon the landing-place without a word and disappears. There is another wrapped in a military cloak asleep. I see his face beneath me, pale and quiet. The *barcaruolo* turns the point in silence. From the darkness they came; into the darkness they have gone. It is only an ordinary incident of coastguard service. But the spirit of the night has made a poem of it.

My gondola followed the course of the small canals; like the mysterious hand of a Genie leading me through the maze of this oriental city, they seemed, as I advanced, to be carving a road for me through the heart of a crowded quarter which they clove asunder, barely dividing with a slender fissure, arbitrarily carved, the tall houses with their tiny Moorish windows; and, as though the magic guide had been holding a candle in his hand and were lighting the way for me, they kept casting ahead of them a ray of sunlight for which they cleared a path . . .

The English critic JOHN ADDINGTON SYMONDS *paid this tribute to the Venetian night in* A Venetian Medley *(1898).*

Wood engraving, 19th century.

In Albertine Disparue *(1925), the seventh novel in his masterpiece,* Remembrance of Things Past, MARCEL PROUST, *in the person of his anonymous narrator, describes the passing show of Venetian life from the vantage of a gondola.*

35

'A narrow canal in the heart of the city . . .'

The sun had barely begun to set when I went to fetch my mother from the Piazzetta. We returned up the Grand Canal in our gondola, we watched the double line of palaces between which we passed reflect the light and angle of the sun upon their rosy surfaces, and alter with them, seeming not so much private habitations and historic buildings as a chain of marble cliffs at the foot of which people go out in the evening in a boat to watch the sunset. In this way, the mansions arranged along either bank of the canal made one think of objects of nature, but of a nature which seemed to have created its works with a human imagination. But at the same time (because of the character of the impressions, always urban, which Venice gives us almost in the open sea, upon those waves whose flow and ebb make themselves felt twice daily, and which alternately cover at high tide and uncover at low tide the splendid outside stairs of the palaces), as we should have done in Paris upon the boulevards, in the Champs-Elysées, in the Bois, in any wide thoroughfare that was a fashionable resort, in the powdery evening light, we passed the most beautiful dressed women, almost all foreigners, who, propped luxuriously upon the cushions of their floating vehicle, took their place in the procession, stopped before a palace in which there was a friend whom they wished to see, sent to inquire whether she was at home; and while, as they waited for the answer, they prepared to leave a card, as they would have done at the door of the Hôtel de Guermantes, they turned to their guide-book to find out the period, the style of the palace, not without being shaken, as though upon the crest of a blue wave, by the thrust of the flashing, prancing water, which took alarm on finding itself pent between the dancing gondola and the slapping marble. And thus any excursion, even when it was only to pay calls or to go shopping, was threefold and unique in this Venice where the simplest social coming and going assumed at the same time the form and the charm of a visit to a museum and a trip on the sea.

'Unexpected winter beauty...'

The English writer OSBERT SITWELL *praised the Venetian winter in his travel book* Winters of Content *(1932).*

Once before I had visited Venice in December, though a week or two earlier and not so near Christmas. But its unexpected winter beauty had made me resolve to return there at this same season. Moreover, one learnt many things about it from seeing it at a new climatic angle and under unaccustomed lights. For example, previously I had never been able to detect any resemblance between the actual city and Canaletto's views of it, but now it became obvious, immediately, that no artist could have rendered it more truthfully or with greater feeling: for Canaletto recorded the aspect of the Venetian winter, while Guardi, whose inspired veracity I had never questioned, depicted the Venetian spring . . . In painting, there is no last vestige of the appearance of a Venetian day that has not been explored and comemorated: but at least the winter, a whole quarter of the year, remains to the writer. And this makes a sojourn in Venice during these months very agreeable to him: for how would he dare to treat of summer among the lagoons after Thomas Mann's wonderful account of it in *Tod in Venedig*, or how venture to treat of the autumn here after the flaming words of a poet have described it once for all in d'Annunzio's *Il Fuoco*? Then, again, spring everywhere is dedicated to the nineteenth-century poets of Germany and England.

'A fantastic vision at the best . . .' – painting by J. M. W. Turner, *c.*1840.

UNREAL CITY

The novelist and social critic
WILLIAM DEAN HOWELLS
*served as United States consul
in Venice from 1860 to 1864,
and published a fascinating
account of the city in his*
Venetian Life *(1869).*

The history of Venice reads like a romance; the place seems a fantastic vision at the best, from which the world must at last awake some morning, and find that after all it has only been dreaming, and that there never was any such city. There our race seems to be in earnest in nothing. People sometimes work, but as if without any aim; they suffer, and you fancy them playing at wretchedness. The Church of St Mark, standing so solidly, with a thousand years under the feet of its innumerable pillars, is not in the least gray with time – no grayer than a Greek lyric.

'All has suffered a sea-change
Into something rich and strange',

in this fantastic city. The prose of earth has risen poetry from its baptism in the sea.

The various portals, the strange projections; in short, the striking irregularity of these stately piles, delighted me beyond idea; and I was sorry to be forced to abandon them so soon, especially as the twilight, which bats and owls love not better than I do, enlarged every portico, lengthened every colonnade, and increased the dimensions of the whole, just as imagination desired. This faculty would have had full scope had I but remained an hour longer. The moon would then have gleamed upon the gigantic forms of Mars and Neptune, and discovered the statues of ancient heroes emerging from the gloom of their niches.

Such an interesting combination of objects, such regal scenery, with the reflection that many of their ornaments once contributed to the decoration of Athens, transported me beyond myself. The *sbirri* thought me distracted. True enough, I was stalking proudly about like an actor in an ancient Grecian tragedy, lifting up his hands to the consecrated fanes and images around, expecting the reply of his attendant chorus, and declaiming the first verses of Œdipus Tyrannus.

In 1780, WILLIAM BECKFORD, the future author of the Gothic romance Vathek, found himself alone as night fell in the courtyard of the Doge's Palace. The sbirri – police – must have found the antics which he recorded in Dreams, Waking Thoughts and Incidents (1783) strange indeed.

If I were to assign the particular quality which conduces to that dreamy and voluptuous existence which men of high imagination experience in Venice, I should describe it as the feeling of abstraction which is remarkable in that city and peculiar to it. Venice is the only city which can yield the magical delights of solitude. All is still and silent. No rude sound disturbs your reveries; Fancy, therefore, is not put to flight. No rude sound distracts your self-consciousness. This renders existence intense. We feel everything. And we feel thus keenly in a city not only eminently beautiful, not only abounding in wonderful creations of art, but each step of which is hallowed ground, quick with associations that, in their more various nature, their nearer relation to ourselves, and perhaps their more picturesque character, exercise a greater influence over the imagination than the more antique story of Greece and Rome.

In his early novel Contarini Fleming *(1832), the future prime minister,* BENJAMIN DISRAELI, *described Venice as haunted by its own past.*

I wonder whether we shall realize Venice this autumn. Lying half asleep, I dream . . . and at last I dream myself into Venice itself. Then I seem to wake up, for when you are at Venice it is like being in a dream, and when you dream about Venice it is like being awake. I do not know how this should be, but Venice seems made to prove that '*La Vita è un sogno.*' What the Venice dream is all the world knows. Motion that is almost imperceptible, colour too deep and gorgeous to strike the eye, gilding so massive and ancient as to wear a mist of amber brown upon its brightness, white cupolas that time has turned to pearls, marble that no longer looks like stone, but like blocks cut from summer clouds, a smooth sea that is brighter and more infinite than the sky it reflects – these are some of the

In this letter written to a friend in 1872, the English literary critic JOHN ADDINGTON SYMONDS *contemplated the paradox of the Venetian dream.*

ingredients of the dream which are too familiar for description. Nothing can describe the elemental warmth of the days, the sea-kisses of the wind at evening, the atmosphere of breathless tepid moonlight in the night. Some people dislike this part of the dream. It just suits me – only I dream of myself in it as dressed in almost nothing and very lazy.

The American poet
HENRY WADSWORTH
LONGFELLOW
wrote his sonnet 'Venice'
in 1842.

White swan of cities, slumbering in thy nest
 So wonderfully built among the reeds
 Of the lagoon, that fences thee and feeds,
  As sayeth thy old historian and thy guest!
White water-lily, cradled and caressed
 By ocean streams, and from the silt and weeds
 Lifting thy golden filaments and seeds,
  Thy sun-illumined spires, thy crown and crest!
White phantom city, whose untrodden streets
 Are rivers, and whose pavements are the shifting
 Shadows of palaces and strips of sky;
I wait to see thee vanish like the fleets
 Seen in mirage, or towers of cloud uplifting
 In air their unsubstantial masonry.

Even the sceptical American
writer MARK TWAIN
succumbed to the Venetian
spell, as he admits in his travel
book The Innocents Abroad
(1869).

Yes, I think we have seen all of Venice. We have seen, in these old churches, a profusion of costly and elaborate sepulchre ornamentation such as we never dreampt of before. We have stood in the dim religious light of these hoary sanctuaries, in the midst of long ranks of dusty monuments and effigies of the great dead of Venice, until we seemed drifting back, back, back, into the solemn past, and looking upon the scenes and mingling with the peoples of a remote antiquity. We have been in a half-waking sort of dream all the time. I do not know how else to describe the feeling. A part of our being has remained still in the nineteenth century, while another part of it has seemed in some unaccountable way walking among the phantoms of the tenth.

In Albertine Disparue
(1925), seventh part of
Remembrance of Things Past,
MARCEL PROUST *evokes*
the vagaries of memory in a city
in which getting lost is more
than just an inconvenience.

After dinner, I went out by myself, into the heart of the enchanted city where I found myself wandering in strange regions like a character in the Arabian Nights. It was very seldom that I did not, in the course of my wanderings, hit upon some strange and spacious piazza of which no guide-book, no tourist had ever told me.

I had plunged into a network of little alleys, *calli* dissecting in all directions by their ramifications the quarter of Venice isolated between a canal and the lagoon, as if it had crystallized along these innumerable, slender, capillary lines. All of a sudden, at the end of one of those little

'White phantom city, whose untrodden streets/Are rivers...'

streets, it seemed as though a bubble had occurred in the crystallized matter. A vast and splendid *campo* of which I could certainly never, in this network of little streets, have guessed the importance, or even found room for it, spread out before me flanked with charming palaces silvery in the moonlight. It was one of those architectural wholes towards which, in any other town, the streets converge, lead you and point the way. Here it seemed to be deliberately concealed in a labyrinth of alleys, like those palaces in oriental tales to which mysterious agents convey by night a person who, taken home again before daybreak, can never again find his way back to the magic dwelling which he ends by supposing that he visited only in a dream.

Marcel Proust.

On the following day I set out in quest of my beautiful nocturnal piazza, I followed *calli* which were exactly like one another and refused to give me any information, except such as would lead me farther astray. Sometimes a vague landmark which I seemed to recognize led me to suppose that I was about to see appear, in its seclusion, solitude and silence, the beautiful exiled piazza. At that moment, some evil genie which had assumed the form of a fresh *calle* made me turn unconsciously from my course, and I found myself suddenly brought back to the Grand Canal. And as there is no great difference between the memory of a dream and the memory of a reality, I ended by asking myself whether it was not during my sleep that there had occurred in a dark patch of Venetian crystallization that strange interruption which offered a vast piazza flanked by romantic palaces, to the meditative eye of the moon.

The poet and critic
ARTHUR SYMONS
*grappled with the unreality
of Venice in his* Cities of Italy
(1904).

Indeed it is difficult to think of Venice as being quite a real place, its streets of water as being exactly real streets, its gondolas as being no more than the equivalent of hansoms, its union of those elsewhere opposed sentiments of the sea, the canal, the island, walled and towered land, as being quite in the natural order of things. I had had my dreams of Venice, but nothing I had dreamed was quite as impossible as what I found. That first night, as I looked at the miraculous, many-coloured façade of St Mark's, the pale, faintly-tinged marble of the Doge's Palace, I seemed, after all, not to have left London, but to be still at the Alhambra, watching a marvellous ballet, and, as it pleases me to be, in the very midst of it, among the glittering 'properties', knocking at every step against some fragment of delicately unreal scenery, losing none of the illusion by being so close to its framework. The Doge's Palace looked exactly like beautifully painted canvas, as if it were stretched on frames, and ready to be shunted into the wings for a fresh 'set' to come forward. Yes, it is difficult to believe in Venice most of all when one is in Venice.

... Mere existence, at Venice, becomes at once romantic and spectacular: it is like living in a room without a blind, in the full sunlight. A realist, in Venice, would become a romantic, by mere faithfulness to what he saw before him.

ITALO CALVINO's *novel*
Invisible Cities *(1972) takes
the form of a dialogue between
the Venetian traveller Marco
Polo and the Great Khan of
China, in whose service he was
employed. Kublai Khan
delights in the Venetian's tales
of the strange cities he has seen
in the course of his journeys,
but wonders why there is one
city of which he never speaks.*

Did you ever happen to see a city resembling this one?' Kublai asked Marco Polo, extending his beringed hand from beneath the silken canopy of the imperial barge, to point to the bridges arching over the canals, the princely palaces whose marble doorsteps were immersed in the water, the bustle of light craft zigzagging, driven by long oars, the boats unloading baskets of vegetables at the market squares, the balconies, platforms, domes, campaniles, island gardens growing green in the lagoon's greyness.

The emperor, accompanied by his foreign dignitary, was visiting Kinsai, ancient capital of deposed dynasties, the latest pearl set in the Great Khan's crown.

'No, sire,' Marco answered, 'I should never have imagined a city like this could exist.'

The emperor tried to peer into his eyes. The foreigner lowered his gaze. Kublai remained silent the whole day.

After sunset, on the terraces of the palace, Marco Polo expounded to the sovereign the results of his missions. As a rule the Great Khan concluded his day savouring these tales with half-closed eyes until his first yawn was the signal for the suite of pages to light the flames that guided the monarch to the Pavilion of the August Slumber. But this time Kublai seemed unwilling to give in to weariness. 'Tell me another city,' he insisted.

'. . . You leave there and ride for three days between the northeast and east-by-northeast winds . . .' Marco resumed saying, enumerating names and customs and wares of a great number of lands. His repertory could be called inexhaustible, but now he was the one who had to give in. Dawn had broken when he said: 'Sire, now I have told you about all the cities I know.'

'There is still one of which you never speak.'

Marco Polo bowed his head.

'Venice,' the Khan said.

Marco smiled. 'What else do you believe I have been talking to you about?'

The emperor did not turn a hair. 'And yet I have never heard you mention that name.'

And Polo said: 'Every time I describe a city I am saying something about Venice.'

'When I ask you about other cities, I want to hear about them. And about Venice, when I ask you about Venice.'

'To distinguish the other cities' qualities, I must speak of a first city that remains implicit. For me it is Venice.'

'You should then begin each tale of your travels from the departure, describing Venice as it is, all of it, not omitting anything you remember of it.'

The lake's surface was barely wrinkled; the copper reflection of the ancient palace of the Sung was shattered into sparkling glints like floating leaves.

'Memory's images, once they are fixed in words, are erased,' Polo said. 'Perhaps I am afraid of losing Venice all at once, if I speak of it. Or perhaps, speaking of other cities, I have already lost it, little by little.'

'The Astrologer', engraving by Giulio Campagnola, 1514.

In his travel book
Pictures from Italy *(1846),*
CHARLES DICKENS
*invested the whole of his
Venetian visit with the logic of
a dream.*

Masquerade, 17th century.

I was awakened after some time (as I thought) by the stopping of the coach. It was now quite night, and we were at the water-side. There lay here, a black boat, with a little house or cabin in it of the same mournful colour. When I had taken my seat in this, the boat was paddled, by two men, towards a great light, lying in the distance on the sea.

Ever and again, there was a dismal sigh of wind. It ruffled the water, and rocked the boat, and sent the dark clouds flying before the stars. I could not but think how strange it was, to be floating away at that hour: leaving the land behind, and going on, towards this light upon the sea. It soon began to burn brighter; and from being one light became a cluster of tapers, twinkling and shining out of the water, as the boat approached towards them by a dreamy kind of track, marked out upon the sea by posts and piles.

We had floated on, five miles or so, over the dark water, when I heard it rippling, in my dream, against some obstruction near at hand. Looking out attentively, I saw, through the gloom, a something black and massive – like a shore, but lying close and flat upon the water, like a raft – which we were gliding past. The chief of the two rowers said it was a burial-place.

Full of the interest and wonder which a cemetery lying out there, in the lonely sea, inspired, I turned to gaze upon it as it should recede in our path, when it was quickly shut out from my view. Before I knew by what, or how, I found that we were gliding up a street – a phantom street; the houses rising on both sides, from the water, and the black boat gliding on beneath their windows. Lights were shining from some of these casements, plumbing the depth of the black stream with their reflected rays; but all was profoundly silent.

So we advanced into this ghostly city, continuing to hold our course through narrow streets and lanes, all filled and flowing with water. Some of the corners where our way branched off, were so acute and narrow, that it seemed impossible for the long slender boat to turn them; but the rowers, with a low melodious cry of warning, sent it skimming on, without a pause. Sometimes, the rowers of another black boat like our own, echoed the cry, and slackening their speed (as I thought we did ours) would come flitting past us, like a dark shadow. Other boats, of the same sombre hue, were lying moored, I thought, to painted pillars, near to dark mysterious doors that opened straight upon the water. Some of these were empty; in some, the rowers lay asleep; towards one, I saw some figures coming down a gloomy archway from the interior of a palace: gaily dressed, and attended by torch-bearers. It was but a glimpse I had of them; for a bridge, so low and close upon the boat that it seemed ready to fall down and crush us: one of the many bridges that perplexed the Dream:

blotted them out, instantly. On we went, floating towards the heart of this strange place – with water all about us where never water was elsewhere – clusters of houses, churches, heaps of stately buildings growing out of it – and, everywhere, the same extraordinary silence. Presently, we shot across a broad and open stream; and passing, as I thought, before a spacious paved quay, where the bright lamps with which it was illuminated showed long rows of arches and pillars, of ponderous construction and great strength, but as light to the eye as garlands of hoar-frost or gossamer – and where, for the first time, I saw people walking – arrived at a flight of steps leading from the water to a large mansion, where, having passed through corridors and galleries innumerable, I lay down to rest; listening to the black boats stealing up and down below the window on the rippling water, till I fell asleep.

The glory of the day that broke upon me in this Dream; its freshness, motion, buoyancy; its sparkles of the sun in water; its clear blue sky and rustling air; no waking words can tell. But, from my window, I looked down on boats and barks; on masts, sails, cordage, flags; on groups of busy sailors, working at the cargoes of these vessels; on wide quays, strewn with bales, casks, merchandise of many kinds; on great ships, lying near at hand in stately indolence; on islands, crowned with gorgeous domes and turrets: and where golden crosses glittered in the light, atop of wondrous churches springing from the sea! Going down upon the margin of the green sea, rolling on before the door, and filling all the streets, I came upon a place of such surpassing beauty, and such grandeur, that all the rest was poor and faded, in comparison with its absorbing loveliness.

It was a great Piazza, as I thought; anchored, like all the rest, in the deep ocean. On its broad bosom, was a Palace, more majestic and magnificent in its old age, than all the buildings of the earth, in the high prime and fulness of their youth. Cloisters and galleries: so light, they might have been the work of fairy hands: so strong that centuries had battered them in vain: wound round and round this palace, and enfolded it with a Cathedral, gorgeous in the wild luxuriant fancies of the East. At no great distance from its porch, a lofty tower, standing by itself, and rearing its proud head, alone, into the sky, looked out upon the Adriatic sea. Near to the margin of the stream, were two ill-omened pillars of red granite; one having on its top, a figure with a sword and shield; the other, a winged lion. Not far from these again, a second tower: richest of the rich in all its decorations: even here, where all was rich: sustained aloft, a great orb, gleaming with gold and deepest blue: the Twelve Signs painted on it, and a mimic sun revolving in its course around them: while above, two bronze giants hammered out the hours upon a sounding bell. An oblong square of lofty houses of the whitest stone, surrounded by a light and beautiful arcade, formed part of this enchanted scene; and, here and there, gay masts for flags rose, tapering, from the pavement of the unsubstantial ground . . .

In the luxurious wonder of so rare a dream, I took but little heed of time, and had but little understanding of its flight. But there were days and nights in it; and when the sun was high, and when the rays of lamps were crooked in the running water, I was still afloat, I thought: plashing the slippery walls and houses with the cleavings of the tide, as my black boat, borne upon it, skimmed along the streets . . .

Floating down narrow lanes, where carpenters, at work with plane and chisel in their shops, tossed the light shaving straight upon the water, where it lay like weed, or ebbed away before me in a tangled heap. Past open doors, decayed and rotten from long steeping in the wet, through which some scanty patch of vine shone green and bright, making unusual shadows on the pavement with its trembling leaves. Past quays and terraces, where women, gracefully veiled, were passing and repassing, and where idlers were reclining in the sunshine, on flag-stones and on flights of steps. Past bridges, where there were idlers too: loitering and looking over. Below stone balconies, erected at a giddy height, before the loftiest windows of the loftiest houses. Past plots of garden, theatres, shrines, prodigious piles of architecture – Gothic – Saracenic – fanciful with all the fancies of all times and countries. Past buildings that were high, and low, and black, and white, and straight, and crooked; mean and grand, crazy and strong. Twining among a tangled lot of boats and barges, and shooting out at last into a Grand Canal! There, in the errant fancy of my dream, I saw old Shylock passing to and fro upon a bridge, all built upon with shops and humming with the tongues of men; a form I seemed to know for Desdemona's, leaned down through a latticed blind to pluck a flower. And, in the dream, I thought that Shakespeare's spirit was abroad upon the water somewhere: stealing through the city . . .

But, close about the quays and churches, palaces and prisons: sucking at their walls, and welling up into the secret places of the town: crept the water always. Noiseless and watchful: coiled round and round it, in its many folds, like an old serpent: waiting for the time, I thought, when people should look down into its depths for any stone of the old city that had claimed to be its mistress.

Thus it floated me away, until I awoke in the old market place at Verona. I have, many and many a time, thought since, of this strange Dream upon the water: half-wondering if it lie there yet, and if its name be Venice.

'Merchants at their Accounts', engraving after a painting by Quentin Masys.

THE MERCHANTS OF VENICE

I passed my time at Venice very pleasantly and restfully, at small expense, and each day I went about seeing many remarkable and delightful things. Every hour there came news from all countries of the world, for the sea-borne traffic is very great, and ships are continually arriving from all parts, and if one desires to have news of any place it is only necessary to enquire of the ships.

PERO TAFUR, *visiting the city in 1436, was awed by its vast commercial network.*

47

WILLIAM SHAKESPEARE, *who never crossed the English Channel, was nonetheless familiar with Venetian dependence on foreign trade, as he demonstrated in* The Merchant of Venice *(I.i. 8–14) (1596–98).*

Y our mind is tossing on the ocean,
There where your argosies with portly sail
Like signiors and rich burghers on the flood,
Or as it were the pageants of the sea,
Do overpeer the petty traffickers
That cur'sy to them (do them reverence)
As they fly by them with their woven wings.

The scholar BERNARDO GIUSTINIANI *described the sound financial practices of the early Venetians in his* History of the Origin of Venice *(1498).*

I n their business affairs they were very careful not in any way to allow foreign injustices to be brought against their merchants, for this reason – that it is incumbent upon those whose entire means of life is engaged in foreign lands, unless they wish to perish together with their goods, to protect themselves and take care that they may be considered everywhere as immune from injury. This was especially true of the succeeding ages, that is, after the number of merchants and the size of the enterprises grew. They had a rule first to demand the things taken, and if they were not returned, then to claim them with force if they were able. If the possibility of force was lacking, then they forbade mutual commerce, so that it rarely happened that what they did not obtain in one way, they did not succeed in getting in another.

'Marvellous affluence and exuberancy' – fish market in Venice, by Ettore Tito (1859–1941).

The envoys waited . . . till the fourth day, as had been appointed them, and entered the palace, which was passing rich and beautiful; and found the Doge and his council in a chamber. There they delivered their message after this manner: 'Sire, we come to thee on the part of the high barons of France, who have taken the sign of the cross to avenge the shame done to Jesus Christ, and to reconquer Jerusalem, if so be that God will suffer it. And because they know that no people have such great power to help them as you and your people, therefore we pray you by God that you take pity on the land oversea, and the shame of Christ, and use diligence that our lords have ships for transport and battle.'

'And after what manner should we use diligence?' said the Doge. 'After all manners that you may advise and propose,' rejoined the envoys, 'in so far as what you propose may be within our means.' 'Certes,' said the Doge, 'it is a great thing that your lords require of us, and well it seems that they have in view a high enterprise. We will give you our answer eight days from to-day. And marvel not if the term be long, for it is meet that so great a matter be fully pondered.'

When the term appointed by the Doge was ended, the envoys returned to the palace. Many were the words then spoken which I cannot now rehearse. But this was the conclusion of that parliament: 'Signors,' said the Doge, 'we will tell you the conclusions at which we have arrived, if so be that we can induce our great council and the commons of the land to allow of them; and you, on your part, must consult and see if you can accept them and carry them through.

'We will build transports to carry four thousand five hundred horses, and nine thousand squires, and ships for four thousand five hundred knights, and twenty thousand sergeants of foot. And we will agree also to purvey food for these horses and people during nine months. This is what we undertake to do at the least, on condition that you pay us for each horse four marks, and for each man two marks.

'And the covenants we are now explaining to you, we undertake to keep, wheresoever we may be, for a year, reckoning from the day on which we sail from the port of Venice in the service of God and of Christendom. Now the sum total of the expenses above named amounts to 85,000 marks.

'And this will we do moreover. For the love of God, we will add to the fleet fifty armed galleys on condition that, so long as we act in company, of all conquests in land or money, whether at sea or on dry ground, we shall have the half, and you the other half. Now consult together to see if you, on your parts, can accept and fulfil these covenants.'

The envoys then departed, and said that they would consult together and give their answer on the morrow. They consulted, and talked

In 1201, the French knight GEOFFROI DE VILLEHARDOUIN arrived in Venice as part of the ill-fated Fourth Crusade. In his Chronicle (c. 1207) Villehardouin recalled the reception given the envoys of the crusading armies by their Venetian hosts, and the clever contract which the Venetians forced on them. The crusade was to lead to the conquest of Constantinople and Venetian dominance in the eastern Mediterranean.

In 1361, the signorie honoured the much-travelled Tuscan poet PETRARCH *by giving him shelter in a house overlooking the Bacino of San Marco, and from there he watched the wealth of the known world spill into Venice's lap, a scene described in a letter to a friend.*

A wine shipment on the canals.

together that night, and agreed to accept the terms offered. So the next day they appeared before the Doge, and said: 'Sire, we are ready to ratify this covenant.'

Experience makes art, says Aristotle. All the arts prove his statement; I have an example under my very eyes – the nautical art. This great city, in which I have lately taken refuge from the storms of the world, owes its remarkable growth to nagivation, next after justice … And now our ships cast off from the Italian strand, some during the grim winter just past, some in this ominous spring weather, amid wintry fogs that belie the coming of summer. Some ships sail for the sunrise, some for the sunset; some head for the north, some for the east; some are bound for Libyan Syrtes; some will turn their backs on Cadiz and the Pillars of Hercules; some will go beyond the double Bosphorus, and Colchos, and Phasis, not in quest of any golden fleece, like the ancient wonder-workers, but tempted by real gold to endure so many adventures and dangers by sea and land. Thus our wines go to slake the Britons' thirst, our honey to the Scythians. Strange, that the timbers of our forests should journey to the Greeks and the Egyptians! Our saffron, oil, and linen travel to the Syrians, the Persians, and the Arabs, and their goods come to us in return!

I will bid you spend an hour with me. Already drowsing, I was writing these words in the dead of night. The clouds hung low. When my tired pen had reached this point, suddenly a great shouting of sailors assailed my ears. Remembering its meaning from other occasions, I got up and climbed to the top floor of my house, which overlooks the harbour. I look down. Good God, what a sight! I was filled with shuddering horror, which was at the same time reverent and uplifting. Here before my door some ships had wintered, moored to the marble quayside. They rival in size the great house which this free and liberal city has granted to my use; their topmasts rise above my twin towers … If you had seen it, you would have called it not a ship but the likeness of a mountain swimming on the sea, so heavily laden, however, that a good part of its bulk was hidden beneath the waves. One vessel was perhaps bound for the river Don, for that is the limit of navigation in the Black Sea; but some of its passengers will there disembark and will not halt until they have crossed the Ganges, and the Caucasus, and have come to the farthest Indies and have reached the Eastern Ocean. Whence comes this fierce, insatiable thirst for possessions that rides the mind of men? My heart bled for them; I understood why the poets well call sailors wretched. And when I could not longer follow the ships through the darkness, I picked up my pen again, moved and stirred. And meditating on their case, I exclaimed: 'Oh, how dear to men is life, and how cheap they hold it!'

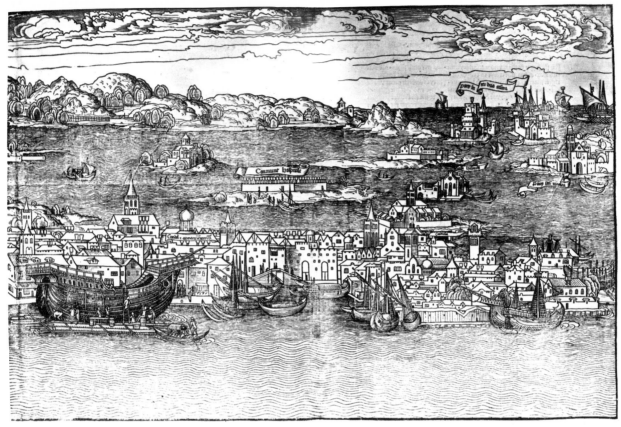

'The likeness of a mountain swimming on the sea' – woodcut, 1480.

The fairest place of all the citie (which is indeed of that admirable and incomparable beauty, that I thinke no place whatsoever, eyther in Christendome or Paganisme may compare with it) is the Piazza, that is, the Market place of St Marke . . . Truely such is the stupendious (to use a strange Epitheton for so strange and rare a place as this) glory of it, that at my first entrance thereof it did even amaze or rather ravish my senses. For here is the greatest magnificence of architecture to be seene, that any place under the sunne doth yeelde. Here you may both see all manner of fashions of attire, and heare all the languages of Christendome, besides those that are spoken by the barbarous Ethnickes; the frequencie of people being so great twise a day, betwixt sixe of the clocke in the morning and eleven, and againe betwixt five in the afternoon and eight, that (as an elegant writer saith of it) a man may very properly call it rather Orbis then Urbis forum, that is, a market place of the world, not of the citie . . .

Amongst many other things that moved great admiration in me in Venice, this was not the least, to consider the marveilous affluence and exuberancy of all things tending to the sustentation of mans life. For albeit they have neyther meadows, nor pastures, nor arable grounds neare their

Venice was the centre of the commercial world, and the Piazza San Marco was the centre of Venice, a 'market place of the world', as the English traveller THOMAS CORYAT *described it in his book* Crudities *(1611).*

51

'Great abundance ... of victuals.'

A trade economy can only flourish where credit is liberal – and debts can be secured. What made a Venetian merchant 'good' was the capital at his disposal, as SHAKESPEARE *well understood in* The Merchant of Venice *(I.iii. 9–24) (1596–98).*

Venetian commerce was in serious decline by the early seventeenth century. The traveller JAMES HOWELL, *in a letter written from Venice in August 1621, explained the principal cause of what was to become an economic crisis.*

city (which is a matter impossible, because it is seated in the sea, and distinguished with such a multitude of channels) to yeeld them corne and victuals: yet they have as great abundance (a thing very strange to be considered) of victuals, corne and fruites of all sorts whatsoever, as any city (I thinke) of all Italy. Their victuals and all other provision being very plenteously ministred unto them from Padua, Vicenza, and other bordering townes and places of Lombardy, which are in their owne dominion. For I have seene their shambles and market places (whereof they have a great multitude) exceedingly well furnished with all manner of necessaries. As for their fruits I have observed wonderful plenty amongst them, as Grapes, Peares, Apples, Plummes, Apricockes ... Figges most excellent of three or foure sorts, as blacke, which are the daintiest, greene, and yellow. Likewise they had another special commodity when I was there, which is one of the most delectable dishes for a Sommer fruite of all Christendome, namely muske Melons. I wondered at the plenty of them; for there was such store brought into the citie every morning and evening for the space of a moneth together, that not onely St Markes place, but also all the market places of the citie were super-abundantly furnished with them ...

SHYLOCK] Three thousand ducats for three months, and Antonio bound.

BASSANIO] Your answer to that.

SHYLOCK] Antonio is a good man.

BASSANIO] Have you heard any imputation to the contrary?

SHYLOCK] Ho no, no, no, no: my meaning in saying he is a good man, is to have you understand me that he is sufficient, – yet his means are in supposition: he hath an argosy bound to Tripolis, another to the Indies, I understand moreover upon the Rialto, he hath a third at Mexico, a fourth for England, and other ventures he hath squand'red abroad, – but ships are but boards, sailors but men, there be land-rats, and water-rats, water-thieves, and land-thieves, (I mean pirates), and then there is the peril of waters, winds, and rocks: the man is notwithstanding sufficient, – three thousand ducats, – I think I may take his bond.

The Wealth of this Republick hath been at a stand, or rather declining, since the Portugal found a Road to the East-Indies, by the Cape of Good-Hope; for this City was used to fetch all those Spices and other Indian Commodities from Grand Cairo down the Nile, being formerly carried to Cairo from the Red Sea upon Camels' and Dromedaries' Backs, sixty Days' Journey: And so Venice us'd to dispense those Commodities thro' all Christendom, which not only the Portugal, but the English and Hollander now transport, and are Masters of the Trade.

German merchants in the courtyard of the Fondaco dei Tedeschi, 1616.

This city stands very convenient for commerce. It has several navigable rivers that run up into the body of Italy, by which they might supply a great many countries with fish and other commodities, not to mention their opportunities for the Levant, and each side of the Adriatic. But, notwithstanding these conveniences, their trade is far from being in a flourishing condition, for many reasons. The duties are great that are laid on merchandizes. Their nobles think it below their quality to engage in traffic. The merchants, who are grown rich, and able to manage great dealings, buy their nobility, and generally give over trade. Their manufactures of cloth, glass, and silk, formerly the best in Europe, are now excelled by those of other countries. They are tenacious of old laws and customs to their great prejudice, whereas a trading nation must be still for new changes and expedients, as different junctures and emergencies arise.

In his Remarks on Several Parts of Italy *(1705), the English essayist* JOSEPH ADDISON *placed some of the blame for Venice's economic decline on the merchants themselves.*

LA SERENISSIMA

La Serenissima, the Most Serene Republic of Venice, survived for a thousand years. In The Stones of Venice *(1851–3),* JOHN RUSKIN *meditated on its history.*

The office of Doge, Venice's elected and largely ceremonial head of state, was unique to the Serenissima. In 1436 Catalan traveller PERO TAFUR *retold the story of the traitorous Doge, Marino Faliero.*

Faliero, engraving, 19th century.

It would be difficult to overrate the value of the lessons which might be derived from a faithful study of the history of this strange and mighty city: a history which, in spite of the labour of countless chroniclers, remains in vague and disputable outline, – barred with brightness and shade, like the far away edge of her own ocean, where the surf and the sandbank are mingled with the sky.

The Doge is never suffered to leave the city for any cause whatever, except to go to the monastery of St George, which is a stone's throw by sea from his palace, and when the city is unhealthy he departs thither. It happened once that a Doge went there to escape a pestilence in the city, and everyone departed for the mainland, so that none remained except the poor people. A kinsman approached the Doge and said to him: 'Lord, you have now such an opportunity as never man had. You have in your possession the treasure of Venice, the chief people have all departed, and none remain except strangers and the poor. Do what you will, take the treasure, place the crown on your head, and call yourself King of Venice, and you will wear the crown for always.' The Doge reproached him greatly for what he had said, and the matter remained secret. But some time later, when certain people spoke ill of the Doge, the kinsman repeated the counsel he had given and said: 'It serves him right since he would not be King of Venice.' Thereupon the kinsman was taken and brought before the Council that they might know the truth, and he was closely examined as to what he had said, and he confessed all. Then the lords of the Council went to the Doge and enquired if it were true, and he replied that it had happened as his kinsman had related. The lords of the Council conferred together, and finally they called the Doge and thanked him much for his loyalty to his country, but in that he had kept silence in a matter which might have threatened great danger to the State, they requested him to await their pleasure. They then ordered that great benefits should be showered upon his wife and children, but directed that he should lose his head, since none might dare to keep silence in any matter affecting the public safety. They have in the great hall ... all the arms of the Doges from the first down to the present, and also those of the Doge whom they killed among the others, these being draped in black velvet.

'The Procession of the Doge on Palm Sunday', engraving by Matteo Pagan, 1559.

Here treason has no place. Here favour in high circles does no wrong to be set right. Here no cruel mistress reigns. Here the insolent and effeminate give no commands. Here no one robs, coerces or murders. O hostelry of all the dispersed and exiled, how much greater would be the woes of Italy if your bounty were any the less! Here stands a refuge for all her nations. Here her wealth may be kept in safety. Venice opens her arms to all whom others shun. She lifts up all whom others abase. She welcomes those whom others persecute. She cheers the mourner in his grief and defends the despised and the destitute with charity and love. And so I bow to Venice with good reason. She is a living reproach to Rome.

The exiled Tuscan wit
PIETRO ARETINO
may have flattered the city which gave him shelter in 1527, but the contrast which he drew (in a letter to the Doge) between just and liberal Venice and oppressive Rome was a commonplace.

The city of Venice has safeguarded itself by having ten citizens who are empowered to punish any citizen without appeal; and, lest the ten should not suffice for the punishing of the powerful, though they have authority to do this, they have set up the tribunal of Forty; and, yet further, have decided that the Court of Rogation, which is the Greater Council, shall have power to punish them; so that there is no shortage of judges there to keep the powerful in check, given that there be no shortage of accusers.

Venice kept a constant check on the power of individuals by its unique constitution, described by
NICCOLO MACHIAVELLI
in his Discourses *(1519).*

PORTIA] It must not be, there is no power in Venice
    Can alter a decree established:
    'Twill be recorded for a precedent,
    And many an error by the same example
    Will rush into the state, – it cannot be.

SHAKESPEARE *was familiar with the Venetian obsession with rigid legality, and dramatized it in* The Merchant of Venice *(IV.i. 214–20) (1596–98).*

Habit of the Duke of Venice, in 1581.

Le Doge de Venise.

Torture by strapado, wood cut, 1541.

Venetian justice could be swift and often cruel, and the Serenissima brooked little dissent. In his Crudities *(1611),* THOMAS CORYAT *observed some luckless Venetian citizens subjected to a particularly horrific form of state torture.*

On the fourth day of August being Thursday, I saw a very Tragicall and dolefull spectacle in Saint Markes place. Two men tormented with the strapado, which is done in this manner. The offender having his hands bound behind him, is conveighed into a rope that hangeth in a pully, and after hoysed up in the rope to a great heigth with two severall swinges, where he sustaineth so great torments that his joynts are for the time loosed and pulled asunder; besides such abundance of bloud is gathered into his hands and face, that for the time he is in the torture, his face and hands doe looke as red as fire.

Let the Secret of the Republick be kept inviolably: And it is fit that our Nobility always remember the great Vogue the Venetian Prudence was in, upon the Condemnation of Carmignola, whose Sentence was kept secret for eight whole Months, notwithstanding it was pronounced in Presence of three hundred Judges; a thing which absolute Princes are not able to find in the Fidelity of only three or four Ministers, altho' excessively loaded by them with Benefits. It was a matter of no less Astonishment, whcn the Doge Foscari was deposed, to see that his Condemnation was conceal'd from him even by his own Brother. It cannot but be a great Affliction to all that wish well to their Country, to see so excellent a Quality, as this of Secrecy, and so peculiar to our Republick, diminish'd, in some measure, by the inconsiderateness of our Youth; who altho' they have no bad Design in what they do, yet out of a heedlessness, and too great freedom of Temper, blab out things of the greatest Importance. It would be necessary that every Father of a Noble Family, at the same time that he instructs his Children in the Christian Religion, should teach them likewise the use of Secrecy. And to avoid the Danger of losing it, it ought not to be allowed to any Persons whatever, not even to the Noblemen that assist in Council, to discourse of the publick Transactions, out of the Council Chamber.

I have now a good while since taken footing in Venice, this admired Maiden-City, so call'd, because she was never defloured by any Enemy since she had a Being, not since her Rialto was first erected, which is now above twelve Ages ago.

I protest to you, at my first landing I was for some days ravished with the high Beauty of this Maid, with her lovely Countenance ... This beauteous Maid hath been often attempted to be vitiated; some have *courted* her, some *bribed* her, some would have *forc'd* her, yet she hath still preserv'd her Chastity entire: and tho' she hath lived so many Ages, and passed so many shrewd brunts, yet she continueth fresh to this very day without the least Wrinkle of old Age, or any symptoms of Decay, whereunto political Bodies, as well as natural, use to be liable. Beside, she hath wrestled with the greatest Potentates upon Earth; the Emperor, the King of France, and most of the other Princes of Christendom, in that famous League of Cambray, would have sunk her; but she bore up still within her Lakes, and broke that League to pieces by her Wit: The Grand Turk hath been often at her, and tho' he could not have his will of her, yet he took away the richest Jewel she wore in her Coronet, and put it in his Turban; I mean the Kingdom of Cyprus, the only Royal Gem she had; he hath set upon her Skirts often since, and tho' she clos'd with him sometimes, yet she came off still with her Maidenhead; tho' some that

'Among all the instances of their politics,' wrote Joseph Addison of the Venetians, 'there is none more admirable than the great secrecy that reigns in their public councils.' For the Venetian scholar, Servite monk, and political scientist PAOLO SARPI, *'secrecy' was also one of the Republic's most prized traditions. In his* Maxims on the Government of Venice *(1610), he advised the* signorie *to maintain it at all costs.*

As Venetian trade declined, its cherished independence, threatened on all sides, was maintained by a combination of diplomatic ingenuity and sheer determination which impressed many visitors, including the seventeenth-century English traveller JAMES HOWELL, *who expressed his admiration in a letter written in 1620.*

envy her happiness would brand her to be of late times a kind of Concubine to him, and that she gives him ready Money once a year to lie with her, which she minceth by the name of Present, tho' it be indeed rather a Tribute.

The English essayist JOSEPH ADDISON, *in his* Remarks on Several Parts of Italy *(1705), traced the origin of the* Serenissima's *decline to its attempt to establish its rule on the Italian mainland.*

It was certainly a mighty error in this state to affect so many conquests on the *terra firma*, which has only served to raise the jealousy of the Christian princes, and, about three hundred years ago, had like to have ended in the utter extirpation of the commonwealth: whereas, had they applied themselves with the same politics and industry to the increase of their strength by sea, they might perhaps have had all the islands of the [Aegean] Archipelago in their hands, and, by consequence, the greatest fleet, and the most seamen of any other state in Europe. Besides, that this would have given no jealousy to the princes their neighbours, who would have enjoyed their own dominions in peace, and have been very well contented to have seen so strong a bulwark against all the forces and invasions of the Ottoman empire.

This republic has been much more powerful than it is at present, as it is still likelier to sink than increase in its dominions.

'Coronation of the Doge on the Giants' Staircase in the Doge's Palace', by Francesco Guardi (1712–93), in the Louvre museum, Paris.

What a strange and unexplained power certain words exercise upon the soul! I, who the evening before so bravely fortified myself with my innocence and courage, by the word tribunal was turned to a stone, with merely the faculty of passive obedience left to me.

My desk was open, and all my papers were on a table where I was accustomed to write.

'Take them,' said I, to the agent of the dreadful Tribunal, pointing to the papers which covered the table. He filled a bag with them, and gave it to one of the *sbirri* [police], and then told me that I must also give up the bound manuscripts which I had in my possession. I shewed him where they were, and this incident opened my eyes ... The books were, 'The Key of Solomon the King', 'The Zecorben', a 'Picatrix', a book of 'Instructions on the Planetary Hours', and the necessary incantations for conversing with demons of all sorts. Those who were aware that I possessed these books took me for an expert magician, and I was not sorry to have such a reputation ...

While Messer-Grande was thus rummaging among my manuscripts, books and letters, I was dressing myself in an absent-minded manner, neither hurrying myself nor the reverse. I made my toilette, shaved myself, and combed my hair; putting on mechanically a laced shirt and my holiday suit without saying a word, and without Messer-Grande – who did not let me escape his sight for an instant – complaining that I was dressing myself as if I were going to a wedding.

As I went out I was surprised to see a band of forty men-at-arms in the ante-room. They had done me the honour of thinking all these men necessary for my arrest, though, according to the axiom *Ne Hercules quidem contra duos*, two would have been enough. It is curious that in London, where everyone is brave, only one man is needed to arrest another, whereas in my dear native land, where cowardice prevails, thirty are required. The reason is, perhaps, that the coward on the offensive is more afraid than the coward on the defensive, and thus a man usually cowardly is transformed for the moment into a man of courage. It is certain that at Venice one often sees a man defending himself against twenty *sbirri*, and finally escaping after beating them soundly. I remember once helping a friend of mine at Paris to escape from the hands of forty bum-bailiffs, and we put the whole vile rout of them to flight ...

In course of time the captain of the men-at-arms came to tell me that he was under orders to take me *under the Leads*. Without a word I followed him. We went by gondola, and after a thousand turnings among the small canals we got into the Grand Canal, and landed at the prison quay. After climbing several flights of stairs we crossed a closed bridge which forms the communication between the prisons and the Doge's palace [Bridge of

As the Republic declined, it gained a sinister reputation for the arbitrary abuse of power. Charged with practising magic, the notorious Italian adventurer and author GIACOMO GIROLAMO CASANOVA *(1725–98) was arrested in 1756 by one Messer-Grande, an agent of the State Inquisition (the 'Tribunal') and sentenced to five years' imprisonment 'under the leads' – that is, the cells under the lead roof of the Doge's Palace. He recounted the event in his posthumous* Memoirs *(1826–38).*

Bust of Casanova.

Sighs], crossing the canal called Rio di Palazzo. On the other side of this bridge there is a gallery which we traversed. We then crossed one room, and entered another, where sat an individual in the dress of a noble, who, after looking fixedly at me, said, '*E quello, mettetelo in deposito.*'

This man was the secretary of the Inquisitors, the prudent Dominic Cavalli, who was apparently ashamed to speak Venetian in my presence as he pronounced my doom in the Tuscan language.

Messer-Grande then made me over to the warden of The Leads, who stood by with an enormous bunch of keys, and accompanied by two guards, made me climb two short flights of stairs, at the top of which followed a passage and then another gallery, at the end of which he opened a door, and I found myself in a dirty garret, thirty-six feet long by twelve broad, badly lighted by a window high up in the roof. I thought this garret was my prison, but I was mistaken; for, taking an enormous key, the gaoler opened a thick door lined with iron, three and a half feet high, with a round hole in the middle, eight inches in diameter, just as I was looking intently at an iron machine. This machine was like a horse shoe, an inch thick and about five inches across from one end to the other. I was thinking what could be the use to which this horrible instrument was put, when the gaoler said, with a smile, –

'I see, sir, that you wish to know what that is for, and as it happens I can satisfy your curiosity. When their excellencies give orders that anyone is to be strangled, he is made to sit down on a stool, the back turned to this collar, and his head is so placed that the collar goes round one half of the neck. A silk band, which goes round the other half, passes through this hole, and the two ends are connected with the axle of a wheel which is turned by someone until the prisoner gives up the ghost, for the confessor, God be thanked! never leaves him till he is dead.'

'All this sounds very ingenious, and I should think that it is you who have the honour of turning the wheel.'

He made no answer, and signing to me to enter, which I did by bending double, he shut me up, and afterwards asked me through the grated hole what I would like to eat.

'I haven't thought anything about it yet,' I answered. And he went away, locking all the doors carefully behind him.

'Grim visages sculptured in marble.'

The Gothic fantasist
WILLIAM BECKFORD
described mouths carved in marble, into which anonymous informers could insert denunciations of their fellow

The walls are covered in most places with grim visages sculptured in marble, whose mouths gape for accusations, and swallow every lie that malice and revenge can dictate. I wished for a few ears of the same kind, dispersed about the Doge's residence, to which one might apply one's own, and catch some account of the mysteries within; some little dialogue between the three Inquisitors, or debate in the Council of Ten.

This is the tribunal which holds the wealthy nobility in continual awe; before which they appear with trembling and terror; and whose summons they dare not disobey. Sometimes, by way of clemency, it condemns its victims to perpetual imprisonment, in close, stifling cells, between the leads and beams of the palace; or, unwilling to spill the blood of a fellow-citizen, generously sinks them into dungeons, deep under the canals which wash its foundations; so that, above and below, its majesty is contaminated by the abodes of punishment. What other sovereign could endure the idea of having his immediate residence polluted with tears? or revel in his halls, conscious that many of his species were consuming their hours in lamentations above his head, and that but a few beams separated him from the scene of their tortures? However gaily disposed, could one dance with pleasure on a pavement, beneath which lie damp and gloomy cavers, whose inhabitants waste away by painful degrees, and feel themselves whole years a-dying? Impressed by these terrible ideas, I could not regard the palace without horror, and wished for the strength of a thousand antediluvians, to level it with the sea, lay open the secret recesses of punishment, and admit free gales and sunshine into every den.

subjects in Dreams, Waking Thoughts and Incidents *(1783). Beckford's awed but hostile attitude is indicative of the reputation as a cruel police state which the* Serenissima *acquired in its last decades.*

Once did She hold the gorgeous east in fee;
And was the safeguard of the west: the worth
Of Venice did not fall below her birth,
Venice, the eldest Child of Liberty.
She was a maiden City, bright and free;
No guile seduced, no force could violate;
And, when she took unto herself a Mate,
She must espouse the everlasting Sea.

And what if she had seen those glories fade,
Those titles vanish, and that strength decay;
Yet shall some tribute of regret be paid
When her long life hath reached its final day:
Men are we, and must grieve when even the Shade
Of that which once was great, is passed away.

In 1796, Napoleon arrived in northern Italy at the head of the French revolutionary armies. In the following year he issued the Serenissima *with an ultimatum: 'I want no more Inquisition, no more Senate; I shall be an Attila to Venice.' In response, the Great Council met for the last time, and decided to abandon power to the French.* WILLIAM WORDSWORTH *commemorated the event in his sonnet 'On the Extinction of the Venetian Republic' (1802).*

'The Canal Tolentini', by Franz Richard Unterberger (1838–1902).

RISORGIMENTO

The spouseless Adriatic mourns her lord;
And, annual marriage now no more renew'd,
The Bucentaur lies rotting unrestored,
Neglected garment of her widowhood!
St Mark yet sees his lion where he stood
Stand, but in mockery of his wither'd power,
Over the proud Place where an Emperor sued,
And monarchs gazed and envied in the hour
When Venice was a queen with an unequall'd dower.

Before St Mark still glow his steeds of brass,
Their gilded collars glittering in the sun;
But is not Doria's menace come to pass?
Are they not bridled? – Venice, lost and won,
Her thirteen hundred years of freedom done,
Sinks, like a seaweed, unto whence she rose!
Better be whelm'd beneath the waves, and shun,
Even in destruction's depth, her foreign foes,
From whom submission wrings an infamous repose.

The Treaty of Vienna, signed by England, Prussia, Russia and Austria, victors over Napoleon, in 1815, assigned Venice to the Austrian Empire. LORD BYRON *made his way to Venice in 1816 and found the spectacle of its once proud citizens bowed under Austrian rule a sad one. Among the first fruits of his stay there was Canto IV of* Childe Harold, *the final instalment of the long self-dramatizing poem which had already won him so many admirers and enemies.*

I missed seeing the new Patriarch's procession to St Mark's the other day (owing to my indisposition) with six hundred and fifty priests in his rear – a 'goodly army'. – The admirable government of Vienna in its edict from thence – authorizing his installation – prescribed as part of the pageant – a '*Coach* & four horses' to show how very very '*German* to the matter' this was – you have only to suppose our Parliament commanding the Archbishop of Canterbury to proceed from Hyde park Corner to St Paul's Cathedral in the Lord Mayor's Barge – or the Margate Hoy. – There is but St Marc's place in all Venice – broad enough for a carriage to move – & it is paved with large smooth flagstones – so that the Chariot & horses of Elijah himself would be puzzled to manoeuvre upon it – those of Pharaoh might do better – for the Canals & particularly the Grand Canal are sufficiently capacious & extensive for his whole host. – of course no coach could be attempted – but the Venetians who are very naive as well as arch – were much amused with the ordinance.

BYRON mocked the absurdities of foreign imperial rule in Venice in this letter to his publisher, John Murray, written in March 1817.

The English poet
PERCY BYSSHE SHELLEY,
*a partisan of liberty and enemy
of tyrants everywhere, detested
the Venetian submission to
foreign rule, as he explained in
a letter to his friend
the novelist Thomas Love Peacock,
dated October 1818.*

Venice, which was once a tyrant, is now the next worse thing, a slave; for in fact it ceased to be free or worth our regret as a nation, from the moment that the oligarchy usurped the rights of the people. Yet, I do not imagine that it was ever so degraded as it has been since the French, and especially the Austrian yoke. The Austrians take sixty per cent in taxes, and impose free quarters on the inhabitants. A horde of German soldiers, as vicious and more disgusting than the Venetians themselves, insult these miserable people. I had no conception of the excess to which avarice, cowardice, superstition, ignorance, passionless lust, and all the inexpressible brutalities which degrade human nature, could be carried, until I had passed a few days at Venice.

In reaction to the degradation described by Byron and Shelley, the movement for Italian national unity and independence, which came to be known as the Risorgimento, *or resurgence, gained strength, at first largely among intellectuals. One of these was* DANIELE MANIN, *a Venetian lawyer, who, with his friend, the scholar Niccolo Tommaseo, agitated for Venetian independence from Austria. Manin, however, was more than just a theorizer; in this entry in his notebook in 1845, he makes clear his readiness to take action.*

I hate disorder, not only with a reasoned but with an instinctive hatred, such as I feel for all discordant elements in nature. Disorder is nevertheless a necessary instrument to begin a revolution.

Daniele Manin.

The year 1848 saw uprisings throughout Europe. In January Manin and Tommaseo presented a petition calling for home rule to the Austrian-appointed puppet-body then ruling Venice. Both were thrown into prison. In March news of a revolt in Vienna

At nine on the morning of the 17th the postal steamer from Trieste . . . entered the lagoon by the Porto di Lido. She was soon within sight of the Piazzetta. On the instant a swarm of gondolas dashed out to meet her and forestall the news, while a dense crowd assembled along the Riva degli Schiavoni to await the issue. A French merchant, well known in the city, leaned over the side of the steamer and shouted to the gondolas that the revolution had triumphed in Vienna, that Metternich had fled and that constitutional Government was to be established throughout the Empire. He held over the bulwarks the charred remains of a portrait of the fallen

Minister, burnt by the mob of Trieste the night before. The gondolas raced back to the quay, shouting the news. The crowd made a rush back to the Piazza, and raised under the Governor's window a clamour such as had not been heard in Venice for centuries. *'Fuori Manine e Tommaseo!'* [Release Manin and Tommaseo!] Fast as men could run or row, the tidings spread, and people from every quarter of the city flung down their work and came thronging into the Piazza, till the great open-air hall and its approaches could hold no more. *'Fuori Manin e Tommaseo!'* It was the voice of Venice, of a new Venice, unknown to Goldoni, to Buonaparte or to Byron.

(later suppressed) reached Venice and spurred the people to their own insurrection. Their first act was to demand the release of Manin and Tommaseo, a scene described by G. M. TREVELYAN *in his* Manin and the Venetian Revolution of 1848 *(1926).*

Citizens, I have yet to learn what are the events which have taken me from the silence of my prison and brought me on men's shoulders to the Piazza of S. Mark. But I see in your faces and by your attitude that love of country and national spirit have made great progress here during my imprisonment. I rejoice at that and thank you in the name of our country. But do not forget that there can be no true liberty, and that liberty cannot last, where there is not order. You must be jealous guardians of order if you hope to preserve freedom.

Freed by the Venetian people, MANIN *found himself addressing a huge crowd in the Piazza San Marco. He appealed to them in the name of a newly awakened national (Venetian) spirit.*

We are free, and we have a double right to boast of it because we have become free without shedding a drop of blood, either our own or our brothers', for I call all men brothers. But it is not enough to have overthrown the old Government; we must put another in its place. The right one, I think, is the Republic. It will remind us of our past glories improved by modern liberties. We do not thereby mean to separate ourselves from our Italian brothers. Rather we will form one of those centres which must bring about the gradual fusion of Italy into one. *Viva la repubblicà! Viva la Libertà! Viva San Marco!*

Days later, again in a crowded Piazza San Marco, MANIN *officially proclaimed the new Republic of Venice.*

The last days of July saw the beginning of the end – the bombardment of the city itself, followed by cholera and famine.

The Austrians had bethought them of a better way than balloons to make the rebel city taste of war. The cannon were dismounted from their carriages, and arranged on beds of timber [on the railway causeway joining Venice to the mainland] with the breeches sunk in the earth, so as to give them an elevation of $45°$. By firing high in the air a greater range was obtained, and projectiles could be thrown into two-thirds of the city – the regions of S. Mark's and the Arsenal remaining still out of range.

On the night of July 29 this new device was sprung on sleeping Venice. The inhabitants of the landward quarters woke to find cannon balls crashing into their bedrooms. For the first time in history Venice was

The Austrians soon restored their power in northern Italy, and gradually encircled the reborn and rebellious Venetian Republic. But as in the past, the sea-city proved nearly unconquerable. Manin, as President of the Revolutionary Republic, lead the resistance. G. M. TREVELYAN *describes the remarkable days of the siege and bombardment.*

Austrian bombardment of Venice – by balloon, 1848.

being bombarded. It was a night of alarm and horror, but not of panic. The poorest families in Venice gathered up their bedding and chattels and fled by alleys and canals, beneath the sky lighted with bursting shells and red-hot balls. They were much more angry than dismayed, and next morning the spirit of resistance was stronger than ever: it was not the bombardment that caused Venice to surrender.

The fugitives were made welcome in the houses of their wealthier neighbours beyond range of the enemy's guns, and were gradually passed on to the islands beyond. But the overcrowding and confusion was an added cause of the spread of cholera and famine in the next three weeks.

As the projectiles could only reach Venice by falling from a height after their force was spent, they seldom penetrated beyond the top floor. The heated balls were dangerous in causing fires, but the firemen worked with a will and it was said that only one house was completely destroyed ...

For three weeks the bombardment continued, and the cholera grew worse. Men, women, and children, weakened by famine, fell an easy prey to disease. By this time medical stores had run out, wine and spirits were finished, fish and flesh were very rare, and the polenta [maize meal] and vegetables on which almost every one had to live could not last for many days. The just distribution of food and the necessary sanitary measures were well organized by Government, in spite of the difficulties created by the emigration of so many fugitives from the bombarded districts. The Swiss Captain Debrunner, who in ten days lost a quarter of his remaining men by cholera, admired the action of the authorities and the spirit of the people. As he hastened along the alleys, meeting a funeral at every turn, and reading on door after door the inscription 'closed for the death of the *padrone*', he was astonished to observe nothing but *Viva Manin* and *Viva la Repubblica*, scrawled on the walls, and never to hear or see a sign that anybody wished to surrender.

At the beginning of the revolution I said ..., 'This people which now cries *Viva Manin* will soon be crying *Morte a Manin'*. And this I said in the full belief that it must be so. I was wrong. The survival of my popularity to the very last has astonished me, moved me and saddened me.

MANIN himself was surprised by the people's steadfastness, as he remarked in his notebook (1848).

If there be more than one opinion among men elsewhere concerning the means by which Austria acquired Venetia and the tenure by which she holds the province, there would certainly seem to be no division on the question in Venice. To the stranger first inquiring into public feeling, there is something almost sublime in the unanimity with which the Venetians appear to believe that these means were iniquitous, and that this tenure is abominable; and though shrewder study and carefuller observation will develop some interested attachment to the present government, and some interested opposition to it; though after-knowledge will discover, in the hatred of Austria, enough meanness, lukewarmness, and selfish ignorance to take off its sublimity, the hatred is still found marvellously unanimous and bitter ... Venice has always hated her masters with an exasperation deepened by each remove from the hope of independence, and she now detests them with a rancor which no concession short of absolute relinquishment of dominion would appease.

In early 1849, the desperate Venetians surrendered and the Austrians re-occupied the city. WILLIAM DEAN HOWELLS, *United States consul in Venice in the 1860s, observed the unyielding hostility between imperious Austrians and rebellious Venetians. He described the accompanying social strains in his book* Venetian Life *(1869).*

Instead, therefore, of finding that public gayety and private hospitality in Venice for which the city was once famous, the stranger finds himself planted between two hostile camps, with merely the choice of sides open to him. Neutrality is solitude and friendship with neither party; society is exclusive association with the Austrians or with the Italians. The latter do not spare one of their own number if he consorts with their masters, and though a foreigner might expect greater allowance, it is seldom shown to him. To be seen in the company of officers is enmity to Venetian freedom, and in the case of Italians it is treason to country and to race. Of course, in a city where there is a large garrison and a great many officers who have nothing else to do, there is inevitably some international love-making, although the Austrian officers are rigidly excluded from association with the citizens. But the Italian who marries an Austrian severs the dearest ties that bind her to life, and remains an exile in the heart of her country. Her friends mercilessly cast her off, as they cast off every body who associates with the dominant race. In rare cases I have known Italians to receive foreigners who had Austrian friends, but this with the explicit understanding that there was to be no sign of recognition if they met them in the company of these detested acquaintance ... As the social life of Italy, and especially of Venice, was in great part to be once enjoyed at the theatres, at the caffè, and at the other places of public resort, so is its absence now to be chiefly noted in those places. No lady of perfect standing among her people goes to the opera, and the men never go in the boxes, but if they frequent the theatre at all, they take places in the pit, in order that the house may wear as empty and dispirited a look as possible. Occasionally a bomb is exploded in the theatre, as a note of reminder, and as means of keeping away such of the nobles as are not enemies of the government. As it is less easy for the Austrians to participate in the diversion of comedy, it is a less offence to attend the comedy, though even this is not good Italianissimism. In regard to the caffè, there is a perfectly understood system by which the Austrians go to one, and the Italians to another; and Florian's, in the Piazza, seems to be the only common ground in the city on which the hostile forces consent to meet. This is because it is thronged with foreigners of all nations, and to go there is not thought a demonstration of any kind. But the other caffè in the Piazza do not enjoy Florian's cosmopolitan immunity, and nothing would create more wonder in Venice than to see an Austrian officer at the Specchi, unless, indeed, it were the presence of a good Italian at the Quadri.

It is in the Piazza that the tacit demonstration of hatred and discontent chiefly takes place. Here, thrice a week, in winter and summer, the military band plays that exquisite music for which the Austrians are famous. The selections are usually from Italian operas, and the attraction is

Giuseppe Garibaldi (1807–82).

the hardest of all others for the music-loving Italian to resist. But he does resist it. There are some noble ladies who have not entered the Piazza while the band was playing there, since the fall of the Republic of 1849 ... they pass from the Piazza when the music begins, and walk upon the long quay at the sea-side of the Ducal Palace; or if they remain in the Piazza they pace up and down under the arcades on either side; for Venetian patriotism makes a delicate distinction between listening to the Austrian band in the Piazza and hearing it under the Procuratie, forbidding the first and permitting the last. As soon as the music ceases the Austrians disappear, and the Italians return to the Piazza.

The city gave Garibaldi a brilliant reception. The Grand Canal was almost transformed into a continuous bridge; to get into our boat when we set out we had to cross dozens of others ... I found Garibaldi neither ill nor any older since our meeting in London in 1864. But he was depressed, worried and not talkative with the Venetians who were presented to him next day. His real retinue was the masses of the people; he grew more lively at Chioggia, where the boatmen and fishermen were expecting him. Mingling with the crowd he said to those poor, simple people:

'How happy and at home I am with you, how deeply I feel that I was born of working folk and have been a working man; the misfortunes of our country tore me away from my peaceful occupations. I too grew up on the sea-coast and know the work of each one of you ...'

A murmur of delight drowned the words of the former boatman and the people rushed upon him.

'Give a name to my newborn child,' cried a woman.

'Bless mine.'

'And mine,' shouted the others.

In 1866 Venice at last secured its independence when the people of Venice and the adjoining mainland voted by 674,426 to 69 in favour of joining the newly formed Kingdom of Italy. In 1869 the Russian radical ALEXANDER HERZEN *was visiting Venice where he was joined by his old comrade Giuseppe Garibaldi, former leader of the Italian revolutionary armies. Herzen reported Garibaldi's reception in the Russian exile periodical* The Bell.

'A Canal Scene', by Santoro Rubens (1859–1942).

VENEZIANI: SIGNORIE E POPOLANI

The condition of the times forced them to belittle and undertake every labour. Whatever the human spirit desires, by indifference to effort, it easily acquires. They did not avoid any perils on the sea; they did not refuse any trials at home. They confronted every difficulty of existence to sustain themselves and their families. It is well enough known that they were especially frugal, for that which is acquired by toil is more carefully retained. Their way of life was poor. Food and drink were simple. They paid no attention to apparel, being scantily dressed, since they could well support heat and cold to which they were inured. Their houses were humble. They were content with little for they were accustomed to the least. Sufficient to each was his own, sufficing also to his wife and children.

BERNARDO GIUSTINIANI celebrated the austere industriousness of the lagoon's early inhabitants in his History of the Origin of Venice *(1498).*

With my thesis that where there are gentry it is impossible to set up a republic, the experience of the Venetian republic may, perhaps, appear to be incompatible, for in that republic no man may hold any office unless he be a 'gentleman'. To which the answer is that this case in no way conflicts with my thesis, since 'gentlemen' in this republic are so in name rather than in point of fact; for they do not derive any considerable income from estates: their great wealth is based on merchandise and movable goods. Moreover, none of them have castles, nor have they any jurisdiction over men. The name 'gentleman' in their case is but a title, indicative of their standing. It is not based on any of the grounds which lead other cities to call people 'gentlemen'. Just as in other republics different classes go by different names, so in Venice the population is divided into 'gentlemen' and 'commoners'; and it has decided that of these the former alone shall hold, or be eligible for, office, from which the latter are wholly excluded.

Other Italian city-states were ruled by great land-owners whose titles and powers were drawn from vast estates. In Venice, of course, there was little land to own, and the ruling class was drawn instead from wealthy merchants, who excluded commoners from all privilege and prestige. NICCOLO MACHIAVELLI *was impressed by the Venetian social system, and contrasted it with other Italian cities in his* Discourses *(1519).*

The Milanese cleric CANON PIETRO CASOLA *visited Venice on his way to the Holy Land in 1494. There he observed the appearance and manners of the Venetian ruling class – the* signorie *or lords – and recorded his observations in the account of his travels which he wrote several years later.*

In Venice, alone among Italian city-states, no single individual or family ever usurped total power. In his Maxims on the Government of Venice *(1610), the scholar and Servite monk* PAOLO SARPI *attributed this to a healthy competition among the* signorie.

As the day of our departure was drawing near, I determined to leave everything else and study the owners of the many beautiful things I have noted – that is, the Venetian gentlemen, who give themselves this title. I have considered the qualities of these Venetian gentlemen. For the most part they are tall, handsome men, astute and very subtle in their dealings, and whoever has to do business with them must keep his eyes and ears well open. They are proud – I think this is on account of their great dominions – and when a son is born to a Venetian gentleman they say themselves, 'A Lord is born into the world.' They are frugal and very modest in their manner of living at home; outside the house they are very liberal.

I dare be bold to prophesy, that the Republick of Venice will never suffer that Fate which has been the end of all other Commonwealths; that is, that the Authority of many having been reduced into the Hands of a few Persons, and from a few into the Hands of one, all Commonwealths have ended in a Monarchy. The Emulation that is, not only between the Nobles of the first Rank, and those who aspire at being greater, but likewise between the Noblemen of one and the same Family, nay even between Brothers, secures us from this Danger. And if ever it should fall out, which is utterly impossible, that the Brothers of one Family should have it in their power to make a Dictator of the Commonwealth, they would never agree in the Choice of any one of themselves; and they would rather chuse to remain Noblemen of a Republick, where they shar'd the Authority with a hundred others, than be Princes of the Blood Royal, and Brothers to the King.

Venetian patricians engaged in *broglio* – political intrigue, 1669.

I have observed a thing amongst the Venetians, that I have not a little wondred at, that their Gentlemen and greatest Senators, a man worth perhaps two millions of duckats, will come into the market, and buy their flesh, fish, fruites, and such other things as are necessary for the maintenance of their family: a token indeed of frugality, which is commendable in all men; but me thinkes it is not an argument of true generosity, that a noble spirit should deject it selfe to these petty and base matters, that are fitter to be done by servants then men of a generose parentage. Therefore I commend mine owne countrey-man, the English Gentleman, that scorneth to goe into the market to buy his victuals and other necessaries for house-keeping, but employeth his Cooke or Cator about those inferior and sordid affaires.

Like many English travellers, THOMAS CORYAT *was surprised to find the great Venetian lords traipsing the streets and markets and rubbing shoulders with the common people. He objected to the practice in his* Crudities *(1611).*

Leaving the horrors of the galley for the ancient home of my ancestors, I palpitated between pleasure at escaping into freedom, hope of being able to make my friend comfortable, and uneasiness lest this hope might prove ill-founded.

We reached the entrance, and my companion gazed with wonder at the stately structure of the mansion, which has really all the appearance of a palace. As a connoisseur of architecture, he complimented me upon its fine design. I answered, what indeed he was about to discover by experience, that attractive exteriors sometimes mask discomfort and annoyance. He had plenty of time to admire the façade, while I kept knocking loudly at the house-door. I might as well have knocked at the portal of a sepulchre. At last a woman, named Eugenia, the guardian-angel of this wilderness, ran to open. To my inquiries she answered, yawning, that the family were in Friuli, but that my brother Gasparo was momently expected. Our luggage had now been brought from the boat, and we began to ascend a handsome marble staircase. No one could have expected that this fine flight of steps would lead to squalor and the haunts of indigence. Yet on surmounting the last stair this was what revealed itself. The stone floors were worn into holes and fissures, which spread in all directions like a cancer. The broken window panes let blasts from every point of the compass play freely to and fro within the draughty chambers. The hangings on the walls were ragged, smirched with smoke and dust, fluttering in tatters. Not a piece remained of that fine gallery of pictures which my grandfather had bequeathed as heirlooms to the family. I only saw some portraits of my ancestors by Titian and Tintoretto still staring from their ancient frames. I gazed at them; they gazed at me; they wore a look of sadness and amazement, as though inquiring how the wealth which they had gathered for their offspring had been dissipated.

The Venetian playwright CARLO GOZZI, *author of* The Love of Three Oranges *and other romantic fantasies popular in the late eighteenth century, was the scion of an old Venetian family. Like many other* signorie *in the declining decades of the* Serenissima, *it had fallen on hard times. In his autobiography,* Useless Memories *(1797), Gozzi describes his unpleasant return home with an army friend, after three years away on military service.*

Whilst the private lives and public pastimes of the Venetian ruling class are extensively recorded in histories, journals, letters and documents, the saga of the majority, the popolani, *the people whose voices were excluded from the Serenissima's councils, is largely hidden from view. At the height of Venice's power and wealth, in the late Middle Ages, both the Venetian workers and the extensive middle class (professionals whose skills were indispensable to the merchant-lords) enjoyed a relatively high standard of living, as observed by the Catalan traveller* PERO TAFUR *in 1436.*

The common people are unusually wealthy, as I saw during the Carnival, at a masquerade in the Doge's Palace. Two galleys came by sea, and they were supposed to bring, the one the Emperor, who came with thirty knights dressed in brocade, and the other the Grand Master of Rhodes who was clad in black velvet. The ladies who received them were attired in brocades, and wore rich jewels, and, of a truth, I saw some who wore three different dresses at that festivity, and even that was not accounted extraordinary. All these people were of the middle classes of the city, and not of the better classes nor the richest.

The *signorie* at play, from a 16th-century woodcut.

16 December 1527. Everything is dear, and every evening, on the Piazza San Marco, in the streets and at Rialto stand children crying 'Bread, bread! I am dying of hunger and cold!', which is a tragedy. In the morning, dead have been found under the portals of the palace. Yet no measures are taken.

2 February 1528. After dinner a Cabinet meeting was held, the city full of feasting and many masquerades; and, by contrast, a great horde of poor by day and by night; and many peasants are beginning to come here with their children, looking for food, because of the great famine outside. Yet this morning we heard that some ships were arrived with corn...

20 February 1528. I must record a notable thing, which I want to be a perpetual memorial of the great famine in this city. Apart from the poor who belong to Venice and are crying in the streets, they have come from the island of Burano, mostly with their clothes upon their heads and children in their arms, asking for charity. And many have come from the provinces of Vicenza and Brescia – a shocking thing. You cannot hear Mass without ten paupers coming to beg for alms, or open your purse to buy something without the poor asking for a farthing. Late in the evening they go knocking at the doors, and crying through the streets 'I am dying of hunger!' Yet no public measures are taken against this.

As a water-bound trading centre, Venice imported most of its food from outlying islands and the mainland. In the first decades of the sixteenth century, warfare laid waste much of northern Italy. Famine raged on the Venetian mainland and soon spread to the island city itself.
MARINO SANUTO, *a Venetian gentleman, part-time politician and obsessive diarist, observed its effects on the* popolani *and the failure of the* Serenissima *to do anything about it, in these diary entries.*

The names Nicolotto and Castellano indicate two factions which have divided the *popolo* – not the aristocracy – of Venice since ever they had a history. The names cannot be younger than the twelfth century, and probably date much further back than that; yet they exist with full life and meaning in modern Venice, and waken her people to a pitch of real enthusiasm...

A match had been arranged between two famous champions. Zatta, the challenger, represented the Nicolotti, while Domenico de Gasparis, commonly called Fighetti, had the sympathy of all good Castellani. The course chosen was from the Lido to Fusina and back again to San Giorgio Maggiore – a distance of some twelve miles. The Nicolotti had won the last regatta. There was, therefore, great excitement on the present occasion. The match was to be rowed in ordinary gondolas, and each champion chose his second man to take the bow oar. The Castellani undoubtedly had the prettier boat; their crew showed the finer form. But the Nicolotti were the stronger, and were also credited with great lasting powers; so that they started favourites...

...Presently comes the thud of a gun, borne muffled and thick upon the wind. There is an indistinguishable moving mass of boats by the point of the gardens; then, in six or seven minutes, the race sweeps by. The

For centuries, the Venetian working classes divided themselves into two factions, the Nicolotti and Castellani, according to which part of the city they were born in. The factions engaged in ritual pitched battles and all manner of competitions, which were pursued at times in deadly earnest. The English expatriate and adoptive Venetian HORATIO BROWN *described their rivalry in* Life on the Lagoons *(1884).*

Castellani are leading, rowing in splendid style; the Nicolotti close behind, plodding heavily, but looking dangerous in their evident strength, so essential for the ten miles of windy watercourse before them. But the Castellani are leading, so the red scarfs may chatter, shout, and rejoice, while the black keep silence. Then all the boats turn round and follow the race, the men rowing with all their might, shouting, gibing, screaming to each other – a mass of floating criticism, crossing and recrossing like black shuttles on the grey web of the water, yet with consummate skill avoiding the slightest touch upon any neighbouring boat. And, looking back, the race and its following is like a comet with a long black tail, taking the curve of the canal by the Redentore . . .

But the speed is too great to allow the spectators to keep up with the race. At the end of the Giudecca the crowd has shouted itself breathless.

Ritual battle between *Nicolloti* and *Castellani*, 16th century.

Most of the boats lie-to, or are moored to the shore, waiting till the race comes back. In a little more than an hour there is a stir far away across the lagoon, by the little island of Saint George-among-the-Seaweed. Then the two white gondolas creep into clearness. They have chosen different courses, one on each side of the wide canal. The Castellani are still ahead, but apparently losing ground, for they have taken the line where the current of the incoming tide flows strongest. Each gondola urges surely forward, followed by the boatmen of their respective factions, shouting advice, objurgations, entreaties, encouragement. The comet's tail, divided now, and not in mass, streams down either side of the Giudecca; and the excitement grows intense, for it is impossible to determine who is winning, the space that separates the racers is too great. But at length the façade of San Giorgio Maggiore is reached. A cry of 'Bravo, Fighetti!' is borne over the water and caught up all round. To the delight of the Castellani, their champion has won. Within five minutes of the finish every boat of all the throng has swiftly and mysteriously disappeared, each about its daily business, leaving the broad and grey lagoon fretted into tiny waves beneath a cold east wind, and the signori just thinking of getting out of bed.

Woodcut from a book by Aldus Manutius.

Apart from six hundred others, there are two things in particular which continually interrupt my work. First, the frequent letters of learned men which come to me from every part of the world and which would cost me whole days and nights if I were to reply. Then there are the visitors who come, partly to greet me, partly to see what new work is in hand, but mostly because they have nothing better to do. 'All right,' they say, 'Let's drop in on Aldus!' So they come in crowds, and sit around with their mouths open, 'Like leeches which will not let go of the skin until they have a bellyfull of blood.' I say nothing of those who come to recite a poem to me or a piece of prose, usually rough and unpolished, which they want me to print for them.

I have at last begun to defend myself from these thoroughly tedious visitors and their interruptions. When those who write to me have nothing very important to say, I do not reply at all: or if it is important, I reply in few words. I ask my friends not to be offended by this, or to take it in any way other than that intended: for it is not pride or scorn that makes me act in this way, but the need to spend what time I have in editing good books. As far as those who come to greet me, or come for any other reason, are concerned: well, I have taken care to warn them with a notice against bothering me any more, or continually breaking in upon my work and study. A notice stands like some sort of an edict above the door of my room, and the words are these: 'Whoever you are, Aldus

In the interests of social stability, the Serenissima *discouraged the hero-worship in which other Italian cities so liberally indulged, and promoted instead a virtual cult of anonymity. As a result, few charismatic characters appear in the annals of Venice. One exception is* ALDUS MANUTIUS *(1449–1515), inventor of elegant typefaces, publisher of Europe's first illustrated printed books, and friend to a generation of humanist scholars. Aldus was not always pleased with the burdens of commercial success and international fame, as he revealed in this preface to one of his fine scholarly editions.*

asks you again and again: if there is anything you want from him, please state your business quickly and get on your way, unless you are going to take his work on your shoulders, as Hercules did for weary Atlas. There will always be something for you, or for anyone else who comes along, to do.'

He seemeth, as in countenance so in spirit, liker to Philip Melanchton than to Luther, and peradventure a fitter instrument to overthrow the falsehood by degrees than on a sudden; which accordeth with a frequent saying on his own, that in these operations *non bisogna far salti* [no need to make jumps]. He is by birth a Venetian, and well skilled in the humours of his own country. For learning, I think I may justly call him the most deep and general scholar of the world, and above other parts of knowledge, he seemeth to have looked very far into the subtleties of the Canonists, which part of skill gave him introduction into the Senate. His power of speech consisteth rather in the soundness of reason than in any other natural ability. He is much frequented, and much intelligenced of all things that pass; and, lastly, his life is the most irreprehensible and exemplar that hath ever been known. These are his parts, set down (I protest unto your Lordship) rather with modesty than excess.

One of the articles for which I was most keenly attacked, was a violation of the purity of the language. I was a Venetian, and I had had the disadvantage of sucking in with my mother's milk the use of a very agreeable and seductive patois, which, however, was not Tuscan.

I learned by principle, and cultivated by reading, the language of the good Italian authors; but first impressions will return at times, notwithstanding every attention used in avoiding them.

I had undertaken a journey into Tuscany, where I remained for four years with the view of becoming familiar with the language; and I printed the first edition of my works at Florence, under the eyes and the criticism of the learned of that place, that I might purify them from errors of lanaguage; all my precautions were insufficient to satisfy the rigorists; I always failed in one thing or other; and I was perpetually reproached with the original sin of Venetianism.

Amidst all this tedious trifling, I recollected one day, that Tasso had been worried his whole life time by the academicians *de la Crusca*, who maintained that his Jerusalem Delivered had not passed through the sieve, which is the emblem of their society.

I was then in my closet, and I turned my eyes towards the twelve quarto volumes of the works of that author, and exclaimed: 'O heavens! must no one write in the Italian language, who has not been born in Tuscany?'

To begin with Goldoni. I recognized in him an abundance of comic motives, truth, and naturalness. Yet I detected a poverty and meanness of intrigue; nature copied from the fact, not imitated: virtues and vices ill-adjusted, vice too frequently triumphant; plebeian phrases of low double meaning, particularly in his Venetian plays; surcharged characters; scraps and tags of erudition, stolen Heaven knows where, and clumsily brought in to impose upon the crowd of ignoramuses. Finally, as a writer of Italian – except in the Venetian dialect, of which he showed himself a master – he seemed to me not unworthy to be placed among the dullest, basest, and least correct authors who have used our idiom.

...I do not think that, with the single exception of his *Beneficent Grumbler*, which he wrote at Paris, which suited the French theatre, but which had no success in its Italian translation here, he ever produced a perfect dramatic piece. At the same time I must add that he never produced on without some excellent comic trait. In my eyes he had always the appearance of a man who was born with the innate sense of how sterling comedies should be composed, but who, by defect of education, by want of discernment, by the necessity of satisfying the public and supplying new wares to the poor Italian comedians through whom he gained his livelihood, and by the hurry in which he produced so many pieces every year to keep himself afloat, was never able to fabricate a single play which does not swarm with faults.

'I shall not die, but live and declare the works of the Lord.' Our lords of state are bound to do all in their power to keep a prisoner under the Leads, and on the other hand the prisoner, who is fortunately not on parole, is bound also to make his escape. Their right to act thus is founded on justice, while the prisoner follows the voice of nature; and since they have not asked him whether he will be put in prison, so he ought not to ask them leave to escape.

Jacques Casanova, writing in the bitterness of his heart, knows that he may have the ill luck to be recaptured before he succeeds in leaving the Venetian territory and escaping to a friendly state; but if so, he appeals to the humanity of the judges not to add to the misery of the condition from which, yielding to the voice of nature, he is endeavouring to escape. He begs them, if he be taken, to return him whatever may be in his cell, but if he succeed he gives the whole to Francis Soradaci, who is still a captive for want of courage to escape, not like me preferring liberty to life. Casanova entreats their excellencies not to refuse the poor wretch this gift. Dated an hour before midnight, in the cell of Count Asquin, on October 31st, 1756.

Goldoni's fierce rival, and harsh critic, the dramatist CARLO GOZZI *(1720–1806), gave this surprisingly balanced account of his enemy's achievements in his autobiography,* Useless Memories *(1797).*

GIACOMO GIROLAMO CASANOVA *(1725–98) became perhaps the most famous – in some quarters infamous – Venetian of all, largely due to his posthumous* Memoirs *(1826–38). During his last moments in the* Serenissima's *prison, just before his escape through an opening in the lead roof of the Doge's Palace, he penned this letter to his jailers.*

Here is the scene at the chief gondola stand — on the quay under the 2 famous columns — 805

Watercolour by R. Caldecott, 1880.

FORESTIERI

*In its heyday as a trading port and pilgrimage post, Venice was host to a large,
ever-changing population of foreigners, or* forestieri. *The prosperity of the State
depended on the confidence of these foreigners and the rigour of the rule of law.*

In WILLIAM SHAKESPEARE's
The Merchant of Venice
*(III. iii. 25–30) (1596–98),
the merchant Antonio despairs of
being released from his debt to
Shylock.*

The duke cannot deny the course of law:
  For the commodity that strangers have
With us in Venice, if it be denied,
Will much impeach the justice of the state,
Since that the trade and profit of the city
Consisteth of all nations.

Give my willing service to our Prior for me; tell him to pray God for me that I may be protected, and especially from the French sickness; I know of nothing that I now dread more than that, for well nigh everyone has got it. Many men are quite eaten up and die of it.

ALBRECHT DÜRER *visited Venice in 1506. In this letter, Dürer voiced a common anxiety among male visitors.*

M. de Montaigne said that he had found Venice different from what he had anticipated, and that, after he had made a diligent visitation of the city, he was somewhat disappointed. The government, the situation, the arsenal, the Place of St Mark, and the vast crowds of foreigners, seemed to him most worthy of remark of anything he saw.

. . . Provisions are as dear here as in Paris, but it is the cheapest town in the world for living, for a train of servants is here quite useless, and every one goes about unattended. The cost of apparel is in like degree moderate; moreover, no one has occasion for a horse.

The French philosopher MICHEL DE MONTAIGNE *was a disgruntled, parsimonious traveller in 1580, as he recorded in his* Journal *(1581), which he wrote in the third person.*

I will also adde that here is great concourse of all nations, as well for the pleasure the City yeeldeth, as for the free conversation; and especially for the commodity of trafficke. That in no place is to be found in one market place such variety of apparell, languages, and manners . . . That no stranger may lie in the City more then a night, without leave of the Magistrates appointed for that purpose; but the next day telling them some pretended causes of your comming to the Towne, they will easily grant you leave to stay longer, and after that you shall be no more troubled, how long soever you stay, onely your Host after certaine daies giveth them account of you. To conclude this most noble City, as well for the situation, freeing them from enemies, as for the freedome of the Common-wealth, preserved from the first founding, and for the freedome which the Citizens and very strangers have, to injoy their goods, and dispose of them, and for manifold other causes, is worthily called in Latine Venetia, as it were *Veni etiam*, that is, come againe.

The English traveller FYNES MORYSON, *who visited Venice in 1596, described its cosmopolitan culture and tolerant but watchful attitude towards foreigners in his* Itinerary *(1617).*

I am impatient to hear good sense pronounced in my native tongue; having only heard my language out of the mouths of boys and governors for these five months. Here are inundations of them broke in upon us this carnival, and my apartment must be their refuge; the greater part of them having kept an inviolable fidelity to the languages their nurses taught them; their whole business abroad (as far as I can perceive) being to buy new clothes, in which they shine in some obscure coffee-house, where they are sure of meeting only one another; and after the important conquest of some waiting gentlewoman of an opera queen, whom perhaps they remember as long as they live, return to England excellent judges of men and manners. I find the spirit of patriotism so

The poet, playwright and diplomat's wife MARY WORTLEY MONTAGU *lived in Venice off and on between 1720 and 1760. Her intimate knowledge of Venetian society made her short-tempered with her tourist compatriots, as she explained in this letter to her friend, the Countess of Pomfret, in February 1740.*

strong in me every time I see them, that I look on them as the greatest blockheads in nature; and, to say truth, the compound a booby and *petit maître* makes up a very odd sort of animal.

In 1765, historian
EDWARD GIBBON,
was unimpressed by his brief experience of Venice.

The spectacle of Venice afforded some hours of astonishment and some days of disgust. Old and in general ill-built houses, ruined pictures, and stinking ditches dignified with the pompous denomination of canals; a fine bridge spoilt by two rows of houses on it, and a large square decorated with the worst architecture I ever yet saw.

The young aristocrat and future Gothic novelist
WILLIAM BECKFORD
*visited Venice in 1780 and was struck – as have been many foreign tourists – by the unique Venetian stench.
He recorded his impressions in*
Dreams, Waking Thoughts and Incidents *(1783).*

I like this odd town of Venice, and find every day some new amusement in rambling about its innumerable canals and alleys. Sometimes I pry about the great church of Saint Mark, and examine the variety of marbles and mazes of delicate sculpture with which it is covered. The cupola, glittering with gold, mosaic, and paintings of half the wonders in the Apocalypse, never fails to transport me to the period of the Eastern empire. I think myself in Constantinople, and expect Michael Paleologus with all his train. One circumstance alone prevents my observing half the treasures of the place, and holds down my fancy just springing into the air: I mean the vile stench which exhales from every recess and corner of the edifice, and which all the incense of the altars cannot subdue.

When no longer able to endure this noxious atmosphere, I run up the Campanile in the piazza, and seating myself amongst the pillars of the gallery, breathe the fresh gales which blow from the Adriatic; survey at my leisure all Venice beneath me, and its azure sea, white sails, and long tracks of islands shining in the sun. Having thus laid in a provision of wholesome breezes, I brave the vapours of the canals, and venture into the most curious and murky quarters of the city, in search of Turks and Infidels, that I may ask as many questions as I please about Cairo and Damascus.

MRS PIOZZI,
literary hostess and friend of Samuel Johnson, visited Venice in 1785, and recorded her disgust with certain Venetian customs in
A Journey Through France, Italy and Germany *(1789).*

But it is almost time to talk of the Rialto, said to be the finest single arch in Europe, and I suppose it is so – very beautiful, too, when looked on from the water, but so dirtily kept and deformed with mean shops, that, passing over it, disgust gets the better of every other sensation. The truth is, our dear Venetians are nothing less than cleanly. St Mark's Place is all covered over in a morning with chicken-coops, which stink one to death, as nobody, I believe, thinks of changing their baskets; and all about the ducal palace is made so very offensive by the resort of human creatures for every purpose most unworthy of so charming a place, that all enjoyment of its beauties is rendered difficult to a person of any delicacy, and poisoned so provokingly, that I do never cease to wonder that so little police and proper regulation are established in a city so particularly lovely to render her sweet and wholesome.

As I walked, I found myself devising sanitary regulations and drawing up a preliminary plan for an imaginary police inspector who was seriously interested in the problem. It shows how eager man always is to sweep his neighbour's doorstep.

I stood in Venice, on the Bridge of Sighs;
A palace and a prison on each hand:
I saw from out the wave her structures rise
As from the stroke of the enchanter's wand:
A thousand years their cloudy wings expand
Around me, and a dying Glory smiles
O'er the far times, when many a subject land
Look'd to the winged Lion's marble piles,
Where Venice sate in state, throned on her hundred isles!

She looks a sea Cybele, fresh from ocean,
Rising with her tiara of proud towers
At airy distance, with majestic motion,
A ruler of the waters and their powers:
And such she was; – her daughters had their dowers
From spoils of nations, and the exhaustless East
Poured in her lap all gems in sparkling showers.
In purple was she robed, and of her feasts
Monarchs partook, and deem'd their dignity increased.

In Venice Tasso's echoes are no more,
And silent rows the songless gondolier;
Her palaces are crumbling to the shore,
And music meets not always now the ear:
Those days are gone – but Beauty still is here.
States fall, arts fade – but Nature doth not die,
Nor yet forget how Venice once was dear,
The pleasant place of all festivity,
The revel of the earth, the masque of Italy!

In his Italian Journey *(1816–17),* GOETHE *meditated on Venice's hygienic inadequacies.*

In 1816, BYRON *rented the Palazzo Mocenigo on the Grand Canal and set himself up in the style, as he imagined, of an old Venetian lord. In the period preceding his arrival in Venice, wandering aimlessly across Europe, he had written little poetry. But he found new inspiration in the ancient queen of the Adriatic and soon completed and published Canto IV of his self-dramatizing epic,* Childe Harold *(1816).*

Bridge of Sighs, engraving, 1829.

Mocenigo Palace, Venice.
from a drawing by Lady Eastlake.

'Here I have pitched my staff' – Byron's residence in Venice, 1816–18.

BYRON's *letters tell the story of his years in Venice with swagger, wit, and candour. He wrote this one to his friend, the English poet Samuel Rogers, on 3 March 1818.*

In Venice I winter, transporting my horses to the Lido bordering the Adriatic (where the fort is) so that I get a gallop of some miles daily along the strip of beach which reaches to Malamocco, when in health – but within these few weeks I have been unwell; – at present I am getting better. – The Carnival was short but a good one. – I don't go out much, except during the time of Masques, – but there are one or two Conversazioni – where I go regularly – just to keep up the system – as I had letters to their Givers – & they are particular on such points – & now & then – though very rarely – to the Governor's. – It is a very good place for women – I have a few like every one else. I like the dialect – & their manner very much – there is a naiveté about them which is very winning – & the romance of the place is a mighty adjunct . . . – The City however is decaying daily – & does not gain in population; – however I prefer it to any other in Italy – & here have I pitched my staff – & here do I purpose to reside for the remainder of my life, – unless events connected with business not to be transacted out of England, compel me to return for that purpose; – otherwise I have few regret – & no desires to visit it again – for it's own sake.

I was always very partial to Venice – and it has not hitherto disappointed me – but I am not sure that the English in general would like it – I am sure that I should not, if *they* did – but by the benevolence of God – they prefer Florence & Naples – and do not infest us greatly here. – In other respects it is very agreeable for Gentlemen of desultory habits – women – wine – and wassail being all extremely fair & reasonable – theatres &c. good – & Society (after a time –) as pleasant as anywhere else (at least to my mind) if you will live with them in their own way – which is different of course from the Ultramontane in some degree. – The Climate is Italian & that's enough – and the Gondolas &c. &c. & habits of the place make it like a romance – for it is by no means even now the most regular & correct *moral* city in the universe. – Young and old – pretty & ugly – high and low – are employed in the laudable practice of Lovemaking – and though most Beauty is found amongst the middling & lower classes – this of course only renders their amatory habits more universally diffused.

BYRON *wrote to his old friend James Wedderburn Webster, on 31 May 1818.*

We passed the laguna in the middle of the night in a most violent storm of wind, rain, and lightning. It was very curious to observe the elements above in a state of such tremendous convulsion, and the surface of the water almost calm; for these lagunas, though five miles broad, a space enough in a storm to sink a gondola, are so shallow that the boatmen drive the boat along with a pole. The sea-water, furiously agitated by the wind, shone with sparkles like stars. Venice, now hidden and now disclosed by the driving rain, shone dimly with its lights. We were all this while safe and comfortable, except that Clare was now and then a little frightened in our cabin ... At three o'clock I called on Lord Byron: he was delighted to see me, and our first conversation of course consisted in the object of my visit ...

Well, my dear Mary, this talk went off, for I did not see in that moment how I could urge it further, and I thought that at least many points were gained in the willingness and good humour of our discussion. So he took me in his gondola – much against my will, for I wanted to return to Clare at the Hoppners', who was anxiously waiting for me, across the laguna to a long sandy island, which defends Venice from the Adriatic. When we disembarked, we found his horses waiting for us, and we rode along the sands of the sea, talking. Our conversation consisted in histories of his wounded feelings, and questions as to my affairs, and great professions of friendship and regard for me.

In August 1818 the poet PERCY BYSSHE SHELLEY *came to Venice with Clare Claremont, his wife's stepsister and the mother of one of Byron's illegitimate children. Shelley's purpose was to visit Byron and persuade him to allow Clare to see her child, whom Byron had placed in the care of a convent. Shelley described his arrival in Venice and his subsequent encounter with Byron in a letter to his wife, Mary.*

SHELLEY *transformed his Venetian encounter with Byron into the poem* Julian and Maddalo, *written months after their meeting in 1818. In the poem, Shelley casts himself as the idealistic Englishman, Julian, and Byron as the cynical Italian, Count Maddalo, and sets their philosophical debate against the evocative background of the then uninhabited Lido and the old canals and palaces of Venice.*

I rode one evening with Count Maddalo
Upon the bank of land which breaks the flow
Of Adria towards Venice: a bare strand
Of hillocks, heaped from ever-shifting sand,
Matted with thistles and amphibious weeds,
Such as from earth's embrace the salt ooze breeds
                              ... the tide makes
A narrow space of level sand thereon,
Where 'twas our wont to ride while day went down.
This ride was my delight. I love all waste
And solitary places; where we taste
The pleasure of believing what we see
Is boundless, as we wish our souls to be:
And such was this wide ocean, and this shore
More barren than its billows; and yet more
Than all, with a remembered friend I love
To ride as then I rode; – for the winds drove
The living spray along the sunny air
Into our faces; the blue heavens were bare,
Stripped to their depths by the awakening north;
And, from the waves, sound like delight broke forth
Harmonizing with solitude, and sent
Into our hearts aëreal merriment.
So, as we rode, we talked ...
Concerning God, freewill and destiny:
Of all that earth has been or yet may be,
All that vain men imagine or believe,
Or hope can paint or suffering may achieve,
We descanted, and I (for ever still
Is it not wise to make the best of ill?)
Argued against despondency, but pride
Made my companion take the darker side.
The sense that he was greater than his kind
Had struck, methinks, his eagle spirit blind
By gazing on its own exceeding light.
Meanwhile the sun paused ere it should alight,
Over the horizon of the mountains; – Oh,
How beautiful is sunset, when the glow
Of Heaven descends upon a land like thee,
Thou Paradise of exiles, Italy!
                              ... 'Ere it fade,'
Said my companion, 'I will show you soon

Percy Bysshe Shelley.

A better station' – so, o'er the lagune
We glided; and from that funereal bark
I leaned, and saw the city, and could mark
How from their many isles, in evening's gleam,
Its temples and its palaces did seem
Like fabrics of enchantment piled to Heaven.
I was about to speak, when – 'We are even
Now at the point I meant,' said Maddalo,
And bade the gondolieri cease to row.
'Look, Julian, on the west, and listen well
If you hear not a deep and heavy bell.'
I looked, and saw between us and the sun
A building on an island; such a one
As age to age might add, for uses vile,
A windowless, deformed and dreary pile;
And on the top an open tower, where hung
A bell, which in the radiance swayed and swung;
We could just hear its hoarse and iron tongue:
The broad sun sunk behind it, and it tolled
In strong and black relief. – 'What we behold
Shall be the madhouse and its belfry tower,'
Said Maddalo, 'and ever at this hour
Those who may cross the water, hear that bell
Which calls the maniacs, each one from his cell,
To vespers.' . . .
              . . . The broad star
Of day meanwhile had sunk behind the hill,
And the black bell became invisible,
And the red tower looked gray, and all between
The churches, ships and palaces were seen
Huddled in gloom; – into the purple sea
The orange hues of heaven sunk silently.
We hardly spoke, and soon the gondola
Conveyed me to my lodging by the way.

The Palazzo Mocenigo, in which Byron lived, is galvanized into ghastly newness by recent repairs, and as it is one of the ugliest palaces on the Grand Canal, it has less claim than ever upon one's interest. The custodian shows people the rooms where the poet wrote, dined, and slept, and I suppose it was from the hideous basket-balcony over the main door that one of his mistresses threw herself into the canal. Another of these interesting relicts is pointed out in the small butter-and-cheese shop

Relics of Byron's days in Venice attracted generations of tourists. The novelist WILLIAM DEAN HOWELLS, *then American consul in Venice, observed some of these in his* Venetian Life *(1869).*

which she keeps in the street leading from Campo Sant' Angelo to San Paterinan: she is a fat sinner, long past beauty, bald, and somewhat melancholy to behold.

The French novelist
GEORGE SAND *visited Venice in 1834 with her young lover, the poet Alfred de Musset. She recalled the event in her autobiography,* Histoire de ma Vie *(1854–55). She omits to mention in this account that her Venetian farewell to de Musset was the end of their relationship, and that his departure was precipitated not so much by his illness as by her affair with the Venetian doctor who was treating him.*

Venice was indeed the city of my dreams, and all that I had already visioned of her still coloured her image in my eyes, both mornings and evenings, upon balmy days and in her darkly mirrored storms. I loved this city for itself, and it is the only one in the world that I can so love, for town life has always produced upon me the effect of a prison which I suffer only on my fellow prisoners' account. But in Venice one could live for a long time; and I understand why, in her hour of splendour and liberty, her children almost personified her in their love, and cherished her not as a thing but as a living being.

Presently I took a fever and then a bad illness with dreadful headaches which I had not previously known, and which have since lodged in my brain in the form of frequent and often unbearable migraines. I expected to remain only a few days in that city, but unexpected events detained me there.

Alfred de Musset was much more gravely affected than I by the air of Venice, which strikes down many foreigners, a fact of which too few are aware. He became seriously ill; a typhoid fever put him within an inch of his life. It was not only the respect due to a noble genius which inspired me with a great solicitude and which gave me – and I so sick myself – unexpected energy; it was also his charm and the moral sufferings continually inflicted upon his poet's constitution. I spent seventeen days at his bedside without taking more than one hour of rest out of twenty-four. His convalescence lasted about as many days, and I recall that directly after his departure my fatigue produced a singular effect upon me. I had accompanied him late in the morning as far as Mestre in a gondola, and I came home through the little canals in the heart of the city. These narrow canals, which serve as streets, are crossed by little one-arch footbridges. I was so blear-eyed after nights of vigil that I saw everything upside down, particularly this arcade of bridges, which rose up before me like a series of inverted arches.

In this letter to her sister, the English poet ELIZABETH BARRETT BROWNING *recounts her trip to Venice in 1851 with her husband, poet Robert Browning, and their child Weideman (later known*

I can't describe what the scene is – the mixture of intricate beauty & open glory, ... the mystery of the rippling streets & soundless gondolas. I could be content to live out my life here. I never saw a place which I could be so glad to live a life in. It fitted my desires in a moment. If Paris turned out ill, & Florence failed us, here would be Venice, ready! Robert & I were sitting outside the caffè in the piazza of St Mark last night at nearly ten, taking our coffee & listening to music, & watching the soundless crowd drift backwards & forwards through that grand square, as if swept by the airs they were listening to. I say 'soundless' – for the absence of carriage or horse removed all ordinary noises. You heard nothing but the music. I was a phantom-sight altogether.

We go to the traiteur to dine – even Wiedeman does. By which you may judge what a good *adaptable* child he really is. He has made friends with the 'holy pigeons', & they were surrounding him like a cloud today for the sake of his piece of bread, . . . he stamping & crying out for rapture in the grand piazza. You have read perhaps about these pigeons, & remember how the whole people of Venice protect them, & how to kill one of them is a crime against the nations. In consequence of which, they are so tame that they mix with the crowd, having no fear of man. You may fancy that Wiedeman is enchanted with the holy pigeons. Also, he has gone with Wilson [his governess], to see all the churches on our route. He shook his head at those of Parma, when I asked him if he thought them beautiful, & said 'No, no'. But nothing has pleased him so much as Venice, & St Mark's – & the gondolas. Only he always wants to get into the water, *'per fare bagno'*. We enquired of him how long he would stay here, and he answered *'Due'* – by which he meant 'a long while', *'Due'* being his idea of more than one . . . in fact of the infinite.

as 'Pen'). The little boy's love of Venice was to be consummated many years later when, with the assistance of his wealthy American wife, he purchased the Palazzo Rezzonico on the Grand Canal.

Robert Browning and his son, on the steps of the Palazzo Rezzonico, 1889.

From 1849 to 1851 John Ruskin lived in Venice, researching his immense study, The Stones of Venice *(completed in 1853). His indefatigable explorations were described by his wife* EFFIE GRAY *in a letter to her mother (1849).*

The Stones of Venice *remains perhaps the most serious extended consideration the city has ever received. It enjoyed popular acclaim and influenced a generation of artists, critics, and tourists.* RUSKIN *himself was dubious about its effect, as he explained in his afterword to the Travellers' Edition of 1877.*

Ruskin's later and increasingly eccentric writings on Venice were collected in St Mark's Rest *(1877).* HENRY JAMES *weighed their excesses and their virtues in the course of his essay 'Venice' (1882).*

John excites the liveliest astonishment to all and sundry in Venice and I do not think they have made up their minds yet whether he is very mad or very wise. Nothing interrupts him and whether the Square is crowded or empty he is either seen with a black cloth over his head taking Daguerr[e]otypes or climbing about the capitals covered with dust, or else with cobwebs exactly as if he had just arrived from taking a voyage with the old woman on her broomstick. Then when he comes down he stands very meekly to be brushed down by Domenico [Ruskin's valet] quite regardless of the scores of idlers who cannot understand him at all.

And her [Venice's] history, so far as it was thus in her desolation graven, is indeed in this book told truly, and, I find on re-reading it, so clearly, that it greatly amazes me at this date to reflect how no one has ever believed a word I said, though the public have from the first done me the honour to praise my manner of saying it; and, as far as they found the things I spoke of amusing to themselves, they have deigned for a couple of days or so to look at them, – helped always through the tedium of the business by due quantity of ices at Florian's, music by moonlight on the Grand Canal, paper lamps and the English papers and magazines at M. Ongania's, with such illumination as those New Lamps contain – Lunar or Gaseous, enabling pursy Britannia to compare, at her ease, her own culminating and co-operate Prosperity and Virtue with the past wickedness and present out-of-pocketness of the umquhile Queen of the Sea.

Fortunately one reacts against the Ruskinian contagion, and one hour of the lagoon is worth a hundred pages of demoralized prose. This queer late-coming prose of Mr Ruskin … is all to be read, though much of it appears addressed to children of tender age. It is pitched in the nursery-key, and might be supposed to emanate from an angry governess. It is, however, all suggestive, and much of it is delightfully just. There is an inconceivable want of form in it, though the author has spent his life in laying down the principles of form and scolding people for departing from them; but it throbs and flashes with the love of his subject – a love disconcerted and abjured, but which has still much of the force of inspiration. Among the many strange things that have befallen Venice, she has had the good fortune to become the object of a passion to a man of splendid genius, who has made her his own and in doing so has made her the world's. There is no better reading at Venice therefore, as I say, than Ruskin, for every true Venice-lover can separate the wheat from the chaff. The narrow theological spirit, the moralism *à tout propos*, the queer provincialities and pruderies, are mere wild weeds in a mountain of flowers.

The church cats are apparently the friends of the sacristans, with whom their amity is maintained probably by entire cession of the spoils of visitors. In these, therefore, they seldom take any interest, merely opening a lazy eye now and then to wink at the sacristans as they drag the deluded strangers from altar to altar, with intense enjoyment of the absurdity, and a wicked satisfaction in the incredible stories rehearsed. I fancy, being Italian cats, they feel something like a national antipathy toward those troops of German tourists, who always seek the Sehenswürdigkeiten in companies of ten or twenty, – the men wearing their beards, and the women their hoops and hats, to look as much like English people as possible; while their valet marshals them forward with a stream of guttural information, unbroken by a single punctuation point. These wise cats know the real English by their 'Murrays' [guidebooks]; and I think they make a shrewd guess at the nationality of us Americans by the speed with which we pass from one thing to another, and by our national ignorance of all languages but English. They must also hear us vaunt the superiority of our own land in unpleasant comparisons, and I do not think they believe us, or like us, for our boastings … The French tourist they distinguish by his evident scepticism concerning his own wisdom in quitting Paris for the present purpose; and the travelling Italian, by his attention to his badly dressed, handsome wife, with whom he is now making his wedding trip.

We have had nothing that we call heat yet – only a delicious sense of sun and a mild breeziness. But we seem to be almost the only persons in our hotel of the *forestière* species, and the Porter opines that everybody is now going to Switzerland. Still we see an occasional group of English or Americans in the churches or on the landing places of other hotels, but we shall not be ashamed if they all leave us behind …

… we live in deep retirement, partly in our rooms and partly in our gondola, never going to sit in the Piazza in the evening – the only place and time when there would be danger of greetings. – We have not yet had the longed-for solemnity of floating in the sunset glory of the lagoon. This we hope to do one evening soon by going to dine on the Lido and coming back just at the right moment … the most modest sunset sends a wondrous light over the watery scene, and every evening we see from our window the white church of S. Giorgio Maggiore and its red tower looking like ivory and coral. This place seems sometimes to me very toy-like with all its costly magnificence of old – as if the doges and grandees had been rich children who pleased themselves with making strange, pretty things on a mimic land in a safe, shallow lake.

In Venetian Life *(1869)*
WILLIAM DEAN HOWELLS
the American consul in Venice, took a jaundiced, cat's-eye view of the tourist trade.

PUNCH'S FANCY PORTRAITS —No. 12.

MR. NARCISSUS RUSKIN.
"WHO IS IT THAT SAYS MOST? WHICH CAN SAY MORE, THAN THIS RICH PRAISE,—THAT YOU ALONE ARE *YOU!*"

Ruskin caricatured in *Punch*, 1880.

In 1880, after a twenty-year absence, and only months before her death, novelist GEORGE ELIOT *revisited Venice in the company of her second husband, J. W. Cross. From there she wrote to her sisters-in-law remarking that though the other tourists had unfortunately uncovered her identity ('I am the criminal usually known under the name of George Eliot') the charms of Venice were undimmed.*

HENRY JAMES,
inveterate traveller and self-styled passionate pilgrim placed the drama of tourism at the centre of novels and stories such as Wings of the Dove *and* The Aspern Papers. *His repeated sojourns in Venice gave rise to several essays, including 'Venice: An Early Impression' (1872).*

There are travellers who think the place odious, and those who are not of this opinion often find themselves wishing that the others were only more numerous. The sentimental tourist's sole quarrel with his Venice is that he has too many competitors there. He likes to be alone; to be original; to have (to himself, at least) the air of making discoveries. The Venice of to-day is a vast museum where the little wicket that admits you is perpetually turning and creaking, and you march through the institution with a herd of fellow-gazers. There is nothing left to discover or describe, and originality of attitude is completely impossible. This is often very annoying; you can only turn your back on your impertinent playfellow and curse his want of delicacy. But this is not the fault of Venice; it is the fault of the rest of the world . . .

. . . Meeting in the Piazza on the evening of my arrival a young American painter who told me that he had been spending the summer just where I found him, I could have assaulted him for very envy. He was painting forsooth the interior of St Mark's. To be a young American painter unperplexed by the mocking, elusive soul of things and satisfied with their wholesome light-bathed surface and shape; keen of eye; fond of colour, of sea and sky and anything that may chance between them; of old lace and old brocade and old furniture (even when made to order); of time-mellowed harmonies on nameless canvases and happy contours in cheap old engravings; to spend one's mornings in still, productive analysis of the clustered shadows of the Basilica, one's afternoons anywhere, in church or campo, on canal or lagoon, and one's evenings in starlight gossip at Florian's, feeling the sea-breeze throb languidly between the two great pillars of the Piazzetta and over the low black domes of the church – this, I consider, is to be as happy as is consistent with the preservation of reason.

In his novel The Desire and Pursuit of the Whole *(1909),* FREDERICK ROLFE, *alias Baron Corvo, celebrated and satirized the British expatriate community in Venice. The hero, Nicholas Crabbe, arrogant, impossible, torn between priesthood and the life of the senses, is clearly a self-portrait of the doomed, eccentric author, who died destitute in Venice in 1913.*

He had walked, so far, as though on definite business; but now he slackened to a leisured dawdle. There was only a night to get through without exciting notice. In the morning, he could arrange better for the future.

The whole quay of the Zattere extended itself before him. He set himself to pace it from end to end. The drizzle ceased, and a warm haze bloomed on the darkness. He kept moving, to dry his drenched clothes.

Midnight sounded, and the stroke of one. The last ferries left the pontoons by the church of the Gesuati. He thought it a pity that that order of Gesuati, which is three centuries older than the Gesuiti, should have become extinct. The Jesuats always had a most respectable reputation. But 'whom the gods love die young.' Had the Jesuats survived, the world might have been spared the word 'Jesuit' as a synonym (with 'Nero' and

'Borgia' and 'Judas') for ultimate turpitude. He chuckled over the witty and very exasperating concept; and thanked the Lord for permitting him the use of his wits.

On the distant bank of the wide canal of Zuecca, the lengthy line of lights along Spinalonga fluttered like little pale daffodils in a night-mist coloured like the bloom on the fruit of the vine. Great quiet reigned. He prayed, to comfort the minutes as they fled by. Holy thoughts were his, and ardent yearnings, in his unhoused loneliness...

About 3½ o'clock, one of the signors of the night addressed him, near the Albergo Calcina. These nocturnal guards are retired *carabinieri*, who reinforce the ordinary *vigili* from dark to dawn. They carry large sticks and a red-striped cap. Everyone pays a penny a week to the private firm which enlists them; and they pervade the city by night, leaving a ticket every three hours in their clients' letter-boxes and prompt to waken would-be early risers. Did the gentleman wish to enter the closed hotel, asked the *guardia notturna*? Crabbe chortled, returning thanks, and saying that (on the contrary) he was out to take the air while studying the effects of night-light and white dawn upon the water. He imparted an atrocious English accent to the vernacular, which assured the watchman that he was merely an admirably mad foreigner nourishing no ugly or burglarious intentions. Dawn, misty, pink and glittering grey like salmon-flesh and scales, came. Very tired and stiff and sodden, he put the night behind him; and crossed Canalazzo, walking by Sanvidal and Sammaurizio and the Piazza to the club.

Before setting foot in Venice one book which every traveller should read is Corvo's *The Desire and Pursuit of the Whole*. It is a very bad novel. It is the most beautiful tribute to Circe ever written, and the truest. This is what happens to people who go to live, and to many who had intended to stay only for a little while, in Venice. They go Corvo. Corvo was taken to Venice for a brief holiday; refused to leave it; piled up debts; was reduced to pauperdom; thrown out of his hotel; rejected by his friends; tramped around his beloved city in the winter night like a homeless cat; got pneumonia; recovered; died and left this, his last, wonderful tribute to the Circe who had killed him.

The Irish writer
SEAN O'FAOLAIN
paid this tribute to one of Venice's strangest immigrants in A Summer in Italy *(1949).*

He delighted, as always, in the scene on the beach, the sight of sophisticated society giving itself over to a simple life at the edge of the element. The shallow grey sea was already gay with children wading, with swimmers, with figures in bright colours lying on the sand-banks with arms behind their heads. Some were rowing in little keelless boats painted red and blue, and laughing when they capsized. A long row of

In THOMAS MANN's
Death in Venice *(1912), the protagonist, writer Gustave von Aschenbach, contemplates the crowd at the Lido from his deck-chair.*

'Sophisticated society giving itself over to a simple life' – the Lido, early 20th century.

capanne ran down the beach, with platforms, where people sat as on verandas, and there was social life, with bustle and with indolent repose; visits were paid, amid much chatter, punctilious morning toilettes hob-nobbed with comfortable and privileged dishabille. On the hard wet sand close to the sea figures in white bath-robes or loose wrappings in garish colours strolled up and down. A mammoth sand-hill had been built up on Aschenbach's right, the work of children, who had stuck it full of tiny flags. Vendors of sea-shells, fruit, and cakes knelt beside their wares spread out on the sand. A row of cabins on the left stood obliquely to the others and to the sea, thus forming the boundary of the enclosure on this side; and on the little veranda in front of one of these a Russian family was encamped; bearded men with strong white teeth, ripe indolent women, a Fräulein from the Baltic provinces, who sat at an easel painting the sea and tearing her hair in despair; two ugly but good-natured children and an old maidservant in a head-cloth, with the caressing, servile manner of the born dependant. There they sat together in grateful enjoyment of their blessings: constantly shouting at their romping children, who paid not the slightest heed; making jokes in broken Italian to the funny old man who sold them sweetmeats, kissing each other on the cheeks – no jot concerned that their domesticity was overlooked.

MICHEL TOURNIER
described the irony of Venetian tourism in Gemini, *(1975).*

When the tourists have had enough of wandering about the narrow streets, the churches and museums, they sit down at a café terrace and look – at other tourists. One of the tourist's principal occupations in

Hotel dining room, the Lido, *c*.1900.

Forestieri on the Lido, 1920s.

Venice is to watch himself in a thousand international avatars, the game consisting in guessing the nationality of the passers-by. This proves that Venice is not merely a spectacular, but also a *specular* city. Specular – from the Latin *speculum*, a mirror – Venice is in more ways than one. She is so because she is mirrored in her waters and her houses are built on nothing but their own reflections. She is so, too, because of her fundamentally *theatrical* nature, by virtue of which Venice and Venice's image are always presented simultaneously, inseparably. Truly, there is enough there to discourage any painter. How can one paint Venice when it is a painting already? There was Canaletto, of course, but he was not the foremost of Italian painters, far from it! On the other hand, there can be no other place in the world on which so much photographic film has been used up. Because the tourist is not creative, he is a born consumer. The images are given him here at every step and he copies them right and left. Moreover, the subject of his snapshots is always himself, in front of the Bridge of Sighs, on the steps of San Stefano, in a gondola. The tourists' 'souvenirs' of Venice are all so many self-portraits.

GORE VIDAL
wrote this paean to one of Venice's most popular hostelries in Vidal in Venice *(1985).*

Harry's Bar may be Venice's most successful invention since Venice itself. In 1931, an American lamented with his favourite hotel bartender, the late Giuseppe Cipriani, that what Venice lacked was a good bar. The American, whose name was Harry, probably was not the first refugee from American Prohibition to make that observation, although the lengthy Venetian chronicles of two other Americans, Henry James and William Dean Howells, carry no mention of the city's lack of saloons. But Harry was the first to follow the inbred American tradition of wanting to set right a wrong. This was done in the form of financial backing to Cipriani, who found a rope storeroom next to the St Mark's *vaporetto* stop and there opened what he called Harry's Bar.

Even without knowing the origin of its history, some American visitors today consider Harry's Bar as being almost extra-territorially *theirs*. Since the closing of the American consulate in the 1970s, it is indeed sometimes the only place for Americans in acute distress to go for comfort and advice. However, Harry's bar was and remains an entirely Venetian operation, though the babble of barbaric voices on summer days and nights is predominantly American. Most important, it is an innovation, perhaps the only one in the ancient city, which has been accepted by the Venetians. It has become one of their own monuments. Like most natives everywhere, they may shy away from actually visiting their monuments (call it the Grant's Tomb or Tower of London syndrome), but they like to know that it is there, and that it is appreciated and frequented by foreign visitors.

DAUGHTERS OF THE ADRIATIC

In times past there were few weeks, or even days, when the fishermen did not take out dead babies from their nets, and this, they say, came from the fact that the merchants were so long separated from their wives. These, urged by their fleshly lusts, gave way to them and became pregnant, and with intent to save their reputations threw the offspring out of window into the sea as soon as they were delivered, the place being aptly disposed therefor. The rulers, in view of such enormous crimes, took counsel together and founded a great and rich hospital, very finely built, and placed in it a hundred wet-nurses to suckle the babes, and now those who would hide their shame take their children there to be reared. The Venetians also obtained a Bull from the Pope that whosoever visited those children in hospital should gain certain pardons. Thus men and women can go there to visit their children, as if to gain pardons.

In Venice, sexual repression gave rise to some curious institutions, as the Catalan traveller PERO TAFUR *observed in his journal on his visit in 1436.*

These Venetian women, especially the pretty ones, try as much as possible in public to show their chests – I mean the breasts and shoulders – so much so, that several times when I saw them I marvelled that their clothes did not fall off their backs. Those who can afford it, and also those who cannot, dress very splendidly, and have magnificent jewels and pearls in the trimming round their collars. They wear many rings on their fingers with great balass rubies, rubies and diamonds. I said also those who cannot afford it, because I was told that many of them hire these things. They paint their faces a great deal, and also the other parts they show, in order to appear more beautiful. The general run of the women who go out of the house, and who are not amongst the number of the pretty girls, go out well covered up and dressed for the most part in black even up to the head, especially in church. At first I thought they were all widows, and sometimes on entering a church at the service time I seemed to see so many nuns of the Benedictine Order. The marriageable girls dress in the same way, but one cannot see their faces for all the world. They go about so completely covered up, that I do not know how they

CANON PIETRO CASOLA, *on his way from Milan to the Holy Land in 1494, cast a censorious eye on Venetian women, as his private journal records.*

can see to go along the streets. Above all – at least indoors – these Venetian women, both high and low, have pleasure in being seen and looked at; they are not afraid of the flies biting them, and therefore they are in no great hurry to cover themselves if a man comes upon them unexpectedly. I observed that they do not spend too much in shawls to cover their shoulders. Perhaps this custom pleases others; it does not please me. I am a priest in the way of the saints, and I had no wish to inquire further into their lives.

FYNES MORYSON's observations of Venice's prostitutes were omitted from the first edition of his Itinerary (1617) and only published at the beginning of this century.

The richer sort dwell in fayre hired howses, and have their owne servants, but the Common sort lodge with Baudes called Ruffians, to whome in Venice they pay of their gayne the fifth parte, as foure Solz in twenty, paying besydes for their bed, linnen and feasting, and when they are past gayning much, they are turned out to begg or turne baudes or servants. And for releife of this misery, they have Nonneryes, where many of them are admitted, and called the converted sisters.

By the end of the sixteenth century, Venice's pimps and prostitutes had become legendary throughout Europe.
THOMAS NASHE, who had never been there, wrote them into a fantastic episode in his picaresque adventure, The Unfortunate Traveller (1594).

We made a long stride and got to Venice in short time; where having scarce lookt about us, a precious supernaturall pandor, apparelled in all points like a gentleman & having halfe a dosen several languages in his purse, entertained us in our owne tongue very paraphrastically and eloquently, & maugre all other pretended acquaintance, would haue us in a violent kinde of curtesie to be the guestes of his appointment. His name was Petro de campo Frego, a notable practitioner in the pollicie of baudrie. The place whether he brought us was a pernicious curtizãs house named Tabitha the Temptresses, a wench that could set as civill a face on it as chastities first martyr Lucrecia. What will you conceit to be in any saints house that was there to seeke? Bookes, pictures, beades, crucifixes, why, there was a haberdashers shop of them in every chamber. I warrant you should not see one set of her neckercher perverted or turned awrie, not a piece of a haire displast. On her beds there was not a wrinkle of any wallowing to be found, her pillows bare out as smooth as a groning wives belly, & yet she was a Turke and an infidel, & had more dooings then all her neighbours besides. Us for our money they used like Emperours.

In his Crudities (1611), the traveller THOMAS CORYAT recounted his assiduous personal investigation into the habits of Venetian courtesans, conducted, he insisted, entirely in the interests of social research.

But since I have taken occasion to mention some notable particulars of their women, I will insist farther upon that matter, and make relation of their Cortezans also, as being a thing incident and very proper to this discourse, especially because the name of a Cortezan of Venice is famoused over all Christendome ... Onely I feare least I shall expose my selfe to the severe censure and scandalous imputations of many carping Criticks, who I thinke will taxe me for luxury and wantonnesse to insert so lascivious a

'Two Venetian Ladies on a Balcony', by Vittore Carpaccio (*c.*1450–1523).

Coryat and the courtesan, 1611.

matter into this Treatise of Venice ...

So infinite are the allurements of these amorous Calypsoes, that the fame of them hath drawen many to Venice from some of the remotest parts of Christendome, to contemplate their beauties, and enjoy their pleasing dalliances. And indeede such is the variety of the delicious objects they minister to their lovers, that they want nothing tending to delight ... As for her selfe shee comes to thee decked like the Queene and Goddesse of love, in so much that thou wilt thinke she made a late transmigration from Paphos, Cnidos, or Cythera, the auncient habitations of Dame Venus. For her face is adorned with the quintessence of beauty. In her cheekes thou shalt see the Lilly and the Rose strive for the supremacy, and the silver tramels of her haire displayed in that curious manner besides her two frisled peakes standing up like pretty Pyramides, that they give thee the true *Cos amoris* [whetstone of love]. But if thou hast an exact judgement, thou maist easily discerne the effects of those famous apothecary drugs heretofore used amongst the Noble Ladies of Rome, even stibium, cerussa, and purpurissum. For few of the Cortezans are so much beholding to nature, but that they adulterate their faces, and supply her defect with one of these three. A thing so common amongst them, that many of them which have an elegant naturall beauty, doe varnish their faces (the observation whereof made me not a little pitty their vanities) with these kinde of sordid trumperies.

...Moreover shee will endevour to enchaunt thee partly with her melodious notes that she warbles out upon her lute, which shee fingers with as laudable a stroake as many men that are excellent professors in the noble science of Musicke; and partly with that heart-tempting harmony of her voice. Also thou wilt finde the Venetian Cortezan (if she be a selected woman indeede) a good Rhetorician, and a most elegant disourser, so that if she cannot move thee with all these foresaid delights, shee will assay thy constancy with her Rhetoricall tongue. And to the end shee may minister unto thee the stronger temptations to come to her lure, shee will shew thee her chamber of recreation, where thou shalt see all manner of pleasing objects, as many faire painted coffers wherewith it is garnished round about, a curious milke-white canopy of needle worke, a silke quilt embrodered with gold: and generally all her bedding sweetly perfumed ... Moreover I will tell thee this newes which is most true, that if thou shouldest wantonly converse with her, and not give her that *salarium iniquitatis*, which thou hast promised her, but perhaps cunningly escape from her company, shee will either cause thy throate to be cut by her Ruffiano, if he can after catch thee in the City, or procure thee to be arrested (if thou art to be found) and clapped up in the prison, where thou shalt remaine till thou hast paid her all thou didst promise her.

This week hath produced here a very unexpected piece of justice, which yet I think will discover more evil than it will amend. On Wednesday last in the night were broken up eleven several doors by the public officer, for the apprehension of so many persons (whereof nine were gentlemen of principal houses) accused to have lasciviously haunted the Nunnery of St Anna, and thence to have transported those votaries to their private chambers, and up and down the town in masking attire at festival assemblies ... Thus far the State hath proceeded already; and having now overpassed the first brunt of the public shame, no doubt they will go forward, if it be but to recover some reputation to the State by exemplar severity. In the meantime it hath occasioned much discourse and introspection into other defects of government, for it is found that the immediate cause of filling cloisters with such willing and wanton creatures, proceeded from their parents, who to spare so much marriage money, impose commonly that life upon three daughters at least if they have five, and so in proportion. The fathers, on the other side, excuse themselves with the excessive rate unto which marriage portions are mounted here; no gentleman's daughter requiring less for the bestowing of her than twenty-five or thirty thousand crowns in present money, which some two hundred years since was a good provision in the public treasury.

HENRY WOTTON, *while serving as English ambassador to the* Serenissima, *noted some of the peculiarities of Venetian sexual mores in a letter to Thomas Edmondes, dated November 1608.*

It was now Ascension-Week, and the great mart, or fair, of the whole year was kept, every body at liberty and jolly. The noblemen stalking with their ladies on *choppines*; these are high-heeled shoes, particularly affected by these proud dames, or, as some say, invented to keep them at home, it being very difficult to walk with them; whence one being asked how he liked the Venetian dames, replied, they were *mezzo carne, mezzo legno*, half flesh, half wood; and he would have none of them. The truth is, their garb is very odd, as seeming always in masquerade; their other habits also totally different from all nations. They wear very long crisp hair, of several streaks and colours, which they make so by a wash, dishevelling it on the brims of a broad hat that has no crown, but a hole to put out their heads by; they dry them in the sun, as one may see them at their windows. In their tire, they set silk flowers and sparkling stones, their petticoats coming from their very arm-pits, so that they are near three quarters and a half apron; their sleeves are made exceeding wide, under which their shift-sleeves as wide, and commonly tucked up to the shoulder, showing their naked arms, through false sleeves of tiffany, girt with a bracelet or two, with knots of points richly tagged about their shoulders and other places of their body, which they usually cover with a kind of yellow veil, of lawn, very transparent. Thus attired, they set their hands on the heads of

JOHN EVELYN *described the strange garb and footwear of Venetian ladies in this 1645 entry in his* Diary.

A Venetian *choppine*.

two matron-like servants, or old women, to support them, who are mumbling their beads. It is ridiculous to see how these ladies crawl in and out of their gondolas, by reason of their *choppines*, and what dwarfs they appear, when taken down from their wooden scaffolds; of these, I saw near thirty together, stalking half as high again as the rest of the world; for courtezans, or the citizens, may not wear *choppines*, but cover their bodies and faces with a veil of a certain glittering taffeta, or lustrèe, out of which they now and then dart a glance of their eye, the whole face being otherwise entirely hid with it; nor may the common misses take this habit; but go abroad barefaced.

Women's regatta, *c.*1600.

As for women, it is not in a city like Venice that a man abstains from them. Have you no confessons to make on this point? someone may ask. Yes, I have something to tell, and I will make this confession as frankly as the rest ...

If there is one circumstance in my life which well describes my character, it is that which I am about to relate. The vividness with which at this moment I recall the purpose of my book will, in this place, make me forget the false feeling of delicacy which would prevent me from fulfilling it. Whoever you may be, who desire to know the inmost heart of a man, have the courage to read the next two or three pages; you will become thoroughly acquainted with Jean-Jacques Rousseau.

I entered the room of a courtesan as if it had been the sanctuary of love and beauty; in her person I thought I beheld its divinity. I should never have believed that, without respect and esteem, I could have experienced the emotions with which she inspired me. No sooner had I recognized, in the preliminary familiarities, the value of her charms and caresses than, for fear of losing the fruit of them in advance, I was anxious to make haste to pluck it. Suddenly, in place of the flame which consumed me, I felt a deathly chill run through my veins; my legs trembled under me; and, feeling ready to faint, I sat down and cried like a child.

Who would guess the reason of my tears, and the thoughts that passed through my head at that moment? I said to myself: This object, which is at my disposal, is the masterpiece of nature and love; its mind and body, every part of it perfect; she is as good and generous as she is amiable and beautiful. The great ones of the world ought to be her slaves; sceptres ought to be laid at her feet. And yet she is a miserable street-walker, on sale to everybody; a merchant captain has the disposal of her; she comes and throws herself at my head, mine, although she knows that I am poor, while my real merits, being unknown to her, can have no value in her eyes. In this there is something incomprehensible. Either my heart deceives me, dazzles my senses, and makes me the dupe of a worthless slut, or some secret defect, with which I am unacquainted, must destroy the effect of her charms, and render her repulsive to those who would otherwise fight for the possession of her. I began to look for this defect with a singular intensity of mind, and it never occurred to me that the possible consequences of having anything to do with her might possibly have something to do with it. The freshness of her skin, her brilliant complexion, her dazzlingly white teeth, the sweetness of her breath, the general air of cleanliness about her whole person, so completely banished this idea from my mind, that, being still in doubt as to my condition since my visit to the *padoana* [Padua women], I rather felt qualms of conscience as to whether I was in sufficiently good health for her, and I am quite

Geneva-born writer and philosopher JEAN-JACQUES ROUSSEAU served as a secretary in the French embassy in Venice from 1743 to 1744. He recalled his ambiguous encounter with a Venetian courtesan in his Confessions *(1770).*

Venetian lady, 1590.

convinced that I was not deceived in my confidence.

These well-timed reflections so agitated me that I shed tears. Zulietta, for whom this was certainly quite a novel sight under the circumstances, was astounded for a moment; but, after having walked round the room and looked in her glass, she understood, and my eyes convinced her, that dislike had nothing to do with this whimsical melancholy. It was an easy matter for her to drive it away, and to efface the slight feeling of shame; but, at the moment when I was ready to sink exhausted upon a bosom, which seemed to permit for the first time the contact of a man's hand and mouth, I perceived that she had only one nipple. I smote my forehead, looked attentively and thought I saw that this nipple was not formed like the other. I immediately began to rack my brains for the reason of such a defect, and, feeling convinced that it was connected with some remarkable natural imperfection, by brooding so long over this idea, I saw, as clear as daylight, that, in the place of the most charming person that I could picture to myself, I only held in my arms a kind of monster, the outcast of nature, of mankind and of love. I pushed my stupidity so far as to speak to her about this defect. At first she took it as a joke, and said and did things in her frolicsome humour, which were enough to make me die of love; but as I was unable to conceal from her that I still felt a certain amount of uneasiness, she at last blushed, adjusted her dress, got up, and without saying a word, went and seated herself at the window. I wanted to sit by her side, but she moved, sat down on a couch, got up immediately afterwards, and, walking about the room and fanning herself, said to me in a cold and disdainful tone '*Zanetto, lascia le donne, et studia la matematica.*'

In the course of his love affair with Teresa Guiccioli, a young woman married to a much older man, LORD BYRON *found himself cast in the role of* cavalier servente*, a peculiar institution which he defines in his long satirical poem* Beppo *(1818).*

Besides, within the Alps, to every woman,
   (Although, God knows, it is a grievous sin,)
'Tis, I may say, permitted to have *two* men;
   I can't tell who first brought the custom in,
But '*Cavalier Serventes*' are quite common,
   And no one notices or cares a pin;
And we may call this (not to say the worst)
A *second* marriage which corrupts the *first*.

The word was formerly a '*Cicisbeo*,'
   But *that* is now grown vulgar and indecent;
The Spaniards call the person a '*Cortejo*,'
   For the same mode subsists in Spain, though recent;
In short, it reaches from the Po to Teio,
   And may perhaps at last be o'er the sea sent:
But Heaven preserve Old England from such courses!
Or what becomes of damage and divorces?

But 'Cavalier Servente' is the phrase
   Used in politest circles to express
This supernumerary slave, who stays
   Close to the lady as a part of dress,
Her word the only law which he obeys.
    His is no sinecure, as you may guess;
Coach, servants, gondola, he goes to call,
And carries fan and tippet, gloves and shawl.

I have seen nothing equal to the formality of this people , who deride colder nations for inflexible manners; and I have certainly never seen society in any small town in America so ill at ease as I have seen society in Venice, writing under self-imposed restraints. At a musical soirée, attended by the class of people who at home would have been chatty and sociable, given to making acquaintance and to keeping up acquaintance, – the young men harmlessly talking and walking with the young ladies, and the old people listening together, while constant movement and intercourse kept life in the assembly, and there was some real pleasure felt amidst a good deal of unavoidable suffering, – I say, I found such a soirée in Venice to be a spectacle of ladies planted in formal rows of low-necks and white dresses around the four sides of one room, and of gentlemen restively imprisoned in dress-coats and white gloves in another ... Amazed at this singular species of social enjoyment, I inquired afterward, of a Venetian lady, if evening parties in Venice were usually such ordeals, and was discouraged to learn that what I had seen was scarcely an exaggeration of prevailing torments. Commonly people do not know each other, and it is difficult for the younger to procure introductions; and when there is previous acquaintance, the presence of some commanding spirit is necessary to break the ice of propriety, and substitute enjoyment for correctness of behaviour. Even at dancing parties, where it would seem that the poetry of motion might do something to soften the rigid bosom of Venetian deportment, the poor young people separate after each dance, and take each sex its appointed prison, till the next quadrille offers them a temporary liberation.

In contrast to the demi-monde frequented by Byron, the official Ventian society of the upper-classes was restrained and formal, as described by the novelist and social critic WILLIAM DEAN HOWELLS in Venetian Life *(1869).*

'The Lute Player', by Giovanni Cariani, *c*.1485–1547.

MUSIC

There was music every where – chorusses, string bands, brass bands, flutes, every thing. I was so surrounded, walled in, with music, magnificence and loveliness, that I became inspired with the spirit of the scene, and sang one tune myself. However, when I observed that the other gondolas had sailed away, and my gondolier was preparing to go overboard, I stopped.

This feast consisted principally of Musicke, which was both vocall and instrumental, so good, so delectable, so rare, so admirable, so superexcellent, that it did even ravish and stupifie all those strangers that never heard the like ... Sometimes there sung sixteene or twenty men together, having their master or moderator to keepe them in order; and when they sung, the instrumentall musitians played also. Sometimes sixteene played together upon their instruments, ten Sagbuts, foure Cornets, and two Violdegambaes of an extraordinary greatness; sometimes tenne, sixe Sagbuts and foure Cornets; sometimes two, a Cornet and a treble violl ... Of the singers there were three or foure so excellent that I thinke few or none in Christendome do excell them, especially one, who had such a peerelesse and (as I may in a maner say) such a supernaturall voice for such a privilege for the sweetnesse of his voice, as sweetnesse, that I think there was never a better singer in all the world, insomuch that he did not onely give the most pleasant contentment that could be imagined, to all the hearers, but also did as it were astonish and amaze them. I alwaies thought that he was an Eunuch, which if he had beene, it had taken away some part of my admiration, because they do most commonly sing passing wel; but he was not, therefore it was much the more admirable. Againe it was the more worthy of admiration, because he was a middle-aged man, as about forty yeares old. For nature doth more commonly bestowe such a singularitie of voice upon boyes and striplings, then upon men of such yeares. Besides it was farre the more excellent, because it was nothing forced, strained, or affected, but came from him with the greatest facilitie that ever I heard. Truly I thinke that had a Nightingale beene in the same roome, and contended with him for the superioritie, something perhaps he might excell him, because God hath granted that little birde such a priviledge for the sweetnesse of his voice, as to none other: but I thinke he could not much.

Music in Venice can be infectious, as the American writer MARK TWAIN *observed in his travel book,* The Innocents Abroad *(1869).*

In the sixteenth century, Venetian music set the standards and style for the whole of Europe. In his Crudities *(1611), the traveller* THOMAS CORYAT *described a Venetian concert, praising the sophistication of the instrumentalists, and the charm of the vocalist.*

Antonio Vivaldi (1678–1741) was one of the great masters of Baroque music, a virtuoso violinist and composer of innumerable instrumental works.

After entering the priesthood, he became an instructor at the Venetian Ospedale della Pietà, an asylum for orphans which sponsored a renowned musical conservatory. Its regular Sunday performances of Vivaldi's latest compositions soon became one of Venice's chief attractions, and his fame spread throughout Europe. The dramatist CARLO GOLDONI *recalled the pleasures and perplexities of working with the great Vivaldi on an opera entitled* Griselda *in his* Memoirs *(1787).*

Goldoni, S. Bartolomeo.

M. Grimani [a producer] sent me to the musician's home in order to make the necessary changes in the opera, be they to shorten the drama or to change the position and the nature of the arias to suit the wishes of the actors and the composer. Therefore, I went to the home of the abbé Vivaldi, I presented myself on behalf of His Excellency Grimani, I found him surrounded by music and with his breviary in hand. He got up, he made a complete sign of the cross, he put his breviary aside, and made me the usual compliments. 'What is the cause of my having the pleasure of seeing you, Monsieur?'

'His Excellency Grimani has entrusted me with the alterations that you think necessary in the opera of the Carnival. I have come to see, Monsieur, what your intentions are.'

'Ah! Ah! Are you entrusted, Monsieur, with the alterations in my opera *Griselda*? Then M. Lalli is no longer connected with M. Grimani's productions?'

'M. Lalli, who is very elderly, will always profit from the dedicatory letters and the sales of the librettos, which does not concern me. I have the pleasure of busying myself in work that ought to amuse me, and I have the honour of beginning under the commands of M. Vivaldi.' The abbé took up his breviary again, made another sign of the cross, and did not answer.

'Monsieur,' I said to him, 'I do not wish to distract you in your religious pursuit; I shall come back at another time.'

'I am well aware, my dear sir, that you have a talent for poetry; I have seen your *Belisario*, which gave me great pleasure. But this is very different. One may be able to create a tragedy or an epic poem, if you please, and not be able to fashion a musical quartrain.'

'Do me the honour of showing me your drama.'

'Yes, yes, I am willing. Where then is *Griselda* tucked away? It was here.... *Deus in adjutorium meum intende … Domine … Domine … Domine....* It was here just now. *Domine ad adjuvandum....* Ah! Here it is. See, Monsieur, this scene between Gualtiere and Griselda; it is an interesting and moving scene. The author has put a pathetic aria at the end, but Mlle Giraud does not like the languid style of singing. She would like a piece with expression and excitement, an aria that expresses emotion by different means, by interrupted words, for example, by heaved sighs, by action and agitation; I don't know if you understand me.'

'Yes, Monsieur, I quite clearly understand you. Moreover, I have had the honour of hearing Mlle Giraud and I know that her voice is not very strong.'

'Why, Monsieur, do you insult my pupil? She is good at everything; she sings everything.'

'Yes, Monsieur, you are right. Give me the book and allow me to do it.'

'No, Monsieur, I cannot give it up, I need it, and I am very hard pressed.'

'Very well, Monsieur, if you are in a hurry, give me a moment and I shall gratify you are once.'

'At once?'

'Yes, Monsieur, at once.'

The abbé, while scoffing at me, held out the drama to me and gave me paper and a writing desk, again took up his breviary and recited his psalms and hymns while walking about. I reread the scene, with which I was already acquainted. I made a summing up of what the musician wanted, and in less than a quarter of an hour I wrote down the text for an aria of eight lines divided into two parts. I called the clergyman and showed him my work. Vivaldi read it and smoothed the wrinkles from his brow; he read it again and uttered cries of joy; he threw his prayer book on the ground and summoned Mlle Giraud. She came.

'Ah!' he said to her, 'Here is an unusual man, here is an excellent poet. Read this aria. It is this gentleman who has done it here without hedging and in less than a quarter of an hour.' And coming back to me, he said, 'Ah! Monsieur, I beg your pardon.' And he embraced me and swore that he would never have another poet but me.

He entrusted me with the drama and ordered the alterations from me. He was always satisfied with me, and the opera succeeded excellently.

'Café Florian, Piazza San Marco', by Richard Doyle, 1854.

The English music historian
CHARLES BURNEY
*visited Venice in 1770, seeking
material for his* History of
Music. *He published the notes
of his trip in* The Present
State of Music in France and
Italy *(1771) including his
meeting with Baldassare
Galuppi (1706–84), at that
time Venice's leading composer
and a master of comic opera.
Galuppi was born in the
lagoons, on the island of
Burano, hence his nickname, il
Buranello.*

The first music which I heard here was in the street, immediately on my arrival, performed by an itinerant band of two fiddles, a violoncello, and a voice, who, though unnoticed here as small-coalmen or oyster-women in England, performed so well, that in any other country of Europe they would not only have excited attention, but have acquired applause, which they justly merited.

My visit to Signor Galuppi this morning, in company with Signor Latilla, was long, profitable, and entertaining. I was very glad to find upon seeing him that time had spared the person as well as genius of this excellent composer. He is still lively and alert, and likely to delight the lovers of music many years. His character and conversation are natural, intelligent, and agreeable. He is in figure little and thin, but has very much the look of a gentleman. Signor Galuppi was a scholar of the famous Lotti, and very early taken notice as a good harpsichord player, and a genius in composition.

He was so obliging as to present me to Signora Galuppi; to shew me his house; an admirable picture of a sleeping child, by P. Veronese, which has been long in his wife's family; and to carry me into his working-room, with only a little clavichord in it, where, he told me, he *dirtied paper*. His family has been very large, but all his children, except three or four, are now well married. He has the appearance of a regular family man, and is esteemed at Venice as much for his private character as for his public talents.

The English poet
ROBERT BROWNING
based his poetic fantasy,
A Toccata of Galuppi's
*(1842), on the Venetian
composer's London sojourn
from 1741 to 1744.*

Oh Galuppi, Baldassaro, this is very sad to find!
I can hardly misconceive you; it would prove me deaf and blind;
But although I take your meaning, 'tis with such a heavy mind!

Here you come with your old music, and here's all the good it brings.
What, they lived once thus at Venice where the merchants were the kings,
Where Saint Mark's is, where the Doges used to wed the sea with rings?

Ay, because the sea's the street there; and 'tis arched by ... what you call
... Shylock's bridge with houses on it, where they kept the carnival:
I was never out of England – it's as if I saw it all.

Did young people take their pleasure when the sea was warm in May?
Balls and masks begun at midnight, burning ever to mid-day,
When they made up fresh adventures for the morrow, do you say?

Was a lady such a lady, cheeks so round and lips so red, –
On her neck the small face buoyant, like a bell-flower on its bed,
O'er the breast's superb abundance where a man might base his head?

Well, and it was graceful of them – they'd break talk off and afford
– She, to bite her mask's black velvet – he, to finger on his sword,
While you sat and played Toccatas, stately at the clavichord?

What? Those lesser thirds so plaintive, sixths diminished, sigh on sigh,
Told them something? Those suspensions, those solutions – 'Must we die?'
Those commiserating sevenths – 'Life might last! we can but try!'

'Were you happy?' – 'Yes.' – 'And are you still as happy?' – 'Yes. And you?'
– 'Then, more kisses!' – 'Did *I* stop them, when a million seemed so few?'
Hark, the dominant's persistence till it must be answered to!

So, an octave struck the answer. Oh, they praised you, I dare say!
'Brave Galuppi! that was music! good alike at grave and gay!
I can always leave off talking when I hear a master play!'

Then they left you for their pleasure: till in due time, one by one,
Some with lives that came to nothing, some with deeds as well undone,
Death stepped tacitly and took them where they never see the sun.

But when I sit down to reason, think to take my stand nor swerve,
While I triumph o'er a secret wrung from nature's close reserve,
In you come with your cold music till I creep thro' every nerve.

Yes, you, like a ghostly cricket, creaking where a house was burned:
'Dust and ashes, dead and done with, Venice spent what Venice earned.
The soul, doubtless, is immortal – where a soul can be discerned.

'Yours for instance: you know physics, something of geology,
Mathematics are your pastime; souls shall rise in their degree;
Butterflies may dread extinction, – you'll not die, it cannot be!

'As for Venice and her people, merely born to bloom and drop,
Here on earth they bore their fruitage, mirth and folly were the crop:
What of soul was left, I wonder, when the kissing had to stop?

'Dust and ashes!' So you creak it, and I want the heart to scold.
Dear dead woman, with such hair, too – what's become of all the gold.
Used to hang and brush their bosoms? I feel chilly and grown old.

The chapel in which we sat to hear the oratorio was dark and solemn; a screen of lofty pillars, formed of black marble and highly polished, reflected the lamps which burn perpetually before the altar. Every tribune was thronged with people, whose profound silence showed them worthy auditors of this master's music. Here were no crackling old women, or groaning Methodists, such as infest our English tabernacles, and scare

WILLIAM BECKFORD *praised the Mendicanti, one of Venice's famous music conservatories in his* Dreams, Waking Thoughts and Incidents *(1783).*

one's ears with hoarse coughs accompanied by the naso obbligato. All were still and attentive, imbibing the plaintive notes of the voices with eagerness; and scarce a countenance but seemed deeply affected with David's sorrows, the subject of the performance. I sat retired in a solitary tribune, and felt them as my own. Night came on before the last chorus was sung, and I still seem to hear its sacred melody.

The singing of the gondolieri, *an ancient tradition, had fallen into some neglect by the time of* GOETHE's *first Venetian visit in 1786. On 7 October of that year he made arrangements to attend a specially staged performance, which he described in his* Italian Journey *(1816–17).*

For this evening I had made arrangements to hear the famous singing of the boatmen, who chant verses by Tasso and Ariosto to their own melodies. This performance has to be ordered in advance, for it is now rarely done and belongs, rather, to the half-forgotten legends of the past. The moon had risen when I took my seat in a gondola and the two singers, one in the prow, the other in the stern, began chanting verse after verse in turns . . .

I shall not go into the question of how the melody evolved. It is enough to say that it is ideal for someone idly singing to himself and adapting the tune to poems he knows by heart.

The singer sits on the shore of an island, on the bank of a canal or in a gondola, and sings at the top of his voice – the people here appreciate volume more than anything else. His aim is to make his voice carry as far as possible over the still mirror of water. Far away another singer hears it. He knows the melody and the words and answers with the next verse. The first singer answers again, and so on. Each is the echo of the other. They keep this up night after night without ever getting tired. If the listener has chosen the right spot, which is halfway between them, the further apart they are, the more enchanging the singing will sound.

To demonstrate this, my boatmen tied up the gondola on the shore of the Giudecca and walked along the canal in opposite directions. I walked back and forth, leaving the one, who was just about to sing, and walking towards the other, who had just stopped.

For the first time I felt the full effect of this singing. The sound of their voices far away was extraordinary, a lament without sadness, and I was moved to tears. I put this down to my mood at the moment, but my old manservant said: '*è singolare, come quel canto intenerisce, e molto più, quando è più ben cantato.*' He wanted me to hear the women on the Lido, especially those from Malamocco and Pellestrina. They too, he told me, sing verses by Tasso to the same or a similar melody, and added: 'It is their custom to sit on the seashore while their husbands are out sea-fishing, and sing these songs in penetrating tones until, from far out over the sea, their men reply, and in this way they converse with each other.' Is this not a beautiful custom? I dare say that, to someone standing close by, the sound of such voices, competing with the thunder of the waves, might not be very agreeable. But the motive behind such singing is so human and genuine that it makes the mere notes of the melody, over which scholars have racked their brains in vain, come to life. It is the cry of some lonely human being sent out into the wide world till it reaches the ears of another lonely human being who is moved to answer it.

I do not much regret that I have heard scarcely any music here as yet; for I suppose I must not include the music of the angels in the 'Assumption', encircling Mary with joyous shouts of welcome, one gaily beating the tambourine, a couple of others blowing away on strange crooked flutes, whilst another charming group is singing – or the music floating in the thoughts of the player. I have only once heard anything on the organ, and that was doleful. I was gazing at Titian's 'Martyrdom of St Peter' in the Franciscan Church. Divine service was going on, and nothing inspires me with more solemn awe than when on the very spot for which they were originally designed and painted, those old pictures with their mighty figures, gradually steal forth out of the darkness in which the long lapse of time has veiled them.

During his visit to Venice in 1830, the composer FELIX MENDELSSOHN *found more inspiration in the city's art than its music, as he explained in a letter to one of his old professors in Venice.*

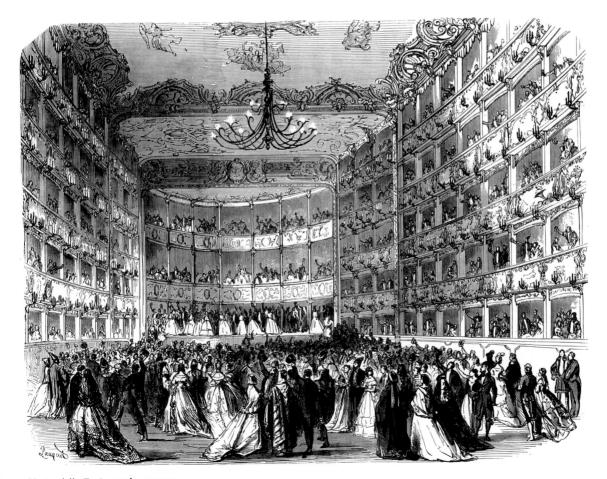

Teatro della Fenice, 19th century.

In 1850, the Teatro Fenice in Venice commissioned an opera from GIUSEPPE VERDI based on a play by Victor Hugo featuring a hunch-backed hero called Triboletto. Before production, the opera was banned on political grounds by the Austrian military rulers. A list of suggested changes was submitted to Verdi. In this letter to the theatre management (dated 14 December 1850), the composer rejects the changes, and defends his original conception. The opera was finally produced at the Fenice, in accord with Verdi's ideas, under the title Rigoletto *on 11 March 1851.*

Let me say I have had very little time to examine the new libretto. I have seen enough, however, to know that in its present form it lacks character, significance, and, in short, the dramatic moments leave one completely cold. If it was necessary to change the characters' names, then the locality should have been changed as well ... The Duke has no character. The Duke must definitely be a libertine: without this there is no justification for Triboletto's fear that his daughter might leave her hiding-place, and the drama is made impossible. What would the Duke be doing in the last act, alone in a remote inn, without an invitation, without a rendezvous? I don't understand why the sack has gone. Why should a sack matter to the police? Are they worried about the effect? But let me say this: why do they think they know better than I do about this? Who is playing the Maestro? Who can say this will make an effect and that won't? We had this kind of difficulty with the horn in *Ernani*. Well, did anyone laugh at the sound of that horn? With that sack removed, it is improbable that Triboletto would talk for an hour to a corpse, before a flash of lightning reveals it to be his daughter. Finally, I see that they have avoided making Triboletto an ugly hunchback!! A hunchback who sings? Why not? ... Will it be effective? I don't know. But, I repeat, if I don't know then they who propose this change don't know either. I thought it would be beautiful to portray this extremely deformed and ridiculous character who is inwardly passionate and full of love. I chose the subject precisely because of these qualities and these original traits, and if they are cut I shall no longer be able to set it to music. If anyone says to me I can leave my notes as they are for this new plot, I reply that I don't understand this kind of thinking, and I say frankly that my music, whether beautiful or ugly, is never written in a vacuum, and that I always try to give it character.

To sum up, an original, powerful drama has been turned into something ordinary and cold. I am extremely sorry that the Management did not reply to my last letter. I can only repeat and beg them to do what I asked then, because my artist's conscience will not allow me to set this libretto to music.

The German composer RICHARD WAGNER, whose politics had made him unwelcome in parts of his homeland, stayed in Venice for several months in 1857, a period he later recalled in My Life *(1870–81).*

There was little to attract my attention in the very oppressed and degenerate life of the Venetian populace, for as far as human activity in the glorious ruins of this wonderful city was concerned, the only impression I was able to form was that it was maintained as a bathing resort for tourists. Strangely enough, it was the thoroughly German element of good military music, so well represented in the Austrian army, that brought me here into a certain contact with public life. The bandmaster of the two Austrian regiments stationed in Venice got the idea of playing overtures of mine, such as those to *Tannhäuser* and *Rienzi*, and invited me to attend rehearsals at the barracks. Here I found the whole officer corps assembled, which on this occasion treated me very respectfully. The two bands took turns playing in the evening in the middle of a brilliantly illuminated St Mark's Square, which offered a truly superb acoustical setting for such music. Several times at the end of dinner I was surprised to hear my overtures all of a sudden; when I sat at the restaurant window abandoning myself to the impressions of the music, I did not know which dazzled me most – the incomparable square in its magnificent illumination filled with countless numbers of moving people, or the music which seemed to be wafting all these phenomena aloft in a resounding transfiguration. But there was one thing utterly lacking here which one would otherwise have certainly expected from an Italian audience: thousands of people grouped themselves around the band and listened to the music with intense concentration; but no two hands ever forgot themselves to the extent of applauding, for any sign of approbation for an Austrian military band would have been looked upon as treason to the motherland ...

Richard Wagner by André Gill.

On a sleepless night that drove me out on the balcony of my apartment at about three o'clock in the morning, I heard for the first time the famous old folksong of the gondolieri. I thought the first call, piercing the stillness of the night like a harsh lament, emanated from the Rialto, barely a quarter hour's distance away, or thereabouts; from a similar distance this would be answered from another quarter in the same way. This strange melancholy dialogue, which was repeated frequently at longish intervals, moved me too much for me to be able to fix its musical components in my mind. Yet on another occasion I learned that this folksong had an indisputably poetic interest. When I was riding back late one evening along the dark canal, the moon came out and illuminated, together with the indescribable palaces, the tall silhouette of my gondolier towering above the stern of his gondola, while he slowly turned his mighty oar. Suddenly from his breast came a mournful sound not unlike the howl of an animal, swelling up from a deep, low note, and after a long-sustained 'Oh', it culminated in the simple musical phrase 'Venezia'. This was followed by some words I could not retain in my memory, being so greatly shaken by the emotion of the moment. Such were the impressions that seemed most characteristic of Venice to me during my stay, and they remained with me until the completion of the second act of *Tristan*, and perhaps even helped to inspire the long-drawn-out lament for the shepherd's horn at the beginning of the third act.

THE STONES

Now when I describe Venice as in essence a stone city, I do not mean to imply that it is entirely, or even largely, made of stone. On the contrary, even on many principal buildings stone rarely comprises more than the bases, and the entrances to the apertures. The area of stone on the walls is probably minute. One thinks of Venice as a stone city because stone is the final material, the head and the fruit of walls of brick and stucco. Emergent from duller surfaces, the white stone glows. Istrian stone is nearly always the boundary as well as the relevant mark upon the wall: not a writing upon the wall but seemingly the nerve and muscle and the limbs of structure . . .

For the rest, stone rebuts the sea at all important points and the stone passages and paved open places display the life and movement there as does a plate the object set upon it. And so, the unhidden brick in Venice, even when it is vast in many campanili including the one of San Marco, in the huge Gothic churches of the Frari and San Zanipolo (they possess, of course, their elaborate stone doors and other facings), suggests a certain domesticity without challenging the image of bright stone. Some of the early Gothic and Renaissance Gothic palaces from which the stucco has peeled are particularly charming. Such rosy brick, like the occasional greenness of enclosed gardens that appears over walls, or like huge Venetian red sails and blinds, suggests an islanded peace, an earth substance matured by the sun, an aged country warmth. Another instance is the Abbazia San Gregorio on the Grand Canal or the huge wall of the salt warehouse on the Zattere, the warmest pitch in Venice on many days of winter.

So much for the brick, a loam in Venice from which the encrusted stone is seen to flower.

As far as my inquiries have extended, there is not a building in Venice, raised prior to the sixteenth century, which has not sustained essential change in one or more of its most important features. By far the greater number present examples of three or four different styles, it may be successive, it may be accidentally associated; and, in many instances, the restorations or additions have gradually replaced the entire structure of the ancient fabric, of which nothing but the name remains, together with a kind of identity, exhibited in the anomalous association of the modernized

'The St Mark's lion, lifted on a blue field covered with stars...' – painting by W. R. Sickert (1860–1942).

portions: the Will of the old building asserted through them all, stubbornly, though vainly, expressive; superseded by codicils, and falsified by misinterpretation; yet animating what would otherwise be a mere group of fantastic masque, as embarrassing to the antiquary as to the mineralogist, the epigene crystal, formed by materials of one substance modelled on the perished crystals of another.

The Russian poet
BORIS PASTERNAK
discovered, like Ruskin, that brick and stone in Venice take on a life of their own – and indeed are transformed by the life lived around them, as he recalled in his memoir Safe Conduct *(1932).*

And so this good fortune came to me too, and I had the happiness of learning that it is just as possible day after day to have rendezvous with a fragment of built-up space as with a living person.

From whatever side one approached the piazza, at every entry there lurked in waiting for one that moment when one's breath was quickened, one's step speeded up, when one's feet without effort carried one on of themselves. Whether from the Merceria side or that of the telegraph building, there is that instant in which the path one has taken turns into a vestibule beyond which the very atmosphere parts from itself, in one gesture to spread forth its own version of the broadly-limned open-skied square and as if at a reception without delay brings forward campanile and Church of St Mark, Doge's Palace and three façaded colonnade.

As you gradually become attached to them, you incline to the impression that Venice is a city inhabited by buildings. The four I have mentioned and still more like them. In this assertion there is no figure of speech. The statement here made in stone by the architects is so lofty that no rhetoric can attain its height. Apart from this, there is the barnacle-like incrustation of centuries of travellers' enthusiasm. That accumulating rapture has squeezed out of Venice the last hint of the declamatory. There is no room left, not a palace unoccupied. Every corner is packed full with beauty.

JOHN RUSKIN
described the approach to the church of San Marco, through the dark portico surrounding the piazza, in The Stones of Venice *(1851–53).*

Beyond those troops of ordered arches there rises a vision out of the earth, and all the great square seems to have opened from it in a kind of awe, that we may see it far away; – a multitude of pillars and white domes, clustered into a long low pyramid of coloured light; a treasure-heap, it seems, partly of gold, and partly of opal and mother-of-pearl, hollowed beneath into five great vaulted porches, ceiled with fair mosaic, and beset with sculpture of alabaster, clear as amber and delicate as ivory, – sculpture fantastic and involved, of palm leaves and lilies, and grapes and pomegranates, and birds clinging and fluttering among the branches, all twined together into an endless network of buds and plumes; and in the midst of it, the solemn forms of angels, sceptred, and robed to the feet, and leaning to each other across the gates, their figures indistinct among the gleaming of the golden ground through the leaves beside them, inter-

Palazzo da Mosto, drawing by John Ruskin.

rupted and dim, like the morning light as it faded back among the branches of Eden, when first its gates were angel-guarded long ago. And round the walls of the porches there are set pillars of variegated stones, jasper and porphyry, and deep-green serpentine spotted with flakes of snow, and marbles, that half refuse and half yield to the sunshine, Cleopatra-like, 'their bluest veins to kiss' – the shadow, as it steals back from them, revealing line after line of azure undulation, as a receding tide leaves the waved sand; their capitals rich with interwoven tracery, rooted knots of herbage, and drifting leaves of acanthus and vine, and mystical signs, all beginning and ending in the Cross; and above them, in the broad archivolts, a continuous chain of language and of life – angels, and the signs of heaven, and the labours of men, each in its appointed season upon the earth; and above these, another range of glittering pinnacles, mixed with white arches edged with scarlet flowers, – a confusion of delight, amidst which the breasts of the Greek horses are seen blazing in their breadth of golden strength, and the St Mark's lion, lifted on a blue field covered with stars, until at last, as if in ecstasy, the crests of the arches break into a marble foam, and toss themselves far into the blue sky in flashes and wreaths of sculptured spray, as if the breakers on the Lido shore had been frost-bound before they fell, and the sea-nymphs had inlaid them with coral and amethyst.

MARK TWAIN,
in characteristically sceptical mood, described the mixed feelings evoked by Venice's great church in his travel memoir, A Tramp Abroad *(1897).*

One lingers about the cathedral a good deal, in Venice. There is a strong fascination about it – partly because it is so old, and partly because it is so ugly. Too many of the world's famous buildings fail of one chief virtue – harmony; they are made up of a methodless mixture of the ugly and the beautiful; this is bad; it is confusing, it is unrestful. One has a sense of uneasiness, of distress, without knowing why. But one is calm before St Mark's, one is calm within it, one would be calm on top of it, calm in the cellar; for its details are masterfully ugly, no misplaced and impertinent beauties are intruded anywhere; and the consequent result is a grand harmonious whole, of soothing, entrancing, tranquillizing, soul-satisfying ugliness. One's admiration of a perfect thing always grows, never declines; and this is the surest evidence to him that it *is* perfect. St Mark's is perfect. To me it soon grew to be so nobly, so augustly ugly, that it was difficult to stay away from it, even for a little while. Every time its squat domes disappeared from my view, I had a despondent feeling; whenever they reappeared, I felt an honest rapture – I have not known any happier hours than those I daily spent in front of Florian's, looking across the Great Square at it. Propped on its long row of low thick-legged columns, its back knobbed with domes, it seemed like a vast warty bug taking a meditative walk.

English essayist
OSBERT SITWELL
visited Venice as a child, and first saw the great piazza shortly after what he called 'the suicide of the Campanile'. In 1902 the famous bell-tower suddenly collapsed in a heap of crumbled brick, leaving an empty, wide open piazza for the first time in centuries. Though Sitwell claimed to prefer the piazza without the Campanile to the piazza with

Yet here it still is, all of it: even St Mark's, the cathedral which has had so many escapes. Its latest feat was to survive an Austrian bomb that fell, just outside it, in the 1914–18 war. Not many years before, there had been the collapse of the Campanile, which might have altogether crushed its fragile grey domes ... even the restorers, with their more subtle, continual, and calculated efforts at destruction – that slow, relentless, insect-like eating away and rebuilding of a mighty church until a new creation is substituted for the old one which we loved, while all the time it is achieved under the cloak of loudly proclaimed necessity and good intentions, and so gradually carried out that many people notice the havoc being wrought no more than they perceive in process the slow decay of their own minds and bodies – cannot entirely spoil its enchantment. Indeed, a visitor is bound on every occasion to discover some new and beautiful effect or detail: for not only is the edifice itself an unrivalled work of art, but it is, in addition, a museum of the first order.

It is as though, whenever the Venetians beheld anything anywhere that they deemed of the finest quality, in bronze, marble, porphyry, or crystal, their first thought was, 'How can we steal this for St Mark's?' Being an ingenious and bold people, untroubled by scruples, they generally succeeded in discovering a method, albeit sometimes they failed to bring it home safely. Thus the Adriatic coast of Italy is sprinkled with objects that the Venetians lost at sea, on their way back from Constantinople, and which eventually, and after the Venetians had forgotten about them, were recovered from the waves. Nevertheless, an immense amount of booty reached the city safely: and, once there, the next thought of the Venetians was, 'Shall we set it in the façade, or upon the sidewalls of our church?' And, by some strange fortune, this haphazard process did actually adorn it. The incongruity of the exhibits is by one means or another banished until they become part of the building, grow in to it, as an orchid flowers from a tropical tree, and even impart to this far shrine a portion of the magic of the places from which they were wrenched.

the Campanile restored (as it was within years of its fall), he nevertheless returned there on many occasions, and marvelled at Venice's staying power in his travel book Winters of Content *(1932).*

The ruins of the Campanile filling Piazza San Marco, 1902.

FYNES MORYSON
charted the movements of the four bronze horses of San Marco in his Itinerary *(1617). Later, in 1798, Napoleon placed them over the gates of the Tuileries in Paris, a symbol of his conquest. They were returned to Venice after Napoleon's defeat in 1815.*

HENRY JAMES
evoked the potent mystery of San Marco's interior in his essay 'Venice' (1882).

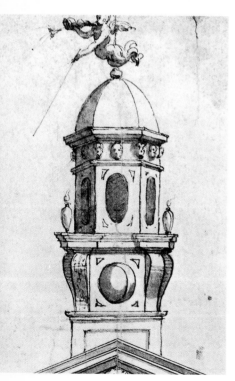

16th-century cupola design.

Over the great doore of the Church, be foure horses of brasse, guilded over, very notable for antiquity and beauty; and they are so set, as if at the first step they would leape into the market place. They are said to be made to the similitude of the Horses of Phœbus, drawing the Chariot of the Sunne, and to have beene put upon the triumphall Arke of Nero, by the people of Rome, when he had overcome the Parthians. But others say that they were given to Nero by Tiridates the King of Armenia, and were made by the hands of the famous engraver Lisippus. These Horses Constantine removed from Rome to Constantinople, and that City being sacked, the Venetians brought them to Venice, but they tooke off the bridles, for a signe that their City had never beene conquered, but enjoied Virgin liberty.

There are moments, after all, when the church is comparatively quiet and empty, and when you may sit there with an easy consciousness of its beauty. From the moment, of course, that you go into any Italian church for any purpose but to say your prayers or look at the ladies, you rank yourself among the trooping barbarians I just spoke of; you treat the place as an orifice in the peep-show. Still, it is almost a spiritual function – or, at the worst, an amorous one – to feed one's eyes on the molten colour that drops from the hollow vaults and thickens the air with its richness. It is all so quiet and sad and faded and yet all so brilliant and living. The strange figures in the mosaic pictures, bending with the curve of niche and vault, stare down through the glowing dimness; the burnished gold that stands behind them catches the light on its little uneven cubes. St Mark's owes nothing of its character to the beauty of proportion or perspective; there is nothing grandly balanced or far-arching; there are no long lines nor triumphs of the perpendicular. The church arches indeed, but arches like a dusky cavern. Beauty of surface, of tone, of detail, of things near enough to touch and kneel upon and lean against – it is from this the effect proceeds. In this sort of beauty the place is incredibly rich, and you may go there every day and find afresh some lurking pictorial nook. It is a treasury of bits, as the painters say; and there are usually three or four of the fraternity with their easels set up in uncertain equilibrium on the undulating floor. It is not easy to catch the real complexion of St Mark's, and these laudable attempts at portraiture are apt to look either lurid or livid. But if you cannot paint the old loose-looking marble slabs, the great panels of basalt and jasper, the crucifixes of which the lonely anguish looks deeper in the vertical light, the tabernacles whose open doors disclose a dark Byzantine image spotted with dull, crooked gems – if you cannot paint these things you can at least grow fond of them. You grow fond even of the old benches of red marble, partly worn away by the breeches of many generations and attached to the base of those wide pilasters of which the precious plating, delightful in its faded brownness, with a faint grey bloom upon it, bulges and yawns a little with honourable age.

St Mark's as a whole, unless seen from a distance or at twilight, is not beautiful. The modern mosaics (seventeenth century) are generally admitted to be extremely ugly, and I myself do not care for some of the Gothic statuary of the pinnacles. The horses, the coloured marble veneers, the Byzantine Madonna of the front, the old mosaic on the left, the marble columns of the portal, the gold encrustations of the top, the five grey domes with their strange ornaments, like children's jacks – these are the details that captivate. As for the rest, it is better not to look too closely, or the whole will begin to seem tawdry, a hodge-podge, as so many critics have said. The whole is not beautiful, and yet again it is. It depends on the light and the time of day or on whether you narrow your eyes, to make it look flat, a painted surface. And it can take you unawares, looking beautiful or horribly ugly, at a time you least expect. Venice, Henry James said, is as changeable as a nervous woman, and this is particularly true of St Mark's façade.

The enigma of San Marco continues to captivate modern visitors like MARY McCARTHY in her Venice Observed *(1956).*

With regard to the magnificence and decoration of the habitation of the aforesaid Doge – as I have seen many other princely palaces in this our time both in Italy and abroad, beginning at Rome – I venture to say that it is the most beautiful in Italy. It is so rich in carved work and everything gilded, that it is a marvel. One of the pages of the aforesaid Doge showed me everything, beginning with the bed in which he sleeps, and proceeding even to the kitchen, and in my opinion nothing could be added. The decorations are not movable, but fixed. There is no lack of marble and porphyry and woodwork subtly carved, and all is of such a nature that one is never weary of looking.

After many modifications and enlargements, the Palazzo Ducale began to take its present, unique form early in the fourteenth century. The building was undergoing one of its periodic renovations when CANON PIETRO CASOLA visited it in 1494.

Now that the materialization of your finest designs is adding the finishing touches to the splendour of the city which we, thanks to its generous hospitality, have chosen as our home (and we have been lucky, for a good foreigner here is accepted not only as Citizen but even as a Gentleman), you see that good has come of the evil of the Sack of Rome, in that your sculpture and your architecture are now being created in this divine place . . .

. . . Anyone who wishes to see the style in which a Republic like this supports the artists who create all its glories, should look at your house, a worthy prison of your art, where the products of your hands and your mind are taking shape all day long.

The Tuscan sculptor and architect Jacopo Sansovino (1486–1570) took refuge in Venice, with other artists and scholars, after the Sack of Rome by the Spanish in 1527. Sansovino made a greater impression on the face of the city than any other single artist before or since. PIETRO ARETINO wrote him this letter in 1537.

Who could fail to praise the way you have restored the church of San Marco to endure for ever?

Who is not stupefied by the huge Corinthian structure of the Misericordia?

Who is not struck dumb by the Rusticated and Doric building of the Zecca?

Façade design by Andrea Palladio.

Who is not dazzled by the sight of the work, started opposite to the Doge's Palace, in carved Doric with a suitably decorated Ionic order above?

How splendid the building to be erected beside it will look, in marble and other types of stone, with its large columns! It will consist of all the finest elements of Architecture, acting as a loggia where members of the nobility will gather . . .

Now may God grant us both long lives, so that you can continue to serve the Venetians, and I to sing their praises.

Looking at the buildings which Palladio completed, in particular at his churches, I have found much to criticize side by side with great excellence. While I was asking myself how far I was right or wrong about this extraordinary man, he seemed to be standing beside me, saying: 'This or that I did against my will, nevertheless I did it because it was the closest approximation to my ideal possible under the circumstances.'

The more I think about him, the more strongly I feel that, when he looked at the height and width of an old church or house for which he had to make a new façade, he must have said to himself: 'How can you give this building the noblest form possible? Because of contradictory demands, you are bound to bungle things here and there, and it may well happen that there will be some incongruities. But the building as a whole will be in a noble style, and you will enjoy doing the work.' It was in this way that he executed the great conception he had in mind, even when it was not quite suitable and he had to mangle it in the details.

There is only one bridge to go over the great channel, which is the same that leadeth from St Marks to the Rialto, and joyneth together both the banks of the channell. This bridge is commonly called Ponte de Rialto, and is the fairest bridge by many degrees for one arch that ever I saw, read, or heard of. For it is reported that it cost about fourescore thousand crownes, which doe make foure and twenty thousand pound sterling. Truely, the exact view hereof ministred unto me no small matter of admiration to see a bridge of that length (for it is two hundred foote long, the channell being at the least forty paces broade as I have before written) so curiously compacted together with one only arch; and it made me presently call to minde that most famous bridge of the Emperour Trajan, so celebrated by the auncient historians . . .

. . . It was first built but with timber (as I heard divers Venetian Gentlemen report) but because that was not correspondent to the magnificent of the other parts of the City, they defaced that, and built this most sumptuous bridge with squared white stone, having two faire rowes

In the sixteenth century, architect Andrea Palladio built beautifully proportioned villas on the Venetian mainland. In Venice itself, his work was restricted to a handful of churches, where his classically-inspired ideas were often constrained by lack of space. GOETHE communed with Palladio's spirit while visiting Venice in 1786 and recalled their dialogue in his Italian Journey *(1816–17).*

The Rialto bridge, spanning the Grand Canal at its deepest point, was for centuries the only means of walking from one end of Venice to the other. The English traveller THOMAS CORYAT gave a detailed account of the celebrated structure in his Crudities *(1611).*

Glass furnace, 16th century.

*The island of Murano has
been a glass-making centre for
centuries.* JAMES HOWELL,
*who worked for a glassware
firm in London, visited Murano
in 1621, and described it in
a letter to his friends at home.*

*Everywhere in Venice one finds
the human visage carved in
stone, usually subjected to a
bewildering variety of grotesque
distortions.
Unlike most modern visitors,*
JOHN RUSKIN *was appalled
by these fantasies, and in*
The Stones of Venice *(1851–53),
he vented his wrath on the huge
head carved at the base of the
Campanile in the Piazza
Santa Maria Formosa.*

of prety little houses for artificers, which are only shops, not dwelling houses. Of these shops there are two rowes in each side of the bridge till you come to the toppe … Moreover this bridge hath two very faire terrasses or railes made at the edge of the same on both sides, to the end to leane over and behold the goodly buildings about the Canal il grande … At the toppe of the bridge directly above those rowes of buildings that I have spoken of, wherein the artificers shops are, there are advanced two faire arches to a pretty convenient heigth which doe greatly adorne the bridge. In those arches I saw the portraiture of the heads of two Hunnicall Gyants that came into Italy with King Attila, very exactly made in the inside of the toppe.

I was, since I came hither, in Murano, a little Island about the distance of Lambeth from London, where Crystal-Glass is made; and 'tis a rare sight to see a whole Street, where on the one side there are twenty Furnaces together at work. They say here, That altho' one should transplant a Glass-Furnace from Murano to Venice herself, or to any of the little Assembly of Islands about her, or to any other part of the Earth besides, and use the same Materials, the same Workmen, the same Fuel, the self-same Ingredients every way, yet they cannot make Crystal-Glass in that perfection, for beauty and lustre, as in Murano: Some impute it to the quality of the circumambient Air that hangs o'er the Place, which is purify'd and attenuated by the concurrence of so many Fires that are in those Furnaces Night and Day perpetually, for they are like the Vestal-fire, which never goes out.

A head, – huge, inhuman, and monstrous, – leering in bestial degradation, too foul to be either pictured or described, or to be beheld for more than an instant: yet let it be endured for the instant; for in that head is embodied the type of the evil spirit to which Venice was abandoned in the fourth period of her decline; and it is well that we should see and feel the full horror of it on this spot, and know what pestilence it was that came and breathed upon her beauty, until it melted away like the white cloud from the ancient field of Santa Maria Formosa.

This head is one of many hundreds which disgrace the latest buildings of the city, all more or less agreeing in their expression of sneering mockery, in most cases enhanced by thrusting out the tongue. Most of them occur upon the bridges, which were among the very last works undertaken by the republic, several, for instance, upon the Bridge of Sighs; and they are evidences of a delight in the contemplation of bestial vice, and the expression of low sarcasm, which is, I believe, the most hopeless state into which the human mind can fall.

We have been treated to it again and again, of course, even if we have never stirred from home; but that is only a reason the more for catching at any freshness that may be left in the world of photography. It is in Venice above all that we hear the small buzz of this vulgarizing voice of the familiar; yet perhaps it is in Venice too that the picturesque fact has best mastered the pious secret of how to wait for us. Even the classic Salute waits like some great lady on the threshold of her saloon. She is more ample and serene, more seated at her door, than all the copyists have told us, with her domes and scrolls, her scolloped buttresses and statues forming a pompous crown, and her wide steps disposed on the ground like the train of a robe. This fine air of the woman of the world is carried out by the well-bred assurance with which she looks in the direction of her old-fashioned Byzantine neighbour; and the juxtaposition of two churches so distinguished and so different, each splendid in its sort, is a sufficient mark of the scale and range of Venice.

In Venice we note particularly any transformation of material. On the sides of some fondamenta, moisture causes the Istrian stone coping to mix with the brickwork below; similarly in the case of layers of stone between the brick. From mortar also, crystallizations appear on brick. Again, the copper dome of the church opposite the station has dripped greenly on the Istrian drum: the bronze statue upon the dome is similarly dyed. This building, the visitor's first sight of Venice, though unlike any other building there, in viridescent form, in a colour most unusual for Venice, symbolizes the prevailing process. This dome confounds the heights with the depths, suggesting in clear and stationary form exalted to an apex, the long tilted lift of the swell against the stone, which subsiding, reveals the greens of seaweed and of slime.

At sunset the water reflects the sky. That which the water reflected all day now it clasps and incorporates. Fusion is complete: the sky itself now rocks beneath the grandeur of yet whiter stone. This same rocking, one feels, sets the more distant churches swaying and swimming, sets their evening bells to roll. The brown prayers of the Redentore are loosed at evening in unmoored sound: and the church slips in upon the sky-and-water, aloft the white embannered Christ upon the dome.

The richness, the salt, the hardness of the water has caked into gleaming and hammered stones, particularly on rough days when the Giudecca's sea-green canal is tipped with foam. The past in Venice seems to be the period taken for crystallization: the store of Venetian history is encased by an image of an accumulated sea-change. So deeply laid are the imaginative foundations of Venice, to such an extent has stone abrogated the meaning of soil in our minds, that decay, as we have seen, takes the form of metamorphosis, and even of renewal.

Baldassare Longhena, Venice's greatest Baroque architect, built his masterpiece, the Church of Santa Maria della Salute, to commemorate Venice's survival of the plague of 1630. He successfully exploited one of the world's great building sites, at the entrance to the Grand Canal, opposite the Piazza San Marco, an achievement celebrated by HENRY JAMES *in his essay* 'The Grand Canal' (1892).

The stones of Venice, as we experience them today, have undergone many mutations since they were put in place by the original masons and architects. Art critic ADRIAN STOKES, *in his* Venice: An Aspect of Art (1945), *found in this process of physical change an emblem of the history of Venice itself.*

L'ARTE DEL PITTORE

To the English traveller
THOMAS CORYAT,
visiting Venice in 1609, the
mosaics of San Marco were a
startling novelty, as he
admitted in his Crudities
(1611).

The inner walles of the Church are beautified with a great multitude of pictures gilt, and contrived in Mosaical worke, which is nothing else but a prety kind of picturing consisting altogether of little pieces and very small fragments of gilt marble, which are square, and halfe as broade as the naile of a mans finger; of which piece there concurreth a very infinite company to the making of one of these pictures. I never saw any of this kind of picturing before I came to Venice, nor ever either read or heard of it, of which Saint Marks Church is full in every wall and roofe. It is said that they imitate the Grecians in these Mosaical workes.

Many travellers to Venice
have found themselves, like
GOETHE in his
Italian Journey (1816–17),
pondering the Venetian scenery
through the eyes of Venetian
painters.

My tendency to look at the world through the eyes of the painter whose pictures I have seen last has given me an odd idea. Since our eyes are educated from childhood on by the objects we see around us, a Venetian painter is bound to see the world as a brighter and gayer place than most people see it. We northerners who spend our lives in a drab and, because of the dirt and the dust, an uglier country where even reflected light is subdued, and who have, most of us, to live in cramped rooms – we cannot instinctively develop an eye which looks with such delight at the world.

As I glided over the lagoons in the brilliant sunshine and saw the gondoliers in their colourful costume, gracefully posed against the blue sky as they rowed with easy strokes across the light-green surface of the water, I felt I was looking at the latest and best painting in the Venetian school. The sunshine raised the local colours to a dazzling glare and even the parts in shadow were so light that they could have served pretty well as sources of light. The same could be said of the reflections in the water. Everything was painted clearly on a clear background. It only needed the sparkle of a white-crested wave to put the dot on the *i*.

The intertwining of Venetian
life and Venetian art fascinated
HENRY JAMES
in his travel book, Italian
Hours (1909).

All the splendour of light and colour, all the Venetian air and the Venetian history are on the walls and ceilings of the palaces; and all the genius of the masters, all the images and visions they have left upon canvas, seem to tremble in the sunbeams and dance upon the waves. That is the perpetual interest of the place – that you live in a certain sort of

'Miracle of the Relic of the Cross', painting by Vittore Carpaccio (1460–1526).

knowledge as in a rosy cloud. You don't go into the churches and galleries by way of a change from the streets; you go into them because they offer you an exquisite reproduction of the things that surround you. All Venice was both model and painter, and life was so pictorial that art couldn't help becoming so. With all diminutions life is pictorial still, and this fact gives an extraordinary freshness to one's perception of the great Venetian works. You judge of them not as a connoisseur, but as a man of the world, and you enjoy them because they are so social and so true. Perhaps of all works of art that are equally great they demand least reflection on the part of the spectator – they make least of a mystery of being enjoyed. Reflection only confirms your admiration, yet is almost ashamed to show its head. These things speak so frankly and benignantly to the sense that even when they arrive at the highest style – as in the Tintoret's 'Presentation of the little Virgin at the Temple' – they are still more familiar.

Art critic and connoisseur
BERNARD BERENSON
tried to account for the singularity of the Venetian style in The Venetian Painters of the Renaissance *(1894).*

The growing delight in life with the consequent love of health, beauty, and joy were felt more powerfully in Venice than anywhere else in Italy. The explanation of this may be found in the character of the Venetian government which was such that it gave little room for the satisfaction of the passion for personal glory, and kept its citizens so busy in duties of state that they had small leisure for learning. Some of the chief passions of the Renaissance thus finding no outlet in Venice, the other passions insisted all the more on being satisfied. Venice, moreover, was the only state in Italy which was enjoying, and for many generations had been enjoying, internal peace. This gave the Venetians a love of comfort, of ease, and of splendour, a refinement of manner, and humaneness of feeling, which made them the first modern people in Europe. Since there was little room for personal glory in Venice, the perpetuators of glory, the Humanists, found at first scant encouragement there, and the Venetians were saved from that absorption in archæology and pure science which overwhelmed Florence at an early date. This was not necessarily an advantage in itself, but it happened to suit Venice, where the conditions of life had for some time been such as to build up a love of beautiful things. As it was, the feeling for beauty was not hindered in its natural development. Archæology would have tried to submit it to the good taste of the past, a proceeding which rarely promotes good taste in the present. Too much archæology and too much science might have ended in making Venetian art academic, instead of letting it become what it did, the product of a natural ripening of interest in life and love of pleasure.

Giovanni Bellini was the universally acknowledged Master of Venetian painting at the turn of the fifteenth century. His altarpieces decorated Venetian churches, and patrons from far and wide vied for his services.

In 1501, MICHELE VIANELLO, *an agent of Isabella d'Este, Marchesa of Mantua, reported to his employer on the progress of her three-year-old commission to Bellini, who was at that time past seventy years of age.*

I have ... already spoken to him several times about your picture. He seems most anxious to serve Your Signory, but does not like the idea of the *Storia* you propose, and is unwilling to paint this, because, if this picture is to be a companion to M. Andrea's [Mantegna] work, he would like to do his best, and is sure that he cannot make anything good out of such a subject. He seems so reluctant to undertake this *Storia* that I doubt if

Your Excellency would be satisfied, and it would, I think, be better to let him do as he pleases.

The storia, *or subject matter, Isabella had proposed to the independent-minded master remains unknown. But in her reply to Vianello, the liberal Marchesa relented.*

If Zuan Bellini objects so much to this *Storia*, I am content to leave the subject to his judgment, as long as he paints a story or fable of his own invention, representing something antique, which has a fine meaning. I should be very glad if he would begin the work at once, so that it may be finished within the year, or even sooner, if possible.

Eventually, the frustrated Isabella demanded the return of her advance. Her agent LORENZO DA PAVIA *wrote to her.*

As for the money, Your Highness must understand that it is difficult to make the painter give back the ducats. Now he pretends that he will paint you a charming *fantasia* after his own fashion, which is, it must be confessed, a rather lengthy fashion! M. Michele begs you to write him a letter which he can show the painter, and will compel him to restore the money.

Bellini's delays drove Isabella to threats of legal action and even an appeal to the Venetian Senate. At last in 1502 LORENZO *was able to despatch the completed picture to Isabella, not without some trepidation.*

It seems to me ... that a thousand years will elapse before I hear how you like this picture. Certainly it is a beautiful work, although I confess, if I had ordered it, I should have preferred the figures to have been larger. And, as I said before, in point of invention no one can rival Andrea Mantegna, who is indeed a most excellent painter, the foremost of our age. But Zuan Bellini excels in colouring, and all who have seen this little picture think it admirable; and it is very highly finished, and will bear close inspection.

Four years later Isabella gave Bellini another commission. The Venetian humanist CARDINAL PIETRO BEMBO *agreed to act on her behalf, but urged her to be patient with the aged painter's moods and methods.*

Bellini, whom I have seen several times of late, is excellently disposed towards Your Excellency, and is only awaiting the measurements of the canvas to begin work. But the invention, which you tell me I am to choose for the picture, must be adapted to the painter's fancy. He does not care to have his imagination fettered by innumerable instructions, but prefers to arrange his composition according to his own ideas, being confident that in this way he can produce the best effect. All the same, I will endeavour to meet your wishes as well as his own.

Vittore Carpaccio (1460–1526), a student of Bellini and creator of his own colourful, highly detailed Venetian genre, barely figures in JOHN RUSKIN's *early writings on Venice. But in his later work, collected in* St Mark's Rest *(1877), the painter became an almost obsessive concern. Ruskin dwelt at length on the Scuola di San Giorgio degli Schiavone, a small building which acted as the offices of a Slav confraternity, and which houses Carpaccio's greatest cycle of paintings.*

The place looks comfortable, and, especially, warm, – the pictures having the effect, you will feel presently, of a soft evening sunshine on the walls, or glow from embers on some peaceful hearth, cast up into the room where one sits waiting for dear friends, in twilight.

In a little while, if you still look with general glance, yet patiently, this warmth will resolve itself into a kind of chequering, as of an Eastern carpet, or old-fashioned English sampler, of more than usually broken and sudden variegation; nay, suggestive here and there of a wayward patch-work, verging into grotesqueness, or even, with some touch of fantasy in masque, into harlequinade, – like a tapestry for a Christmas night in a home a thousand years old, to adorn a carol of honoured knights with honouring queens.

. . . go forward a little, please, to the second picture on the left, wherein, central, is our now accustomed friend, St George: stiff and grotesque, even to humorousness, you will most likely think him, with his dragon in a singularly depressed and, as it were, water-logged, state. Never mind him, or the dragon, just now: but take a good opera-glass, and look therewith steadily and long at the heads of the two princely riders on the left – the Saracen king and his daughter – he in high white turban, she beyond him in the crimson cap, high, like a castle tower.

Look well and long. For truly, – and with hard-earned and secure knowledge of such matters, I tell you, through all this round world of ours, searching what the best life of it has done of brightest in all its times and years, – you shall not find another piece quite the like of that little piece of work, for supreme, serene, unassuming, unfaltering sweetness of painter's perfect art. Over every other precious thing, of such things known to me, it rises, in the compass of its simplicity; in being able to gather the perfections of the joy of extreme childhood, and the joy of a hermit's age, with the strength and sunshine of mid-life, all in one.

The German artist ALBRECHT DÜRER, *intent on mastering the techniques of the Italian Renaissance, made his second visit to Venice in 1506. He recounted his ambitions, frustrations, and triumphs there*

How I wish you were here at Venice! There are so many nice men among the Italians who seek my company more and more every day – which is very pleasing to one – men of sense and knowledge, good luteplayers and pipers, judges of painting, men of much noble sentiment and honest virtue, and they show me much honour and friendship. On the other hand there are also amongst them some of the most false, lying, thievish rascals; I should never have believed that such were living in the world. If one did not know them, one would think them the nicest men the earth could show. For my own part I cannot help laughing at them whenever they talk to me. They know that their knavery is no secret but they don't mind.

Amongst the Italians I have many good friends who warn me not to eat and drink with their painters. Many of them are my enemies and they copy my work in the churches and wherever they can find it; and then they revile it and say that the style is not *antique* and so not good. But Giovanni Bellini has highly praised me before many nobles. He wanted to have something of mine, and himself came to me and asked me to paint him something and he would pay well for it. And all men tell me what an upright man he is, so that I am really friendly with him. He is very old, but is still the best painter of them all.

in letters to his lifelong friend and patron Wilibald Pirckheimer, a Nuremberg merchant and humanist scholar. Bellini remained his model, as he confessed in this letter, dated 7 February 1506.

'Here I am a gentleman, at home only a parasite' – self-portrait by Albrecht Dürer, 1498.

In this letter of 2 April 1506, DÜRER *depicts himself besieged by jealous Venetian painters and demanding German merchants.*

The painters here, let me tell you, are very unfriendly to me. They have summoned me three times before the magistrates and I have had to pay four florins to their school. You must also know that I might have gained a great deal of money if I had not undertaken to paint the German picture. There is much work in it and I cannot get it quite finished before Whitsuntide. Yet they only pay me 85 ducats for it. Now you know how much it costs to live, and then I have bought some things and sent some money away, so that I have not much before me now. But don't misunderstand me, I am firmly purposed not to go away hence till God enables me to repay you with thanks and to have a hundred florins over besides. I should easily earn this if I had not got the German picture to paint, for all men except the painters wish me well.

At last, DÜRER *completed the German merchants' commission. He boasted of his achievements in this letter of 8 September 1506.*

My picture, you must know, says it would give a ducat for you to see it, it is well painted and beautifully coloured. I have earned much praise but little profit by it. In the time it took to paint I could easily have earned 220 ducats, and now I have declined much work, in order that I may come home. I have stopped the mouths of all the painters who used to say that I was good at engraving but, as to painting, I did not know how to handle my colours. Now everyone says that better colouring they have never seen.

DÜRER *relished the status enjoyed by artists in Venice, and contrasted it with the low esteem in which they were held in Germany, in this letter of 13 October 1506.*

In reply to your question when I shall come home, I tell you ... that I shall have finished here in ten days; after that I should like to ride to Bologna to learn the secrets of the art of perspective, which a man is willing to teach me. I should stay there eight or ten days and then return to Venice. After that I shall come with the next messenger. How I shall freeze after this sun! Here I am a gentleman, at home only a parasite.

GIORGIO VASARI *depicted the short-lived but immensely influential artist, Giorgione di Castelfranco (1478–1510) in his* Lives of the Artists *(1550). To the Tuscan Vasari, the intuitive, painterly Venetian style was clearly inferior to that of the self-conscious intellectualism of the Florentine school. But in the case of the prodigious Giorgione, he made an exception.*

While Florence was winning fame through the works of Leonardo no less glory was conferred on Venice by the talents and achievements of one of her citizens, who greatly surpassed not only the Bellini (whom the Venetians regarded so highly) but also every other Venetian painter up to that time.

This artist was called Giorgio; he was born in 1478 at Castelfranco near Treviso, when the doge was Giovanni Mocenigo, Doge Piero's brother. Because of his physical appearance and his moral and intellectual stature he later came to be known as Giorgione [big George]; and although he was of humble origin throughout his life he was nothing if not gentle and courteous. He was brought up in Venice. He was always a very amorous man and he was extremely fond of the lute, which he played so beautifully to accompany his own singing that his services were often used at music recitals and social gatherings. He also studied and derived tremendous pleasure from the arts of design, in which he was highly gifted by nature; and he fell so deeply in love with the beauties of nature that he would represent in his works only what he copied directly from life. He always imitated and followed nature so faithfully that he was recognized not only as having surpassed Gentile and Giovanni Bellini but also as rivalling those who were working in Tuscany and creating the modern style.

At last, with final mastery of all the technical secrets of his art, and with somewhat more than 'a spark of the divine fire' to his share, comes Giorgione. He is the inventor of genre, of those easily movable pictures which serve neither for uses of devotion, nor of allegorical or historic teaching – little groups of real men and women, amid congruous furniture or landscape – morsels of actual life, conversation or music or play, but refined upon or idealized, till they come to seem like glimpses of life from afar. Those spaces of more cunningly blent colour, obediently filling their places, hitherto, in a mere architectural scheme, Giorgione detaches from the wall. He frames them by the hands of some skilful carver, so that people may move them readily and take with them where they go, as one might a poem in manuscript, or a musical instrument, to be used, at will, as a means of self-education, stimulus or solace, coming like an animated presence, into one's cabinet, to enrich the air as with some choice aroma, and, like persons, live with us, for a day or a lifetime. Of all art such as this, art which has played so large a part in men's culture since that time, Giorgione is the initiator. Yet in him too that old Venetian clearness or justice, in the apprehension of the essential limitations of the pictorial art, is still undisturbed. While he interfuses his painted work with a high-strung sort of poetry, caught directly from a singularly rich and high-strung sort of life, yet in his selection of subject, or phase of subject, in the subordination of mere subject to pictorial design, to the main purpose of a picture, he is typical of that aspiration of all the arts towards music, which I have endeavoured to explain, – towards the perfect identification of matter and form.

The essayist and art critic WALTER PATER *celebrated Giorgione's achievement in his* Renaissance Studies *(1877).*

I ... turned to look upon the sky. Never since God created it had it seemed to me so beautiful in its subtle pattern of light and shade. Anyone who wished to record the quality of that atmosphere would have been consumed with envy at not being you. Read on and you will understand why.

To begin with, the houses, though they were of stone, appeared phantasmal. The air in some directions looked transparent and alive, in others thick and dead. You must imagine, if you can, how I wondered at the clouds, which after all were nothing but condensed humidity. In the

PIETRO ARETINO, *contemplating the beauty of a Venetian sunset, wrote enviously to his friend, the master painter Titian (c.1490–1576).*

middle distance some seemed to touch the roofs, while others retreated far away. To the right they resembled a poised mass of greyish-black smoke.

I was amazed at the variety of their hues. Those near at hand burned like fiery suns. Those in the distance glowed dully, like half-molten lead. The world's ingenious brush-strokes lent perspective to the atmosphere in recession behind the palaces, just as in one of your own landscapes. The bluish-green in some places and the greenish-blue in others seemed really to have been composed by nature with a capricious yet wonderfully skilled hand, lightening or subduing the tones in accordance, it appeared, with a personal choice.

'Death of St Peter Martyr', engraving after an alterpiece by Titian destroyed by fire in 1867.

I who know your brushes to be the soul itself of nature exclaimed three or four times in succession: 'Ah Titian, where are you?' I would take an oath by all that I hold sacred that if you had painted what I have just described men would have stood rooted to the spot with the same stunning admiration I felt as I beheld the scene and realized that its miracle would not last.

The pictures Titian was painting ten years after his companion's death have not only many of the qualities of Giorgione's, but something more, as if done by an older Giorgione, with better possession of himself, and with a larger and firmer hold on the world. At the same time, they show no diminution of spontaneous joy in life, and even an increased sense of its value and dignity. What an array of masterpieces might be brought to witness! In the 'Assumption', for example, the Virgin soars heavenward, not helpless in the arms of angels, but borne up by the fullness of life within her, and by the feeling that the universe is naturally her own, and that nothing can check her course. The angels seem to be there only to sing the victory of a human being over his environment. They are embodied joys, acting on our nerves like the rapturous outburst of the orchestra at the end of 'Parsifal'. Or look at the 'Bacchanals' in Madrid, or at the 'Bacchus and Ariadne' in the National Gallery. How brim-full they are of exuberant joy! You see no sign of a struggle of inner and outer conditions, but life so free, so strong, so glowing, that it almost intoxicates. They are truly Dionysiac, Bacchanalian triumphs – the triumph of life over the ghosts that love the gloom and chill and hate the sun.

Titian and Giorgione were contemporaries, and in their youth Giorgione seemed the more innovative and dominant of the two. After his early death, his mantle passed to Titian, who developed his friend's style and surpassed it in his large-scale masterpieces, such as the 'Assumption' on the high altar of the Frari Church in Venice, celebrated by BERNARD BERENSON *in* The Venetian Painters of the Renaissance *(1894).*

It is certainly true that the method used by Titian for painting these last pictures is very different from the way he worked in his youth. For the early works are executed with incredible delicacy and diligence, and they may be viewed either at a distance or close at hand; on the other hand, these last works are executed with bold, sweeping strokes, and in patches of colour, with the result that they cannot be viewed from near by, but appear perfect at a distance. This method of painting is the reason for the clumsy pictures painted by the many artists who have tried to imitate Titian and show themselves practised masters; for although Titian's works seem to many to have been created without much effort, this is far from the truth and those who think so are deceiving themselves. In fact, it is clear that Titian has retouched his pictures, going over them with his colours several times, so that he must obviously have taken great pains. The method he used is judicious, beautiful, and astonishing, for it makes pictures appear alive and painted with great art, but it conceals the labour that has gone into them.

In his last years Titian developed a new, freer style of working which left the brushstroke visible on the canvas. GIORGIO VASARI *describes it in the life of Titian included in the second edition of his* Lives of the Artists *(1568).*

Drawing by Tintoretto.

Venice, *Sept. 23.* – I have been quite overwhelmed to-day by a man whom I never dreamed of – Tintoret. I always thought him a good and clever and forcible painter; but I had not the smallest notion of his enormous powers … It is marvellous lucky I came here, or I might have disgraced myself for ever by speaking slightly of Tintoret. I look upon Tintoret now, though as a less perfect painter, yet as a far greater man than Titian ipse …

Sept. 24. – I have had a draught of pictures to-day enough to drown me. I never was so utterly crushed to the earth before any human intellect as I was to-day – before Tintoret. Just be so good as to take my list of painters and put him in the school of Art at the top – top – top of everything, with a great big black line underneath him to stop him off from everybody; and put him in the school of Intellect, next after Michael Angelo. He took it so entirely out of me to-day that I could do nothing at last but lie on a bench and laugh … Tintoret don't seem able to stretch himself till you give him a canvas forty feet square, and then – he lashes out like a leviathan, and heaven and earth come together … Just imagine the audacity of the fellow – in his Massacre of the Innocents one of the mothers has hurled herself off a terrace to avoid the executioner and is falling head foremost and backwards – holding up the child still.

And such a Resurrection as there is – the rocks of the Sepulchre cracked all to pieces and roaring down upon you, while the Christ soars forth into a torrent of angels, whirled up into heaven till you are lost ten times over. And then to see his touch of quiet thought in his awful Crucifixion. There is an *ass* in the distance, feeding on the remains of palm leaves. If that isn't a master's stroke, I know not what is. As for painting, I think I didn't know what it meant till to-day; the fellow outlines you your figure with ten strokes, and colours it with as many more. I don't believe it took him ten minutes to invent and paint a whole length. Away he goes, heaping host on host, multitudes that no man can number – never pausing, never repeating himself. Clouds and whirlwinds and fire and infinity of earth and sea, all alike to him …

Sept. 25. – Is this really the 25th? I don't know at all what to do. I am so divided between Tintoret and the Grand Canal. I had a good two hours' sit before him this morning, and it did me mighty good and made me feel bigger, taken up into him as it were. I am in a great hurry now to try my hand at painting a real, downright, big oil picture. I think I am up to a dodge or two that I wasn't, and I must have some tries in it. Tintoret has shown me how to paint leaves. My word, he does *leave* them with a vengeance. I think you would like to see how he does the trunk, too, with two strokes; one for the light side and one for the dark side, all the way down; and then on go the leaves: never autumn swept them off as he sweeps them on; and then to see his colossal straws; and his sublime rush-bottomed chairs; and his stupendous donkey in the Flight into Egypt – such a donkey, such a donkey, with ears that look as if they heard the Massacre of the Innocents going on in Palestine all the way from Egypt; and well he might if it had been Tintoret's instead of Herod's. I looked at it to-day till I heard the women shriek – there they are – tumbling all over each other, executioners' swords and all – one mass of desperation and agony, nothing disgusting, nothing indecent, no blood, no cutting of throats; but the most fearful heap of human grief and madness and struggle that ever man's mind conceived.

Titian was assuredly a mighty poet, but Tintoret – well, Tintoret was almost a prophet. Before his greatest works you are conscious of a sudden evaporation of old doubts and dilemmas, and the eternal problem of the conflict between idealism and realism dies the most natural of deaths. In his genius the problem is practically solved; the alternatives are so harmoniously interfused that I defy the keenest critic to say where one begins and the other ends. The homeliest prose melts into the most ethereal poetry – the literal and the imaginative fairly confound their identity.

HENRY JAMES also caught the Tintoretto mania, but he exorcized it in more cerebral fashion in his Italian Hours (1909).

INQUISITOR] What does the image of the man with the nose bleed signify?

VERONESE] I made him as a servant, who by some accident, has got a nose bleed.

INQUISITOR] What do the armed men dressed in German fashion with halberds signify?

VERONESE] We painters take the same licence as poets and madmen . . . it seemed fitting that the master of the house, whom I was told was great and rich, would have such servants.

INQUISITOR] The one dressed as a buffoon with a parrot in his fist, why is he in this picture?

VERONESE] As an ornament . . .

INQUISITOR] Do you really believe you would find such figures at the Last Supper?

VERONESE] I believe you would find Christ and his apostles, but in a picture with so much space, I added other figures, as they occurred to me.

INQUISITOR] Did any other person commission you to put in Germans and buffoons and similar things?

VERONESE] No, signor. But the commission was to ornament the

The third in the great triumvirate of Venetian sixteenth-century masters was Paolo Caliari, known as VERONESE (1528–88). Less introspective and intellectual than either Titian or Tintoretto, Veronese was nonetheless summoned, in 1573, to appear before the much-feared Church Inquisition, which was disturbed by some of the details the painter had included in his recent rendering of The Last Supper. The ensuing dialogue survives in the state archives in Venice.

picture, which was large and had space for many figures, as seemed best to me.

INQUISITOR] Do you usually try to make the subordinate figures in your picture in keeping with the main figures, or do you just put them in without any discretion or judgement?

VERONESE] I made the picture in a way that seemed suitable to me, according to my understanding of it.

INQUISITOR] Did it seem suitable to you to paint the Last Supper of the Lord with buffoons, drunks, Germans and other scurrilities?

VERONESE] No, signor.

INQUISITOR] Don't you know that in Germany and other places infected with heresy they are using pictures full of scurrilities and other inventions to attack and make a joke of the Catholic Church, teaching bad doctrine to stupid and ignorant people?

VERONESE] Signor, yes it's bad, but as I have said before, I was obliged to follow the example of my masters.

INQUISITOR] What have your masters done? Have they done similar things?

VERONESE] Michelangelo in Rome, in the Papal Chapel, has painted Jesus Christ, his Holy Mother, Saint John, Saint Peter and the celestial court in the nude, in different positions, with little reverence.

INQUISITOR] Don't you know that in painting the Last Judgement one doesn't paint clothes and such things, because they do not appear in clothes? In spiritual matters one doesn't find buffoons and food and weapons and other nonsense. Doesn't it seem to you that it would have been better to paint this picture in the proper fashion, and then you could have defended it better?

VERONESE] I do not want to defend it, and I hope to do better. I did not consider many things, because I hoped not to make a disordered effect. It would have been better to put the buffoons outside the place where the Lord was.

Veronese was commanded to alter the picture within three months. He conformed to the Inquisition's verdict without exerting himself further, simply by changing the picture's title. The Last Supper *became* Supper at the House of Levi, *and hangs today in the Accademia Gallery in Venice.*

In 1727 OWEN MCSWINEY, *negotiated with the artist Canaletto on behalf of the future Duke of Richmond. He warned his patron of the artist's antics in a letter.*

The fellow is whimsical and vary's his prices every day and he that has a mind to have any of his work, must not seem to be too fond of it, for he'l be the worse treated for it, both in the price and the painting too. He has more work than he can doe, in any reasonable time, and well: but by the assistance of a particular friend of his, I get once in two months a piece sketch'd out and a little time after finished, by force of bribery . . . I

Drawing of the Piazza S. Giacomo di Rialto, by Antonio Canale, known as Canaletto (1697–1768).

shall have a view of the Rialto Bridge, done by Canal in twenty days, and I have bespoke another view of Venice for, by the by, his excellence lyes in painting things which fall immediately under his eyes.

It constantly happens, that public bodies who will not pay five pounds to preserve a picture, will pay fifty to repaint it: and when I was at Venice in 1846, there were two remedial operations carrying on, at one and the same time, in the two buildings which contain the pictures of greatest value in the city (as pieces of colour, of greatest value in the world), curiously illustrative of this peculiarity in human nature. Buckets were set on the floor of the Scuola di San Rocco, in every shower, to catch the rain which came through the pictures of Tintoret on the ceiling; while, in the Ducal Palace, those of Paul Veronese were themselves laid on the floor to be repainted; and I was myself present at the re-illumination of the breast of a white horse, with a brush, at the end of a stick five feet long, luxuriously dipped in a common house-painter's vessel of paint.

Much of Venice's pictorial heritage was neglected in the eighteenth and nineteenth centuries. JOHN RUSKIN, *who struggled for years to preserve its artistic treasures, was appalled by this scene, described in* The Stones of Venice *(1851–53).*

A Jewish wedding in Venice, 18th century.

THE CITY OF SAINT MARK

According to legend, an angel appeared to St Mark, who had sought shelter in a deserted spot in the then uninhabited Venetian lagoon, and told him that, one day, his body would rest here. The legend was fulfilled – by force – in AD 828, when two Venetian merchants stole the saint's remains from Alexandria, and transported them back to the small settlement on the island of Rialto. The infant city then adopted Mark as its patron and his lion as its emblem.

There are many notable monasteries at Venice, which are very sumptuous and magnificent, there being more than eighty for men and women, and above fifty churches. There are likewise many relics and holy bodies: the body of St Helena, that of St Marina, and a leg of St Christopher from the knee downwards, as well as many bones of the Innocents, with an infinite number more which the Venetians brought from Constantinople when they took it.

I will only say, speaking generally, that the poorest parish church of Venice is more ornate than the finest at Milan. Almost all the Venetian churches – the parish churches I mean – have a beautiful choir and an organ, and no expense is spared to decorate them; everything is gilded, and they are well served. This makes me think strongly that the Venetians must be greatly aided by God in all their affairs, because they are very solicitous with regard to divine worship in all their churches.

Two lay lords, great personages in this kingdom, inquired of me whence it came that your Excellency [the government of Venice] was of such slippery faith, now favouring one party and then the other? Although these words might reasonably have provoked me, I answered them with all discretion, that you did keep, and ever have kept your faith, the maintenance of which has placed you in great trouble, and subjected you to wars of longer duration than you would otherwise have experienced; descending to particulars in justification of your Sublimity; whereupon, one of them replied, '*Isti Veneti sunt piscatores!*' [those Venetians are fishermen!]. Marvellous was the command I then had over myself in not giving vent to expressions which might have proved

In 1436, PERO TAFUR, a Catalan pilgrim on his way to the Holy Land, was impressed by Venice's religious monuments and collection of relics.

Another pilgrim, PIETRO CASOLA, Canon of Milan Cathedral, and a proud Milanese patriot, described the opulence of the Venetian churches during his visit in 1494.

SEBASTIANO GIUSTINIANI *served as Venetian ambassador to the Court of Henry VIII. Venice was at this time trying to steer a course between Pope and Protestants. Giustiniani was driven by Henry's partisan courtiers to defend the honour of his homeland, as he reported in this despatch, dated 15 April 1516.*

injurious to your Signory, and with extreme moderation, I rejoined that had he been at Venice and seen our senate and the Venetian nobility, he perhaps would not speak thus; and, moreover, were he well read in our history, both concerning the origin of our city and the grandeur of your Excellency's feats, neither the one nor the other would seem to him those of fishermen; yet, said I, did fishermen found the Christian faith, and we have been those fishermen who defended it against the forces of the infidel, our fishing-boats being galleys and ships, our hooks the treasure of St Mark, and our bait the life-blood of our citizens who died for the Christian faith . . .

For centuries the Venetian clergy, especially monks, enjoyed a widespread reputation for irreligious behaviour, a stereotype exploited by the Tuscan writer GIOVANNI BOCCACCIO *in this tale from his* Decameron *(1355).*

There lived at Imola a man of a very bad life, called Berto della Massa, whose evil works had gained him such a character there that nobody could believe him even when he spoke the truth. Finding, therefore, that all his quirks and cunning would stand him in no farther stead at Imola, he removed, in a kind of despair, to Venice, the common receptacle of all sorts of wickedness, when he resolved to manage his ill doings in a quite different manner; and, as if he felt some remorse of conscience for his past life, pretending also to be seized with uncommon zeal and devotion, he joined a religious order, calling himself Brother Alberto of Imola. In this habit, he seemed to lead a mighty sanctified life, highly commending penance and abstinence, eating no flesh and drinking no wine, – at least when he could get neither to please him; insomuch that, before any one had taken notice of the matter, he was changed from a thief, a ruffian, and homicide, into a preacher of righteousness, without abandoning his vices, if he could enact them in secrecy. Besides this, when he was officiating at the altar at any time, if he were taken notice of by many people, he would be sure to weep over our Saviour's passion, having tears enough at command whenever he pleased. To be short, what with his preaching and weeping together, he had so far insinuated himself into the good graces of the people of Venice that there was scarcely a will made but he was left executor; he had the care also and disposal of many people's money, and was the chief adviser and confessor to the greatest part both of men and women; so that from a wolf he became the shepherd, and the fame of his sanctity was greater than ever was that of Saint Francis.

ROGER ASCHAM, *passionate Protestant and pedagogue, railed against the irreligion of Venetian Catholicism in* The Scholemaster *(1570).*

I was once in Italie my selfe: but I thanke God, my abode there was but ix. dayes: And yet I sawe in that litle tyme, in one Citie, more libertie to sinne, than ever I hard tell of in our noble Citie of London in ix. yeare. I sawe, it was there as free to sinne, not onelie without all punishment, but also without any mans marking, as it is free in the Citie of London to chose without all blame, whether a man lust to weare Shoo or pantocle.

And good cause why: For being unlike in troth of Religion, they must nedes be unlike in honestie of living. For blessed be Christ, in our Citie of London commonlie the commandementes of God be more diligentlie taught, and the service of God more reverentlie used, and that daylie, in many private mens houses, than they be in Italie once a weeke in their common Chirches: where masking Ceremonies to delite the eyes, and vaine soundes to please the eare, do quite thrust out of the Chirches all services of God in spirit and troth ... I learned, when I was at Venice, that there it is counted good pollicie, when there be foure or five brethren of one familie, one onelie to marie: and all the rest to waulter with as litle shame in open lecherie, as Swyne do here in the common myre.

Mine associate and I, were no sooner landed, and perceiving a great throng of people, and in the midst of them a great smoake; but we begun to demaund a Venetian what the matter was? who replied, there was a gray Frier burning quicke at S. Markes pillar, of the reformed order of S. Francis, for begetting fifteene young Noble Nunnes with child, and all within one yeare; he being also their Father confessor. Whereat, I sprung forward through the throng, and my friend followed me, and came just to the pillar as the halfe of his body and right arme fell flatlings in the fire; The Frier was forty six yeares old, and had bene Confessor of that Nunnery of Sancta Lucia five yeares: Most of these young Nunnes were Senators daughters; and two of them were onely come in to learne vertue, and yet fell in the midst of vice.

These fifteene with child, were all re-cald home to their fathers Pallaces; the Lady Prioresse, and the rest of her voluptuous crew, were banished for ever from the precincts of Venice. The Monastery was razed to the ground, their rents were allowed to be bestowed upon poore families, and distressed age, and their Church to be converted to an Hospitall.

12 May 1606. The Jesuits here finally refusing (though at first they gave some hope of the contrary) to perform any ecclesiastical duties when the Pope's *interdictum* should come actually in force, the State hereupon, three days since, did pass a decree in Senate to banish them out of all their dominion, with this notorious circumstance comprehended in the decree, that an under secretary of the Senate, with a *Comandatore* or pursuivant, should take an inventory of their movables, not permitting them to transport with them anything but their quotidian habit, and their breviaries; which hath accordingly been executed here. Now before their going, one of the principalest and boldest of them (called *Il Padre* Barone), having obtained a private access unto the Prince [the Doge], made offer unto him of interposing his Society for the reconcilement of the Pope.

The Scottish adventurer
WILLIAM LITHGOW,
in his travel book Rare
Adventures and Painefull
Peregrinations *(1632), found
the Venetian clergy's ill repute
confirmed by his first
impressions of the city.*

*For centuries Venice had
resisted the territorial claims
and worldly aspirations of the
Vatican. In 1606 the long-
simmering feud came to a head
when the Venetians took the
unprecedented step of
prosecuting two monks, charged
with petty crimes, in the secular
courts. The Pope placed the city
under an Interdict, forbidding
the clergy to celebrate the Mass*

*in its territories, and
excommunicating the Doge and
the entire Senate. Venice defied
the Pope's authority, ably
defended in treatises and tomes
by the monk and scholar, Paolo
Sarpi. After a tense year, the
Vatican climbed down and an
accord was reached reconciling
Venice to the Catholic Church.
The temper of events during
the critical weeks can be
followed in the despatches sent
home by the English ambassador
in Venice, Sarpi's friend,
HENRY WOTTON,
who hoped to persuade the
Venetians to join the Protestant
camp.*

This was on Saturday last in the morning; at which time he had from the Prince this noble answer, that 'the State of Venice had never before used such instruments and would not now begin'; and therefore he willed him 'to forbear the employment of themselves either much or little in this matter, and rather to spend their time in considering that they had been already too busy in the world'. And so he departed.

19 May 1606. The differences between the Pope and State of Venice being now grown so far, that neither of the parties can retire without notable loss of reputation . . . Now, in the dependency of this business, many things have been done here provisionally; some in judgement, some in passion, some in earnest, some in sport, some in contempt, and nothing (that I have yet seen) in fear: which I will set down by way of rhapsody, like the very nature of the time itself. First, the ambassadors are departed from both sides, the Nuncio first, and with leave demanded and granted civilly and easily. The Venetian from Rome with violence, for the Pope by a bishop commanded him to be gone, unless he would remain there in private quality, which he refused; and is this very day expected here from a town but five miles from hence, where he lay the last night.

26 May 1606. Yesterday was the Feast of Corpus Christi, celebrated by express commandment of the State (which goeth farther than devotion), with the most sumptuous procession that ever had been seen here, wherein the very basins and ewers were valued in common judgement at 200,000 pound sterling, besides many costly and curious pageants, adorned with sentences of Scripture fit for the present, as *Omnis potestas est a Deo, Date Caesari quae Caesaris et Deo quae Dei, Omnis anima subdita sit potestatibus sublimioribus, Regnum meum non est de hoc mundo* and the like. The reasons of this extraordinary solemnity were two, as I conceive it. First, to contain the people still in good order with superstition, the foolish band of obedience. Secondly, to let the Pope know (who wanteth not intelligencers) that notwithstanding his interdict, they had friars enough and other clergymen to furnish out the day.

The process of the Jesuits dependeth still before the Council of Ten as a criminal cause.

The monks of St Benedict (which draw 200,000 crowns of yearly revenue out of the Venetian State) have found a notable way to delude the Pope's authority, not yet daring to deny it, which is this: they have caused a chest to be made without a lock, fast nailed on all sides, and in the top thereof a little hole, into which they throw all letters that are directed to their convent without exception, lest they might receive some prohibition from their General, and so mean to save their consciences by the way of ignorance: which point of subtle discretion is likely to be imitated by other orders.

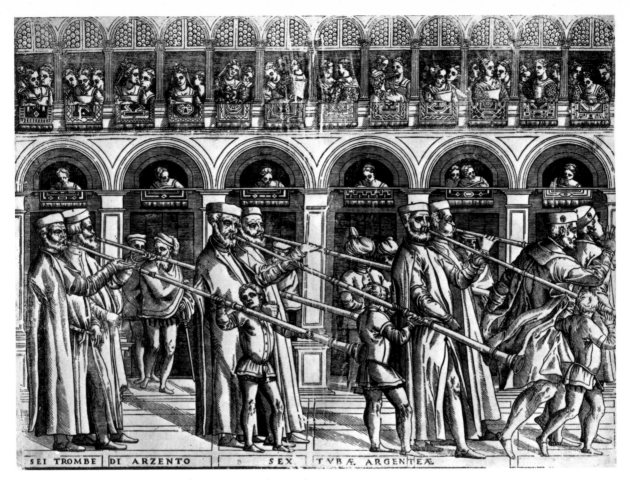

SEI TROMBE | DI ARZENTO | | SEX | TVBÆ ARGENTEÆ

'Procession of the Doge on Palm Sunday', engraving by Matthew Pagan, 1559.

The other ffest was oon Corpis xpi [Christi] Day, wher was the most Solemne pcession that ever I saw. Ther went Pagents of the old law and the new law Joynyng to gedyr ... And over that it was a grett merveyle to se the grett nowmbre of Religius ffolkes and of Scolys that we call Bachelors or ffelachippys Clothid all in white garmens with Diverse bags on ther brestis which bar all lights of wondyr goodly facion, And be twyne every of the Pagents went lityll childern of both kynds, gloriusly and rechely Dressed beryng in ther handys ryche Cuppes or other vessales of gold and silver Rychely inamelyd and gylt ffull of plesaunt fflowers and well Smellying which chyldern kest the flowers upon the lords and pylgrymes. They war Dressed as Aungellis with clothe of gold and crymsyn velvet to order the seyd procession. The forme and manner therof excedyd all other that ever I Saw, so much that I canne nott wryte it.

The Duke Satt in Seynt Markes Churche in ryght hys astate in the Qwer on the ryght syd with senyoryte which they call lords in Riche aparell as purpyll velvet, cremsyn velvet, ffyne Scarlett.

The Venetian calendar was full of grand religious festivals, in which nobility, commoners, and foreigners all took part. In 1517, the English knight RICHARD TORKINGTON, *in the course of his pilgrimage to Jerusalem, witnessed one of the most elaborate, the Feast of Corpus Christi, celebrated in honour of the Eucharist, on the Thursday after Pentecost; he recorded the event in his travel journal.*

Also all the pylgrymes war commandyd to com in to the ffor seyd Qwer and ther we Satt all on the left syd on the quere. The Duke thus Syttyng with hys lords, the seyd procession be ganne to com be hym a bowte viii of the clok and it was xii or the seyd pression myght Com oonys a bowt pessyng by as faste as they myght goo but on tyme.

Thanne the Duke rose vp with hys lords and company to folow the fforsayd procession. He commaundyd hys lordys that they shuld in the procession every oon of them take a Pylgryme on his Right-hande hys servaunts gevyng to vs grett Candyls of wax, whych Candelys every Pylgrim bar a-way the procession Doon at hys owen plesur. We procedyd owt of Seynt Markes Churche, in to the Dukys pales, and so went procession with inne the seyd place because it was Reyne wedyr, And so retornyed in the Churche a geyne of Seynt Marke and ther made ende of the seyde Procession.

In 1630, Venice was devastated by plague. In the space of sixteen months, 50,000 people died. The church of Santa Maria della Salute was then begun as a thanks-offering to the Virgin for her intercession, which was alleged to have brought the plague to an end. The Feast of the Salute soon became one of Venice's premier public occasions.

The English expatriate HORATIO BROWN described it in Life on the Lagoons (1884).

On three occasions only in the year are pontoon bridges thrown across the Grand Canal – on the Day of St Anthony, the Day of the Redentore, and this Festival of the Salute ... On the Day of the Salute there are two bridges – one for going and one for coming. The crowds that pass backwards and forwards all day are very large, for the inhabitants of Venice, even those who are ordinarily indifferent to the Mass, feel bound to visit the church upon this festival.

From the very earliest morning the tramp of feet begins below one's window, and sleep is impossible. It is best to get up and go with the crowd. The cloaked and muffled throng look dim and ghostly and unwonted in the doubtful morning light, as they stream across the bridges. All round the open space by the church, stalls are set up, and a small fair goes actively forward with the sale of hot fish, coffee, statuettes of the saints in plaster, rosaries, 'portraits' of Madonna, pamphlets of her miracles, but above all *gallani*, a mixture the Venetians delight in at this season. *Gallani* is made of flour, lard, and white of egg, raised to a froth, like whipped cream, by the yeast that is beaten up in it. They serve it to you in little conical cups of pastry; but those who expect the flavour of whipped cream would probably be disappointed.

At half-past ten the great function takes place. The procession of all the parishes musters in the piazza. The priests of each parish wear different coloured stoles to distinguish them from one another; and the procession, when seen from the steps the façade as it moves slowly over the bridge, looks like some huge serpent with bands of various hues upon his skin. Inside the church, the devout light the candles they have carried, one taking the fire from another, and press forward after the priests up to the altar rails; there the tapers are handed over to the sacristans and placed

The church of S. Maria della Salute, designed by Baldassare Longhena.

Sketch of a Venetian tomb.

beside the high altar, where Madonna stands, triumphing over a figure of the plague. Thousands and thousands of candles are passed over the rails until the whole space by the altar seems like one solid wall of embossed gold as the flames waver and flicker in the draught. In return for their candles and some centesimi, the pious receive a picture of Madonna, which is devoutly kissed and put away inside their shirts or shawls . . .

The services go on all day long, one succeeding the other, till the final vespers and benediction at five o'clock.

But the Venetians do not end their festa there; they keep it up far beyond midnight; and from the wine-shops and eating-houses come bursts of laughter and of song . . .

149

The scuola *was a unique Venetian institution, part lay religious order, part charitable body, and part state-supervised social club. The English traveller* FYNES MORYSON *described it in his* Itinerary *(1617).*

The Venetians have six fraternities or great schooles, such as be also at Rome, and the Gentlemen and Citizens all give their names to one of them, as in England at London, the Citizens have companies, into which the King, Queene, and Nobles, many times vouchsafe to be admitted. And in these schooles, as it were in Universities, they use to have exercises of religion. The first of them is called Saint Mary of Charity, after the rule whereof, the rest are framed, and the great Guardian thereof is chosen yeerly, and weares a skarlet gowne with large sleeves, which they call Ducall sleeves, and he hath the title of Magnifico by priviledge. These schooles give dowries yeerely to 1500. Virgins, and distribute among the poore much money, meale, and clothes: for besides many gifts by last testaments daily given to those uses, each of the schooles hath some five or six thousand duckets in yeerely revenew, and they are governed like common wealthes. In the said schoole, the Images of the Apostles, and the pictures, especially one of the blessed Virgin, and another of the foure Doctors of the Church, are very faire. In the schoole of Saint John the Evangelist, the passion of Christ is wonderfully figured, and Phillip the second King of Spaine, and his sonne Ferdinand, and Don John of Austria, and other Princes, have beene of this fraternity. The third is of mercy. The fourth of Saint Marke. The fifth of Saint Rocco, passing the rest in ceremonies & pompe, and number of brethren. The sixth is of Saint Theodore, and each of these hath his Church and Pallace, and precious monuments and these are subject to the counsell of ten . . .

Because of its commercial traditions and dependence on foreign trade, Venice was more tolerant of minorities than other European cities. Its Jewish community was long-established and highly respected. When WILLIAM SHAKESPEARE *wrote of it in* The Merchant of Venice *(1. iii) (1596–98), Jews were still banned from England.*

ANTONIO] Well Shylock, shall we be beholding to you?
SHYLOCK] Signior Antonio, many a time and oft
In the Rialto you have rated me
About my moneys and my usances:
Still have I borne it with a patient shrug,
(For suff'rance is the badge of all our tribe)
You call me misbeliever, cut-throat dog,
And spet upon my Jewish gaberdine,
And all for use of that which is mine own.
Well then, it now appears you need my help:
Go to then, you come to me, and you say,
'Shylock, we would have moneys,' you say so:
You that did void your rheum upon my beard,
And foot me as you spurn a stranger cur
Over your threshold, moneys is your suit.
What should I say to you? Should I not say
'Hath a dog money? is it possible
A cur can lend three thousand ducats?' or

Shall I bend low, and in a bondman's key
With bated breath, and whisp'ring humbleness
Say this:
'Fair sir, you spat on me on Wednesday last,
You spurn'd me such a day, another time
You call'd me dog: and for these courtesies
I'll lend you thus much moneys'?

Had I, Marino Sanuto, been a member of the Senate as I was last year, I would have spoken, though not to speak for the Jews, because I could describe many sharp practices of theirs in connexion with their loans. I would have spoken ... proving that Jews are even more necessary to a city than bakers are, and especially to this one, for the sake of the general welfare. I would have referred to laws, and to what our ancestors have always done, and to the opinion of the Doctors Alessandro of Imola, Pietro of Ancarano, Baldus and others, who advise us that Jews can be kept to lend upon interest. And thus I would have spoken on the question at issue. It is true that I would not have wished them to keep shops dealing in second-hand goods, so as not to deprive Christians of a living, even though if they kept them goods could be sold very profitably. Our countrymen have never wanted Jews to keep shops to trade in this city, but to buy and sell and go away again. But there should be none of this humbug in our State about expelling the Jews when there is no Monte di Pietà [lending bank] ... There is very little trade in the city. Shopkeepers are complaining that they are not selling their goods, and it will not be forgotten that a man can on his property borrow from the Jews at 15 per cent in order to fulfil his own needs and feed and maintain his family.

In the sixteenth century, with the growth of the Inquisition, Jews were expelled from many Italian cities. The Venetian Senate debated the question in 1519, and decided to allow them to stay, though confined within the walls of what became known as the Ghetto Nuovo. The Venetian signor, one-time senator, and compulsive diarist, MARINO SANUTO, weighed the case against the Jews and found in their favour, largely because of their powerful lending banks, as he explained in this entry in his diary, November 1519.

I was at a place where the whole fraternity of the Jews dwelleth together, which is called the Ghetto, being an Iland: for it is inclosed round about with water. It is thought there are of them in all betwixt five and sixe thousand ... They have divers Synagogues in their Ghetto, at the least seven, where all of them, both men, women and children doe meete together upon their Sabboth, which is Saturday, to the end to doe their devotion, and serve God in their kinde, each company having a several Synagogue ...

... In the roome wherin they celebrate their divine service, no women sit, but have a loft or gallery proper to themselves only, where I saw many Jewish women, whereof some were as beautiful as ever I saw, and so gorgeous in their apparel, jewels, chains of gold, and rings adorned with previous stones, that some of our English Countesses do scarce exceed them, having marvailous long traines like Princesses that are borne up by

For early English travellers like THOMAS CORYAT, the Jews of the Venetian ghetto were an exotic, incomprehensible breed. With blind self-assurance, he narrated his encounter with them in his Crudities *(1611).*

waiting women serving for the same purpose. An argument to prove that many of the Jewes are very rich . . .

For when as walking in the Court of the Ghetto, I casually met with a certaine learned Jewish Rabbin that spake good Latin, I insinuated my selfe after some fewe termes of complement into conference with him, and asked him his opinion of Christ, and why he did not receive him for his Messias; he made me the same answere that the Turke did at Lyons, of whom I have before spoken, that Christ forsooth was a great Prophet, and in that respect as highly to be esteemed as any Prophet amongst the Jewes that ever lived before him . . .

But to shut up this narration of my conflict with the Jewish Rabbin, after there had passed many vehement speeches to and fro betwixt us, it happened that some forty or fifty Jewes more flocked about me, and some of them beganne very insolently to swagger with me, because I durst reprehend their religion: Whereupon fearing least they would have offered me some violence, I withdrew my selfe by little and little towards the bridge at the entrance into the Ghetto, with an intent to flie from them, but by good fortune our noble Ambassador Sir Henry Wotton passing under the bridge in his Gondola at that very time, espyed me somewhat earnestly bickering with them, and so incontinently sent unto me out of his boate one of his principall Gentlemen Master Belford his secretary, who conveighed mee safely from these unchristian miscreants, which perhaps would have given mee just occasion to forsweare any more comming to the Ghetto.

ARTHUR HUGH CLOUGH's *poem* Dipsychus *(1852) is a verse drama which considers, among much else, the conflicting attractions of Christian faith and the life of the senses. Set in Venice, it exploits the city's ambiguous tradition of religious celebration and sensual indulgence.*

Spirit
Nay –
'Twas well enough once in a way;
Such things don't fall out every day.
Having once happened, as we know,
In Palestine so long ago,
How should it now at Venice here?
Where people, true enough, appear
To appreciate more and understand
Their ices, and their Austrian band,
And dark-eyed girls –

Dipsychus
The whole great square they fill,
From the red flaunting streamers on the staffs,
And that barbaric portal of St Mark's,
To where, unnoticed, at the darker end,
I sit upon my step. One great gay crowd.

The Campanile to the silent stars
Goes up, above – its apex lost in air.
While these – do what?

Spirit
Enjoy the minute,
And the substantial blessings in it;
Ices, *par exemple*; evening air;
Company, and this handsome square;
Some pretty faces here and there;
Music! Up, up; it isn't fit
With beggars here on steps to sit.
Up – to the café! Take a chair
And join the wiser idlers there.
Aye! what a crowd! and what a noise!
With all these screaming half-breeched boys.
Partout dogs, boys, and women wander –
And see, a fellow singing yonder;
Singing, ye gods, and dancing too –
Tooraloo, tooraloo, tooraloo, loo;
Fiddle di, diddle di, diddle di da
Figaro sù, Figaro giù –
Figaro quà, Figaro là!
How he likes doing it! Ah, ha, ha!

Dipsychus
While these do what – ah heaven!

Spirit
If you want to pray
I'll step aside a little way.
Eh? But I will not be far gone;
You may be wanting me anon.
Our lonely pious altitudes
Are followed quick by prettier moods.
Who knows not with what ease devotion
Slips into earthlier emotion?

Dipsychus
While these do what? Ah, heaven, too true, at Venice
Christ is not risen either!

'Interior of San Marco', drawing by Canaletto (1697–1768).

INDULGENCE

A nd
I came here in my young youth
                    and lay there under the crocodile
By the column, looking East on the Friday,
And I said: Tomorrow I will lie on the South side
And the day after, south west.
And at night they sang in the gondolas
And in the barche with lanthorns;
The prows rose silver on silver
                    taking light in the darkness. 'Relaxetur!'

Upon my word, I have spoken my real thoughts in relation to Venice; but I will be more particular in my description, lest you should find the same reason of complaint you have hitherto experienced. It is impossible to give any rule for the agreeableness of conversation; but here is so great a variety, I think 'tis impossible not to find some to suit every taste … It is the fashion for the greatest ladies to walk the streets, which are admirably paved; and a mask, price sixpence, with a little cloak, and the head of a domino, the genteel dress to carry you everywhere. The greatest equipage is a gondola, that holds eight persons, and is the price of an English chair. And it is so much the established fashion for everybody to live their own way, that nothing is more ridiculous than censuring the actions of another. This would be terrible in London, where we have little other diversion; but for me, who never found any pleasure in malice, I bless my destiny that has conducted me to a part where people are better employed than in talking of the affairs of their acquaintance. It is at present excessive cold (which is the only thing I have to find fault with); but in recompense we have a clear bright sun, and fogs and factions things unheard of in this climate.

It appeared to me that the lamps of Venice formed a decoration both useful and agreeable, and the more deserving of praise, as the burden does not fall on individuals, but is defrayed by an additional drawing of

'All this Moorish architecture in white marble, set in limpid waters...' – painting by Frederico del Campo, 19th century.

the lottery every year.

Besides this general illumination, there is that of the shops, which at all seasons remain open till ten o'clock in the evening, and a great number are not shut till midnight, and several are never shut at all.

Every thing eatable is to be found displayed at midnight in Venice, the same as in the middle of the day; all the taverns are open, and suppers are in preparation in every inn and hotel; for company dinners and suppers are not common in Venice, but parties of pleasure and pic-nics bring together individuals with greater liberty and gaiety.

In summer the square of St Mark and its environs are frequented by night as much as by day. The coffee-houses are full of fashionable company, males and females of every description.

In every square, street, and canal, singing is to be heard. The shop-keepers sing while they sell their wares; the workmen sing on quitting their labours; the gondoleers sing while waiting for their masters. The essential character of the people is gaiety, and the character of the Venetian language is pleasantry.

in the neighbouring countryside. On his return to his native city, he found it 'a city still more wonderful by night than by day', as he recalled in his Memoirs *(1787).*

PERCY BYSSHE SHELLEY
savoured the pleasures of his
days in Venice with Byron in
his poem Julian and Maddalo
(1818).

If I had been an unconnected man
I, from this moment, should have formed some plan
Never to leave sweet Venice, – for to me
It was delight to ride by the lone sea;
And then, the town is silent – one may write
Or read in gondolas by day or night,
Having the little brazen lamp alight,
Unseen, uninterrupted; books are there,
Pictures, and casts from all those statues fair
Which were twin-born with poetry, and all
We seek in towns, with little to recall
Regrets for the green country. I might sit
In Maddalo's great palace, and his wit
And subtle talk would cheer the winter night
And make me know myself, and the firelight
Would flash upon our faces, till the day
Might dawn and make me wonder at my stay:
But I had friends in London too . . .

While visiting Venice in 1834
with the poet Alfred de Musset,
French novelist
GEORGE SAND
described its attractions in a
letter to her half-brother.

I was not much taken with Tuscany but there is nothing in all the world more beautiful than Venice. What more can one desire than all this Moorish architecture in white marble, set in limpid waters under a superb sky; than these gay, unthinking people, so witty and so full of song, these gondolas, churches, picture galleries, pretty women and smart women; than the sea breaking with a whisper in one's ears, moonlight such as one gets nowhere else, gondolier-choruses which are really well-trained, serenaders under every window, cafés full of Turks and Armenians, fine theatres where Porta and Donzelli sing, magnificent palaces, Gustave Malus' *polichinelle* theatre which runs ten feet underground, delicious oysters which can be fished from the steps of any of the houses, Cyprus wine at fivepence a bottle, excellent chickens for about a franc, flowers in mid-winter, and the warmth of May in February; I say again, what more could you desire?

The stillness of a city
where the clatter of horses
was unheard was one of the
delights of Venice to
FRANCES TROLLOPE,
travel writer (and mother of the
novelist), who praised it in
A Visit to Italy *(1842).*

But the deepest impression of all, perhaps, has been made by the trifling circumstance of doing and seeing everything without noise. After a good deal of travelling in search of sights, one gets a habit of preparing oneself for noise and tumult at the gates of every city; and the finding the stillness of night amidst the splendour of day produces a sort of wonder from which I have not yet recovered. I have, moreover, two sources of gratification here, not only distinct, but in absolute contrast to each other. The one consists in seeking with industrious avidity for the pictures, the statues, the *relievi*, the architecture, and the antiquities of Venice; and the other in avoiding every species of research and abandoning myself in delicious idleness to the gentle movement of our gondola, floating here, and floating there, without any other end or object than the enjoyment of that waking dream of beauty which, go in what direction we will, can never fail. The best hour perhaps for this last species of delight is when the moon rides triumphant, and in all the fullness of her meridian glory over the towers and domes, the bridges, the palaces, and the dark waters of Venice.

Venice is quite exquisite; it wrapt me round with a spell at first sight, and I longed to live and die there – never to go away. The gondolas, and the glory they swim through, and the silence of the population, drifted over one's head across the bridges, and the fantastic architecture and the coffee-drinking and music in the Piazza San Marco, everything fitted into my lazy, idle nature and weakness of body, as if I had been born to the manner of it and to no other. Do you know I expected in Venice a

The poet ELIZABETH BARRETT BROWNING, *pleasantly surprised by the indolence of Venice, described it in a letter to John Kenyon (1851).*

'The essential character of the people is gaiety' – café scene, 19th century.

dreary sort of desolation? Whereas there was nothing melancholy at all, only soothing, lulling, rocking atmosphere . . .

For the English essayist and translator JOHN ADDINGTON SYMONDS, *Venice was an endless source of passing delights, which he recorded in his journal in 1862.*

I wish I could give some notion of the luxury we enjoyed in gliding through the narrow canals. There, though the sun was blazing in an unclouded sky, those tall houses almost meeting overhead gave a delicious shade. From light to shadow we passed as the gondola swung round the corners to the warning cry of the oarsmen. To feel the air so soft and warm upon one's cheek, to feel the undulation of the green smooth water, to see those ancient palaces and profound glooms of deep-cast shadows over marble traceries of vines and eagled lions and angels was truly Venice. Sometimes our black gondola, like a great crocodile, dispersed a troop of little swimmers. The boys here are amphibious, and run about quite naked, but for a wrapper round the middle. They leapt and ran on land, broadening their chests with play. In the water they dived and swam and flung themselves about like ducks. Without shame or restraint, fair to look upon, but oh, how animal.

In his essay 'Venice' (1882), HENRY JAMES *evoked the casual pleasures of an idle spring in the city.*

Exquisite hours, enveloped in light and silence, to have known them once is to have always a terrible standard of enjoyment. Certain lovely mornings of May and June come back with an ineffaceable fairness. Venice isn't smothered in flowers at this season, in the manner of Florence and Rome; but the sea and sky themselves seem to blossom and rustle. The gondola waits at the wave-washed steps, and if you are wise you will take your place beside a discriminating companion. Such a companion in Venice should of course be of the sex that discriminates most finely. An intelligent woman who knows her Venice seems doubly intelligent, and it makes no woman's perceptions less keen to be aware that she can't help looking graceful as she is borne over the waves. The handsome Pasquale, with uplifted oar, awaits your command, knowing, in a general way, from observation of your habits, that your intention is to go to see a picture or two. It perhaps doesn't immensely matter what picture you choose: the whole affair is so charming. It is charming to wander through the light and shade of intricate canals, with perpetual architecture above you and perpetual fluidity beneath. It is charming to disembark at the polished steps of a little empty *campo* – a sunny shabby square with an old well in the middle, an old church on one side and tall Venetian windows looking down. Sometimes the windows are tenantless; sometimes a lady in a faded dressing-gown leans vaguely on the sill. There is always an old man holding out his hat for coppers; there are always three or four small boys dodging possible umbrella-pokes while they precede you, in the manner of custodians, to the door of the church.

'The boys here are amphibious . . .'

This was a holiday-place of all holiday-places. The Lido, with its acres of sun-pinked or pyjamaed bodies, was like a strand with an endless heap of seals come up for mating. Too many people in the piazza, too many limbs and trunks of humanity on the Lido, too many gondolas, too many motor-launches, too many steamers, too many pigeons, too many ices, too many cocktails, too many men-servant wanting tips, too many languages rattling, too much, too much sun, too much smell of Venice, too many cargoes of strawberries, too many silk shawls, too many huge, raw-beef slices of water-melon on stalls: too much enjoyment, altogether far too much enjoyment!

For some, the pleasures of Venice were too many, and the opportunities for self-indulgence too frequent. In Lady Chatterley's Lover *(1928),* D. H. LAWRENCE *expressed his disgust with the place.*

The days passed, one by one, for weeks, and I had never been so content, never so much at ease, never so purely animal. I had let the surf of sensation roll me over and over on their sands. I had basked like a seal on the rocks of Nepenthe. The things I most enjoyed are the things least communicable; slivers of sunlight on water; a gondola passing; a white sail; a blissful sense, less sensual than a sense, a half-awareness of a pleasing ambience that can never now be defined, since I was only half aware of it and did not question it; odd things like the great noise at half-past nine each evening, when all the blessed bells in the Piazza rang together, why I do not know, and the demons with the raffle under the Ducal Palace – they didn't care about ART! roared through their loud-speaker, and Florian's and Quadri's played their Austrian tunes in disunison. . . Altogether a wonderful medley of noise such as went, I make no doubt, right to the heart of every Italian present. Or I enjoyed the talk of a stone-cutter about the various stones used in Venice; enjoyed *pesce di spada al pomodoro con piselli*; and the little squashy purple figs with the ham; and the thick cream in chocolate with creamy cakes; and enjoyed comparing peperonati and zucchini and melassane and never getting them clear; and going one by one through the countless kinds of fish; and hearing the padrone curse the municipal authorities because they let the clergy stop them from having a casino in the Palazzo Dandolo where Casanova once gambled, although, he cried, Venice used to be full of these gaming-clubs, and as Londoners cool off in the dawn at Covent Garden's coffee-stalls, and Parisians at Les Halles, the Venetians used to relax at the Vegetable Market; or I enjoyed the old waiter I call Pop who looked like a dreadful Hun and was a perfect baby. I enjoyed all the odds and ends that every traveller enjoys, adds up, remembers and forgets.

In A Summer in Italy *(1949), the Irish writer* SEAN O'FAOLAIN *tried to catalogue the innumerable subliminal pleasures of Venice.*

Shrovetide, when all the world repair to Venice, to see the folly and madness of the Carnival; the women, men, and persons of all conditions disguising themselves in antique dresses, with extravagant

JOHN EVELYN *described the Carnival of 1640 in his* Diary.

music and a thousand gambols, traversing the streets from house to house, all places being then accessible and free to enter. Abroad, they fling eggs filled with sweet water, but sometimes not over-sweet. They also have a barbarous custom of hunting bulls about the streets and piazzas, which is very dangerous, the passages being generally narrow. The youth of the several wards and parishes contend in other masteries and pastimes, so that it is impossible to recount the universal madness of this place during this time of licence. The great banks are set up for those who will play at bassett; the comedians have liberty, and the operas are open; witty pasquils are thrown about, and the mountebanks have their stages at every corner.

LORD BYRON

treated his English readers to a mock lecture on the history and purpose of Carnival in his long satirical narrative poem Beppo *(1818).*

'Tis known, at least it should be, that throughout
  All countries of the Catholic persuasion,
Some weeks before Shrove Tuesday comes about,
  The people take their fill of recreation,
And buy repentance, ere they grow devout,
  However high their rank, or low their station,
With fiddling, feasting, dancing, drinking, masking,
  And other things which may be had for asking.

The moment night with dusky mantle covers
  The skies (and the more duskily the better),
The time less liked by husbands than by lovers
  Begins, and prudery flings aside her fetter;
And gaiety on restless tiptoe hovers,
  Giggling with all the gallants who beset her;
And there are songs and quavers, roaring, humming,
Guitars, and every other sort of strumming.

'Fiddling, feasting, dancing, drinking, masking...'

This feast is named the Carnival, which being
    Interpreted, implies 'farewell to flesh':
So call'd, because the name and thing agreeing,
    Through Lent they live on fish both salt and fresh.
But why they usher Lent with so much glee in,
    Is more than I can tell, although I guess
'Tis as we take a glass with friends at parting,
In the stage-coach or packet, just at starting.

Of all the places where the Carnival
    Was most facetious in the days of yore,
For dance, and song, and serenade, and ball,
    And masque, and mime, and mystery, and more
Than I have time to tell now, or at all,
    Venice the bell from every city bore, –
And at the moment when I fix my story,
That sea-born city was in all her glory.

It is the height of the Carnival – and I am in the estrum & agonies of a new intrigue – with I don't know exactly whom or what – except that she is insatiate of love – & won't take money – & has light hair & blue eyes – which are not common here – & that I met her at the Masque – & that when her mask is off I am as wise as ever. – I shall make what I can of the remainder of my youth – & confess – that like Augustus – I would rather die *standing*.

I have hardly had a wink of sleep this week past. We are in the agonies of the Carnival's last days, and I must be up all night, as well as to-morrow. I have had some curious masking adventures this Carnival; but, as they are not yet over, I shall not say on. I will work the mine of my youth to the last veins of the ore, and then – good night. I have lived, and am content.

I do think the Turkish sailor gave an admirable account of a carnival when he told his Mahometan friends at his return that those poor Christians were all disordered in their senses and nearly in a state of actual madness, while he remained among them, till one day, on a sudden, they luckily found out a certain gray powder that cured such symptoms, and, laying it on their heads one Wednesday morning, the wits of all the inhabitants were happily restored at a stroke; the people grew sober, quiet and composed, and went about their business just like other folks. He meant the ashes strewed on the heads of all one meets in the streets

For BYRON, *all the pleasures of Venice were concentrated in the madness of Carnival. He recounted his adventures in a letter to his publisher John Murray, dated 27 January 1818.*

BYRON *wrote to his friend the poet Thomas Moore, on 2 February 1818.*

On Ash Wednesday, the revelry of Carnival came to an end and the self-denial of Lent began. MRS PIOZZI *described the transformation in* A Journey Through France, Italy and Germany *(1789).*

In Venice Observed *(1956),*
American novelist and critic
MARY McCARTHY
showed how the spirit of
Carnival lives on in modern
Venice.

through many a Catholic country, when all masquerading, money-making, etc., subside for forty days, and give, from the force of the contrast, a greater appearance of devotion and decorous behaviour in Venice than almost anywhere else during Lent.

Now that the carnival is over, the Venetians have adjusted themselves with a good grace. There are no acrobats any more to slide down a rope on Shrove Tuesday and alight at the doge's feet in the loggia of the Ducal Palace, no bullfights in the Piazza, no Ascension Day fair. But there are still regattas, with the *sestieri* competing, and there is still the bridge of boats thrown across the Giudecca Canal to Palladio's church on the Feast of the Redentore. On the night of the Redentore (the eve of the third Sunday in July) there is a tremendous fireworks display. Boats of all kinds, hung with Chinese lanterns – gondolas, barges, rowboats, a float carrying the orchestra of the Fenice theatre, motorboats, an old Venetian galleon – mass in the dark Giudecca Canal to watch the rockets and Roman candles go off from the Piazzale Roma, near the station. For an hour, the sky is illuminated by bursts of coloured stars; the *palazzi* rock with the explosions; greens and golds, reds and violets are reflected in the water and in the darkened windows of the houses. It is a picture, everyone agrees, or rather a series of pictures; shades of Guardi, of the Bassano night-scenes, even of Carpaccio, pass across the Canal. Everyone seeks for a comparison, and all comparisons seem true: I myself think of the 'Embarkation of the Queen of Cyprus' in a painting in the Correr Museum. When the fireworks are over, nobody starts for home; a second show (how typical of Venice) is about to begin, the duplicate, the twin, of the first, at the other end of the Canal, on the island of San Giorgio, where the other Palladian church is lit up. All the boats move off in procession, accompanied by music. Traditionally, after the second fireworks display, you are supposed to be rowed to the Lido to see the sunrise. As a gondolier explained to me, gravely, the true colours of nature ('*i veri colori della natura*') refresh the eye after the fires of artifice.

There spoke Venice, the eternal connoisseur, in the voice of her eternal gondolier.

DEATH AND DECAY

Since first the dominion of men was asserted over the ocean, three thrones, of mark beyond all others, have been set upon its sands: the thrones of Tyre, Venice, and England. Of the First of these great powers only the memory remains; of the Second, the ruin; the Third, which inherits their greatness, if it forget their example, may be led through prouder eminence to less pitied destruction.

The exaltation, the sin, and the punishment of Tyre have been recorded for us, in perhaps the most touching words ever uttered by the Prophets of Israel against the cities of the stranger. But we read them as a lovely song; and close our ears to the sternness of their warning: for the very depth of the Fall of Tyre has blinded us to its reality, and we forget, as we watch the bleaching of the rocks between the sunshine and the sea, that they were once 'as in Eden, the garden of God'.

Her successor, like her in perfection of beauty, though less in endurance of dominion, is still left for our beholding in the final period of her decline: a ghost upon the sands of the sea, so weak – so quiet, – so bereft of all but her loveliness, that we might well doubt, as we watched her faint reflection in the mirage of the lagoon, which was the City, and which the Shadow.

I would endeavour to trace the lines of this image before it be for ever lost, and to record, as far as I may, the warning which seems to me to be uttered by every one of the fast-gaining waves, that beat like passing bells, against the Stones of Venice.

Sing to me, Gondolier!
  Sing words from Tasso's lay;
While blue, and still, and clear,
  Night seems but softer day:
The gale is gently falling,
  As if it paused to hear
Some strain the past recalling –
  Sing to me, Gondolier!

Writers have found all manner of lessons in Venice's decline, none more insistently than JOHN RUSKIN *in* The Stones of Venice *(1851–53).*

John Ruskin.

In 'Sing to Me, Gondolier' (1825), the English poet, FELICIA HEMANS *(1793–1835) mourned the passing of Venice's glory, symbolized in the silence of its gondoliers, who seemed to have forgotten the legendary songs of Tasso.*

163

'Oh, ask me not to wake
  The memory of the brave;
Bid no high numbers break
  The silence of the wave.
Gone are the noble-hearted,
  Closed the bright pageants here;
And the glad song is departed
  From the mournful Gondolier!'

LORD BYRON
*relished Venice's decay, as he
explained in a letter to the poet
Thomas Moore in 1816.*

It is my intention to remain at Venice during the winter, probably, as it
has always been (next to the East) the greenest island of my imagination. It has not disappointed me; though its evident decay would,
perhaps, have that effect upon others. But I have been familiar with ruins
too long to dislike desolation. Besides, I have fallen in love, which, next to
falling into the canal, (which would be of no use, as I can swim.) is the best
or the worst thing I could do.

BYRON'S Ode on Venice
*(1816) both mourns and
celebrates the city's decline.*

Oh Venice! Venice! when thy marble walls
  Are level with the waters, there shall be
A cry of nations o'er thy sunken halls,
A loud lament along the sweeping sea!
If I, a northern wanderer, weep for thee,
What should thy sons do? – anything but weep:
And yet they only murmur in their sleep.
In contrast with their fathers – as the slime,
The dull green ooze of the receding deep,
Is with the dashing of the spring-tide foam
That drives the sailor shipless to his home,
Are they to those that were; and thus they creep,
Crouching and crab-like, through their sapping streets.
Oh! agony – that centuries should reap
No mellower harvest! Thirteen hundred years
Of wealth and glory turn'd to dust and tears;
And every monument the stranger meets,
Church, palace, pillar, as a mourner greets;
And even the Lion all subdued appears,
And the harsh sound of the barbarian drum,
With dull and daily dissonance, repeats
The echo of thy tyrant's voice along
The soft waves, once all musical to song,
That heaved beneath the moonlight with the throng
Of gondolas – and to the busy hum
Of cheerful creatures, whose most sinful deeds
Were but the overbeating of the heart...

'I have been familiar with ruins too long to dislike desolation' – painting by Frank Fox, 1918.

For some, Venice's stagnant atmosphere was suffocating. RALPH WALDO EMERSON *recorded his discontent in his* Journal *in 1837.*

I am speedily satisfied with Venice. It is a great oddity – a city for beavers – but to my thought a most disagreeable residence. You feel always in prison, & solitary. Two persons may live months in adjoining streets & never meet, for you go about in gondolas and all the gondolas are precisely alike & the persons within commonly concealed; then there are no Newsrooms; except St Mark's piazza, no place of public resort. – It is as if you were always at sea. And though, for a short time, it is very luxurious to lie on the eider down cushions of your gondola & read or talk or smoke, drawing to now the cloth lined shutter, now the venetian blind, now the glass window, as you please, yet there is always a slight smell of bilgewater about the thing, & houses in the water remind me of a freshet & of desolation – any thing but comfort. I soon had enough of it.

PERCY BYSSHE SHELLEY'S *infant daughter died in Venice in 1818. Months later, he composed* Lines Written Among the Euganaean Hills, *in which, contemplating Venice from afar, he mingles his personal grief with political despair at the spectacle of the once-independent Republic in the thrall of Austrian rule.*

Sun-girt City, thou hast been
Ocean's child, and then his queen;
Now is come a darker day,
And thou soon must be his prey,
If the power that raised thee here
Hallow so thy watery bier.
A less drear ruin then than now,
With thy conquest-branded brow
Stooping to the slave of slaves
From thy throne, among the waves
Wilt thou be, when the sea-mew
Flies, as once before it flew,
O'er thine isles depopulate,
And all is in its ancient state,
Save where many a palace gate
With green sea-flowers overgrown
Like a rock of Ocean's own,
Topples o'er the abandoned sea
As the tides change sullenly.
The fisher on his watery way,
Wandering at the close of day,
Will spread his sail and seize his oar
Till he pass the gloomy shore,
Lest thy dead should, from their sleep
Bursting o'er the starlight deep,
Lead a rapid masque of death
O'er the waters of his path.

This Venice, which was a haughty, invincible, magnificent Republic for nearly fourteen hundred years; whose armies compelled the world's appplause whenever and wherever they battled; whose navies well nigh held dominion of the seas, and whose merchant fleets whitened the remotest oceans with their sails and loaded these piers with the products of every clime, is fallen a prey to poverty, neglect and melancholy decay. Six hundred years ago, Venice was the Autocrat of Commerce; her mart was the great commercial centre, the distributing-house from whence the enormous trade of the Orient was spread abroad over the Western world. Today her piers are deserted, her warehouses are empty, her merchant fleets are vanished, her armies and her navies are but memories. Her glory is departed, and with her crumbling grandeur of wharves and palaces about her she sits among her stagnant lagoons, forlorn and beggared, forgotten of the world. She that in her palmy days commanded the commerce of a hemisphere and made the weal or woe of nations with a beck of her puissant finger, is become the humblest among the peoples of the earth, – a peddler of glass beads for women, and trifling toys and trinkets for school-girls and children.

In his travel book
The Innocents Abroad *(1869),*
an uncharacteristically solemn
MARK TWAIN *addressed*
Venice's palpable decline.

It is a fact that almost every one interesting, appealing, melancholy, memorable, odd, seems at one time or another, after many days and much life, to have gravitated to Venice by a happy instinct, settling in it and treating it, cherishing it, as a sort of repository of consolations; all of which today, for the conscious mind, is mixed with its air and constitutes its unwritten history. The deposed, the defeated, the disenchanted, the wounded, or even only the bored, have seemed to find there something that no other place could give.

For HENRY JAMES,
in his essay 'Casa Alvisi'
(1902), the association of
Venice with death and decay
was one of its charms.

There was a hateful sultriness in the narrow streets. The air was so heavy that all the manifold smells wafted out of houses, shops, and cook-shops – smells of oil, perfumery, and so forth – hung low, like exhalations, not dissipating. Cigarette smoke seemed to stand in the air, it drifted so slowly away. Today the crowd in these narrow lanes oppressed the stroller instead of diverting him. The longer he walked, the more was he in tortures under that state, which is the product of the sea air and the sirocco and which excites and enervates at once. He perspired painfully. His eyes rebelled, his chest was heavy, he felt feverish, the blood throbbed in his temples. He fled from the huddled, narrow streets of the commercial city, crossed many bridges, and came into the poor quarter of Venice. Beggars waylaid him, the canals sickened him with their evil exhalations. He reached a quiet square, one of those that exist at the city's heart, forsaken of God and man; there he rested awhile on the margin of a

In his novella
Death in Venice *(1912),*
THOMAS MANN's
hero Von Aschenbach feels both
the repulsion and attraction of
the moribund city.

'When thy marble walls/Are level with the waters...' – photograph by Snowdon.

fountain, wiped his brow, and admitted to himself that he must be gone.

... He resolved, he rose to his feet and sought the nearest gondola-landing, where he took a boat and was conveyed to San Marco through the gloomy windings of many canals, beneath balconies of delicate marble traceries flanked by carven lions; round slippery corners of wall, past melancholy façades with ancient business shields reflected in the rocking water. It was not too easy to arrive at his destination, for his gondolier, being in league with various lace-makers and glass-blowers, did his best to persuade his fare to pause, look, and be tempted to buy. Thus the charm of this bizarre passage through the heart of Venice, even while it played upon his spirit, yet was sensibly cooled by the predatory commercial spirit of the fallen queen of the seas.

The island of San Michele, lying a few hundred yards to the north of Venice, is given over entirely to the burial of the dead. In her essay 'All Souls' Day in Venice' (1903) the writer VERNON LEE

They had put a bridge of boats from the northermost quay of Venice to the cemetery island. A dense crowd, coming and going across it, black over the black anchored barges, each two with their yard of pale water between their tarred hulls. And, as we draw near, as we go beneath, the seeming silence turns into a murmur, a shuffle, and a rumble.

For this one day in all the year the cemetery island is bridged on to the islands of the living. This is no mere coincidence, but a real symbol.

The cloisters and the gardens are full as for a fair, crowds coming and going, buying tapers, lighting them at the glittering waxlights before the chapel, bringing a few flowers; and the smell of trodden sods and drenched, bruised chrysanthemums mingles, funereal, with the stifle of all these poor, down-at-heel, recently drenched, unwashed live folk in the warm, moist air . . .

But all this squalor is oddly solemn. And the presence of work-a-day clothes, of babies carried, and children dragged along; nay, the very provisions unpacked and consumed among the graves, brings home the importance and universality of this yearly meeting of the dead and the living . . .

Part of the crowd are people merely doing vague honour to vague dead, whose little numbered headstones have perhaps been long pulled out; their bones, years ago, thrown behind the gate marked 'Ossuario', and their brief resting-place given to others; or gaping, a long trench of freshly turned earth, in readiness for those still of this life. These multitudes of vague mourners tramp round the burial squares, looking about, stopping here and there, subdued by mere general contact with the fact of death.

But the real mourners fill the squares themselves, and attend to their own business. Some are doing their year's gardening, weeding, as I have said, or dividing and replanting iris bulbs or arranging cut flowers in patterns . . .

. . .But there were less active yet more impressive ways of honouring the dead: people kneeling for an indefinite time before those little numbered cubes of stone, or sitting on the ground alongside. Several old women thus – squatting, not praying, but just staying there. Some had brought scraps of food; and one was taking snuff out of a bit of paper; all of them keeping the dead one company, staring before them into space and time. At one poor grave there was a group of four, one at each corner: an old woman, a younger one, a man and a sickly child; all silent, blurred-looking. Surely for these poor folk there is a reality, if only a negative one, in this suspending of the labour, cares, the empty grind of life; and their hour of watching by the dead may be, in some way deeper than words can say, an hour of communing with the eternities . . .

As we got back into the gondola the crowd was streaming only one way along the black bridge; away from the cemetery, back into life.

The cult of death is still powerful among the Venetians, and a constant flow of visitors moves silently among the graves, or meditates among the pleasant flower-beds of the place. Many of the grander tombs, already inscribed and shuttered, are not yet occupied, but await a death in the family. Others are so spacious, well built and frequented that they are

depicts the annual mass pilgrimage to the cemetery island.

JAMES MORRIS *described a visit to the cemetery isle of San Michele in* Venice *(1960).*

San Michele, photograph by Snowdon.

more like nightmare summer-houses than tombs, and remind me of the hospitable mausoleums in Cairo's City of the Dead. Inside others again there hang, in the Italian manner, portraits of the departed, giving them rather the feelings of well-polished marble board-rooms, awaiting a quorum. There is an annual pilgrimage of ballet-lovers to the modest tomb of Diaghilev; and an increasing trickle of visitors finds its way to the obscure burial-place, high in a tomb-terrace, of Frederick William Serafino Austin Lewis Mary Rolfe, 'Baron Corvo', He died, according to British Consulate records, in October 1913, in the Palazzo Marcello, at the age of 53: his life in Venice had sunk from eccentricity to outrage to depravity, but he refused ever to leave the city, wrote some incomparable descriptions of it, died in poverty and obloquy, and was buried (characteristically) at his brother's expense. Silently this multitude of shades lies there beneath the dark trees of San Michele; and at night-time, I am told, a galaxy of little votive lamps flutters and twinkles on ten thousand tombstones, like so many small spirits.

At the eastern corner of San Michele is an old Protestant graveyard of very different temper. It is like a Carolina churchyard, lush, untended and overgrown, shaded by rich gnarled trees, with grassy walks and generations of dead leaves. Most of its graves are obscured by weeds, earth and foliage, and it is instructive to wander through all this seductive desolation, clearing a gravestone here and there, or peering through the thickets at a worn inscription. There are many Swiss and Germans in these graves; and many British seamen who died on their ships in the port of Venice. There is an English lady, with her daughter, who perished in a ferry disaster off the Lido in the early 1900s; and several Americans with names such as Horace, Lucy or Harriet; and one or two diplomats, among whose flowery but almost illegible epitaphs you may discern a plethora of adjectives like 'noble-minded', 'lofty', 'much-respected', 'eminent'. There is a long-forgotten English novelist, G. P. R. James, whose merits as a writer, we are ironically assured, 'are known where the English language is spoken'; and there is an unfortunate Mr Frank Stanier, of Staffordshire, whose mourners wrote of him in a phrase that might be kindlier put, that he 'Left Us In Peace, Febry 2nd 1910'.

In an untitled poem written in 1920, OSIP MANDELSTAM *turned Venice's decay into a metaphor for the condition of Europe after the First World War.*

Venice, the stagnant, barren life –
it's plain what it means.
Look at it, peering with its cold smile
into the blue decayed glass.

Faint scent of leather. Fine veins in blue ink.
White snow. Green brocade.

They ride in cypress sedan chairs
and emerge from their cloaks, warm and dozing.

And candles still burn, burn, in baskets:
as if the dove had flown back into the Ark.
And on stage and among the listless assembly
man is dying.

For there's no way out of love and terror:
the ring of Saturn is heavier than platinum.
The block is draped in black velvet
and so is the beautiful face.

O Venice, the weight of your garments
and of your mirrors in their cypress frames!
Your air is cut in facets, and mountains
of blue decayed glass melt in the bedchamber.

A rose or a phial between fingers –
green Adriatic, farewell!
Why are you silent? Lady of Venice,
how can one escape this festivity of death?

The evening star flashes black in the mirror.
Everything passes. Truth is dark.
Man is born. Pearl dies.
Susanna will have to wait for the elders.

A Venetian hearse.

He had almost reached the end of the alley, and the bridge was in sight, when he saw the child. It was the same little girl with the pixie-hood who had leapt between the tethered boats the preceding night and vanished up the cellar steps of one of the houses. This time she was running from the direction of the church the other side, making for the bridge. She was running as if her life depended on it, and in a moment he saw why. A man was in pursuit, who, when she glanced backwards for a moment, still running, flattened himself against a wall, believing himself unobserved. The child came on, scampering across the bridge, and John, fearful of alarming her further, backed into an open doorway that led into a small court.

He remembered the drunken yell of the night before which had come from one of the houses near where the man was hiding now. This is it, he thought, the fellow's after her again, and with a flash of intuition he connected the two events, the child's terror then and now, and the murders reported in the newspapers, supposedly the work of some

DAPHNE DU MAURIER
set her macabre tale
Don't Look Now *(1970) in*
haunted, death-obsessed,
off-season Venice.

madman. It could be coincidence, a child running from a drunken relative, and yet, and yet ... His heart began thumping in his chest, instinct warning him to run himself, now, at once, back along the alley the way he had come – but what about the child? What was going to happen to the child?

Then he heard her running steps. She hurtled through the open doorway into the court in which he stood, not seeing him, making for the rear of the house that flanked it, where steps led presumably to a back entrance. She was sobbing as she ran, not the ordinary cry of a frightened child, but the panic-stricken intake of breath of a helpless being in despair. Were there parents in the house who would protect her, whom he could warn? He hesitated a moment, then followed her down the steps and through the door at the bottom, which had burst open at the touch of her hands as she hurled herself against it.

'It's all right,' he called. 'I won't let him hurt you, it's all right,' cursing his lack of Italian, but possibly an English voice might reassure her. But it was no use – she ran sobbing up another flight of stairs, which were spiral, twisting, leading to the floor above, and already it was too late for him to retreat. He could hear sounds of the pursuer in the courtyard behind, someone shouting in Italian, a dog barking. This is it, he thought, we're in it together, the child and I. Unless we can bolt some inner door above he'll get us both.

He ran up the stairs after the child, who had darted into a room leading off a small landing, and followed her inside and slammed the door, and, merciful heaven, there was a bolt which he rammed into its socket. The child was crouching by the open window. If he shouted for help someone would surely hear, someone would surely come before the man in pursuit threw himself against the door and it gave, because there was no one but themselves, no parents, the room was bare except for a mattress on an old bed, and a heap of rags in one corner.

'It's all right,' he panted, 'it's all right,' and held out his hand, trying to smile.

The child struggled to her feet and stood before him, the pixie-hood falling from her head on to the floor. He stared at her, incredulity turning to horror, to fear. It was not a child at all but a little thick-set woman dwarf, about three feet high, with a great square adult head too big for her body, grey locks hanging shoulder-length, and she wasn't sobbing any more, she was grinning at him, nodding her head up and down.

Then he heard the footsteps on the landing outside and the hammering on the door, and a barking dog, and not one voice but several voices, shouting, 'Open up! Police!' The creature fumbled in her sleeve, drawing a knife, and as she threw it at him with hideous strength, piercing his throat, he stumbled and fell, the sticky mess covering his protecting hands.

And he saw the vaporetto with Laura and the two sisters steaming down the Grand Canal, not today, not to-morrow, but the day after that, and he knew why they were together and for what sad purpose they had come. The creature was gibbering in its corner. The hammering and the voices and the barking dog grew fainter, and, 'Oh, God,' he thought, 'what a bloody silly way to die...'

'The Aviary of Death', engraving by Giovanni Paola Cimerlini, *c.*1568.

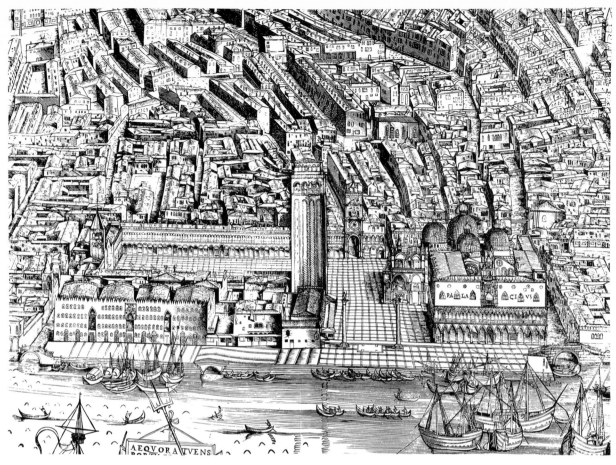

Part of Jacopo de' Barbari's vast woodcut, 'Bird's Eye View of Venice', 1500.

PAEAN

In 1362 a coalition of local inhabitants and expatriate Venetian patricians rebelled against Venetian rule in Crete. Two years later the revolt was crushed. The Tuscan poet PETRARCH, *then an honoured guest of the* Serenissima, *described the victory celebrations in a letter to Pietro da Muglio of Bologna in 1364.*

The august city of Venice rejoices, the one home today of liberty, peace and justice, the one refuge of honourable men, the one port to which can repair the storm-tossed, tyrant-hounded craft of men who seek the good life. Venice – rich in gold but richer in fame, mighty in her resources but mightier in virtue, solidly built on marble but standing more solid on a foundation of civil concord, ringed with salt waters but more secure with the salt of good counsel! Do not think that Venice exults merely for the recovery of the island of Crete, which, though great in antiquity, is poor in great spirits – and all great things are small in comparison with virtue. Venice rejoices at the outcome, which is as it should be – the victory not of its arms but of justice. For it is no remarkable achievement for men of might, with the power of Venice and a great leader, and with mastery of sea and land warfare, to have

174

vanquished a swarm of unarmed, cowardly, runaway Greeklings. The important thing is that even in our age fraud yields so speedily to fortitude, vices succumb to virtue, and God still watches over and fosters man's affairs . . .

A universal thanksgiving and praise of God . . . took place throughout the city, but noteworthily in the basilica of the blessed Mark the Evangelist. I think there is nothing more beautiful on earth. There was done everything that man can do for God's honour. The rites were sumptuously celebrated, and there was a mighty procession around the church. Not only the populace and all the clergy were present, but there were high prelates from afar, who happened to be in the city or who were attracted by eagerness to participate or by the news of the great ceremony.

When religion had amply received its due, everyone turned to games and spectacles.

I declare that it is impossible to tell or write fully of the beauty, the magnificence or the wealth of the city of Venice. Something indeed can be told and written to pass the time as I do, but it will be incredible to anyone who has not seen the city.

I do not think there is any city to which Venice, the city founded on the sea, can be compared: nevertheless I appeal always to the judgment of every person who has been there some time. Although this city is built entirely in the water and the marshes, yet it appears to me that whoever desires to do so can go everywhere on foot, as it is well kept and clean. Anyone, however, who does not want to endure the fatigue can go by water, and will be entreated to do so, and it will cost him less than he would spend elsewhere for the hire of a horse. As to the size of the city, I may say that it is so large, that, after being there so many days as I was, I made but little acquaintance with the streets. I cannot give the dimensions of this city, for it appears to me not one city alone but several cities placed together.

CANON PIETRO CASOLA, on his way from Milan to the Holy Land in 1494, passed several months in Venice and sang its praises in an account of his pilgrimage which remained unpublished for four hundred years.

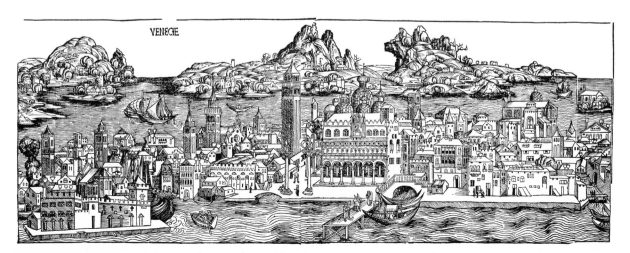

'The Paragon of all Cities in the World' – woodcut, 16th century.

I am now in carefree, liberal and just Venice, where neither sickness, death, hunger nor war oppresses the citizens. It is my opinion that if Eden, where Adam dwelt with Eve, had resembled Venice she would have had a hard time trying to tempt him out of that earthly paradise with her fruit. For to lose a place like Venice, where so much is lovely, would be a very different matter from losing the Garden of Eden, for all its figs, melons and grapes. For my part, as I have said before, I should wish God to change me into a gondola when I die, or else into its canopy, or if that is considered beyond my deserts into one of its oars, rowlocks or cleaning rags. Even a baling scoop would do. A sponge would be still more appropriate. And I would love, just so as not to have to leave Venice, to become one of those little copper coins with which people here pay the ferrymen. If I were a rat that feeds in the Venetian Treasury I would feel like one of heaven's cherubim. Nor would I change my condition for that which popes are said to have in paradise, though I doubt whether any are really there, if I could only be the door leading into the Tower of St Mark. For, to sum up, Venice is not only more eternal than or rather as eternal as the world itself but also the refuge, the delight and the consolation of all who live there.

The Richesse, the sumptuous buyldyng, The religius howses and the stabelyssyng of ther Justyces and Counceylles, with all other thynges that makyth a Cite glorius Surmownteth in Venys a bove all places that ever I Sawe.

This City is seven miles in compasse, and from so base an abject beginning, it is growne (as it were) to be the chiefe bulwarke of Europe. The lawes of this City permit not the younger sonnes of the best Gentry to marrie, least the number increasing should deminish the dignity: Yet neverthelesse they permit them unlawfull pleasures, and for their sakes allow publicke stewes. The Jewes here, and in Rome, weare red, and yellow hats for notice sake, to distinguish them from others: which necessary custome (would to God) were enjoyned to all the Papists here in England, so should we easily discerne them from the true Christians. And finally, to discourse upon the provision of their magnificent Arsenall, Artillery, Munition and Armor, the division of streetes with channels, the innumerable bridges of stone and timber, their accustomable kind of living, apparell, curtesies, and conventions; and finally, the glory of Gallants, Galleries, Gallies, Galleasses and Gallouns, were a thing impossible for me briefly to relate. Wherefore, I desist, concluding thus; this incomparable mansion is the Paragon of all Cities in the World.

This race did not seek refuge in these islands for fun, nor were those who joined later moved by chance; necessity taught them to find safety in the most unfavourable location. Later, however, this turned out to their greatest advantage and made them wise at a time when the whole northern world still lay in darkness; their increasing population and wealth were a logical consequence. Houses were crowded closer and closer together, sand and swamp transformed into solid pavement. The houses grew upward like closely planted trees and were forced to make up in height for what they were denied in width. Avid for every inch of ground and cramped into a narrow space from the very beginning, they kept the alleys separating two rows of houses narrow, just wide enough to let people pass each other. The place of street and square and promenade was taken by water. In consequence, the Venetian was bound to develop into a new kind of creature, and that is why, too, Venice can only be compared to itself. The Canal Grande, winding snakelike through the town, is unlike any other street in the world, and no square can compete with the vast expanse of water in front of the Piazza San Marco, enclosed on one side by the semicircle of Venice itself. Across it to the left is the island of San Giorgio Maggiore, to the right the Giudecca with its canal, and still further to the right the Dogana with the entrance to the Canal Grande, where stand some great gleaming marble temples. These, in brief, are the chief objects which strike the eye when one leaves the Piazza San Marco between the two columns.

After dinner I hurried out without a guide and, after noting the four points of the compass, plunged into the labyrinth of this city, which is intersected everywhere by canals but joined together by bridges. The compactness of it all is unimaginable unless one has seen it. As a rule, one can measure the width of an alley with one's outstretched arms; in the narrowest, one even scrapes one's elbows if one holds them akimbo; occasionally there is a wider lane and even a little square every so often, but everything is relatively narrow.

I easily found the Canal Grande and its principal bridge, the Ponte Rialto, which is a single arch of white marble. Looking down, I saw the Canal teeming with gondolas and the barges which bring all necessities from the mainland and land at this point to unload...

... Everything around me is a worthy, stupendous monument, not to one ruler, but to a whole people. Their lagoons may be gradually silting up and unhealthy miasmas hovering over their marshes, their trade may be declining, their political power dwindling, but this republic will never become a whit less venerable in the eyes of one observer. Venice, like everything else which has a phenomenal existence, is subject to Time.

JOHANN WOLFGANG VON GOETHE *visited Venice in 1786, and analysed the city's greatness in his* Italian Journey *(1816–17).*

The English essayist and critic
WILLIAM HAZLITT
marvelled at Venice in his
Notes of a Journey through
France and Italy *(1826).*

For an hour and a half, that it takes you to cross from the last point of land to this Spouse of the Adriatic, its long line of spires, towers, churches, wharfs is stretched along the water's edge, and you view it with a mixture of awe and incredulity. A city built in the air would be something still more wonderful; but any other must yield the palm to this for singularity and imposing effect. If it were on the firm land, it would rank as one of the first cities in Europe for magnificence, size, and beauty; as it is, it is without a rival ... The effect is certainly magical, dazzling, perplexing. You feel at first a little giddy: you are not quite sure of your footing as on the deck of a vessel. You enter its narrow, cheerful canals, and find that instead of their being scooped out of the earth, you are gliding amidst rows of palaces and under broad-arched bridges, piled on the sea-green wave. You begin to think that you must cut your liquid way in this manner through the whole city, and use oars instead of feet. You land, and visit quays, squares, market-places, theatres, churches, halls, palaces; ascend tall towers, and stroll through shady gardens, without being once reminded that you are not on *terra firma* ...

... Venice is loaded with ornament, like a rich city-heiress with jewels. It seems the natural order of things. Her origin was a wonder: her end is to surprise. The strong, implanted tendency of her genius must be to the showy, the singular, the fantastic. Herself an anomaly, she reconciles contradictions, liberty with aristocracy, commerce with nobility, the want of titles with the pride of birth and heraldry. A violent birth in nature, she lays greedy, perhaps ill-advised, hands on all the artificial advantages that can supply her original defects. Use turns to gaudy beauty; extreme hardship to intemperance in pleasure. From the level uniform expanse that forever encircles her, she would obviously affect the aspiring in forms, the quaint, the complicated, relief and projection. Her eye for colours and costume she would bring with conquest from the East. The spirit, intelligence, and activity of her men, she would derive from their ancestors: the grace, the glowing animation and bounding step of her women, from the sun and mountain-breeze!

*In the course of his long
and often obscure poem*
Sordello *(1840),*
ROBERT BROWNING
*paused to celebrate the ineffable
power of Venice.*

Venice seems a type
Of life, – 'twixt blue and blue extends, a stripe,
As Life, the somewhat, hangs 'twixt nought and nought
'Tis Venice, and 'tis Life – as good you sought
To spare me the Piazza's slippery stone,
Or keep me to the unchoked canals alone,
As hinder Life the evil with the good
Which makes up living, rightly understood.

'Venice seems a type of life, – 'twixt blue and blue extends...' – painting by Arthur Meadows (1843–1907).

Have you ever thought what a world his eyes opened on – fair, searching eyes of youth? What a world of mighty life, from those mountain rocks to the shore; of loveliest life, when he went down, yet so young, to the marble city – and became himself as a fiery heart to it?

A city of marble, did I say? nay, rather a golden city, paved with emeralds. For truly, every pinnacle and turret glanced or glowed, overlaid with gold, or bossed with jasper. Beneath, the unsullied sea drew in deep breathing, to and fro, its eddies of green wave. Deep-hearted, majestic, terrible as the sea, – the men of Venice moved in sway of power and war; pure as her pillars of alabaster, stood her mothers and maidens; from foot to brow, all noble, walked her knights; the low bronzed gleaming of sea-rusted armour shot angrily under their blood-red mantle-folds. Fearless, faithful, patient, impenetrable, implacable, – every word a fate – sate her senate. In hope and honour, lulled by flowing of wave around their isles of

JOHN RUSKIN
*pictured Venice as it would
have appeared to the young
Gorgione, fresh from the
countryside, in* Modern
Painters, *Volume V (1860).*

179

sacred sand, each with his name written, and the cross graved at his side, lay her dead. A wonderful piece of world. Rather, itself a world. It lay along the face of the waters, no larger, as its captains saw it from their masts at evening, than a bar of sunset that could not pass away; but for its power, it must have seemed to them as if they were sailing in the expanse of heaven, and this a great planet, whose orient edge widened through ether, a world from which all ignoble care and petty thoughts were banished, with all the common and poor elements of life. No foulness, nor tumult, in those tremulous streets, that filled or fell beneath the moon; but rippled music of majestic change or thrilling silence.

Russian political activist and writer ALEXANDER HERZEN *wrote his essay 'Venezia la Bella' in Venice in 1867, a tribute to the city's rebirth after decades of Austrian oppression.*

There is no such magnificent absurdity as Venice. To build a city where it is impossible to build a city is madness in itself; but to build there one of the most elegant and grandest of cities is the madness of genius. The water, the sea, their sparkle and glitter, call for a peculiar sumptuousness. Molluscs embellish their cabins with mother-of-pearl and pearls.

A single superficial look at Venice shows one that it is a city of strong will, of vigorous intellect, republican, commercial, oligarchical; that it is the knot that ties something together across the waters, a warehouse for merchandise under a military flag, a city with a noisy popular assembly and a soundless city of secret councils and measures; in its squares the whole population is jostling from morning till night, while the rivers of its streets flow silently to the sea. While the crowd clamours and shouts in St Mark's Square, a boat glides by and vanishes unobserved. Who knows what is under its black awning? Was not this the very place to drown people, within hail of lovers' trysts.

The men who felt at home in the Palazzo Ducale must have been of an eccentric cast. They stuck at nothing. There is no earth, there are no trees, what does it matter? Let us have still more carved stones, more ornaments, gold, mosaics, sculptures, pictures and frescoes. Here an empty corner has been left; into the corner with a thin sea-god with a long, wet beard! Here is an empty recess; put in another lion with wings and a gospel of Saint Mark! There it is bare and empty; put down a carpet of marble and mosaic! and here, lacework of porphyry! Is there a victory over the Turks or over Genoa? does the Pope seek the friendship of the city? then more marble; cover a whole wall with a curtain of carving, and above all, more pictures. Let Paul Veronese, Tintoretto, Titian fetch their brushes and mount the scaffolding: every step in the triumphal progress of the Beauty of the Sea must be depicted for posterity in paint or sculpture. And so full of life was the spirit that dwelt in these stones that new routes and new seaports, Columbus and Vasco da Gama, were not enough to crush it. For its destruction the 'One and Indivisible' republic had to rise up on the ruins of the French throne, and on the ruins of that republic the soldier who in Corsican fashion stabbed the lion with a stiletto poisoned by Austria. But Venice has digested the poison and proves to be alive once more after half a century.

'No foulness, no tumult, in those tremulous streets' – wood engraving, *c*.1889.

'A superb, barbaric patchwork', painting by Mortimer Menpes, 1916.

The Russian dramatist and master of the short story ANTON CHEKHOV *praised Venice in a letter to his sister-in-law written from there in 1891.*

Ravishing, blue-eyed Venice sends greetings to all of you. Ah, *Signori e Signorine*, what a wondrous city this Venice is! Picture to yourselves a city made up of houses and churches such as you have never seen: an inebriating architecture in which everything is as graceful, light, as the birdlike gondola. Such houses and churches can be built only by men possessing enormous artistic and musical taste and endowed with a leonine temperament. Now imagine that on the streets and in the lanes instead of pavement there is water; picture a city in all of which there is not a single horse, imagine that instead of cabbies you are seeing gondoliers on their astonishing boats, light, dainty, beaky birds which barely touch the water and twitch at the least wave. And everything, from sky to earth, is inundated by sun.

There are streets as wide as Nevsky Prospekt, and there are some where, by spreading your arms, the whole street can be blocked. The centre of the city is the Piazza of St Mark with its famous Cathedral named after the same saint. The Cathedral is magnificent, especially from the outside. Alongside it is the Palazzo of the Doges, where Othello had his explanation with the Doge and the Senators.

Generally speaking, there isn't the least spot which fails to stir up recollections or to move you. The small house where Desdemona lived, for instance, creates an impression that is difficult to get rid of.

The best time in Venice is the evening. First of all, there are the stars; secondly, the long canals, in which the stars and lights are reflected; thirdly, gondolas, gondolas, and gondolas – when it is dark they seem alive. Fourthly, you want to weep, because you can hear music and superb singing coming from every side. Here's a gondola floating by, with little multicolored lanterns hanging all over it; there is light enough to make out a double bass, a guitar, a mandolin, a violin. – Here's just such another gondola – with men and women singing – and how they sing! Grand opera, absolutely.

Fifthly, the weather is warm....

In short, he who doesn't go to Venice is a fool. Living here is cheap. Room and board come to 18 francs a week per person (i.e., 6 rubles and, by the month, 25 rubles); a gondolier charges 1 franc (i.e., 30 copecks) per hour. Admission to museums, the Academy, and so on, is free. Ten times cheaper than the Crimea, and yet the Crimea stacks up against Venice as a cuttlefish against a whale ...

What glass they have here, what mirrors! Why am I not a millionaire?

Next year we will all take a country house in Venice for the summer.

All Venice is a piece of superb, barbaric patchwork in which the East and the West have an equal share. The lion of St Mark's, his head and shoulders in one piece, his hind-quarters in another, is a symbol of the construction of Venice, just as the bronze horses, which have seen the downfall of Nero, the splendours of Constantinople, and, at Paris, the First Empire, are a symbol of its history. Venice is as near to the East as it is to Italy; you are reminded of the East at every step; yet, after all, its interest is precisely that it is not Eastern, that it is really of the West, and that it has given a new touch of the fantastic to the fantasy which we call Oriental, an arrangement of lines and colours which, in its own country, has a certain air of being at home, but which, out of its country, frankly admits itself barbaric, a bastard.

The English critic and poet ARTHUR SYMONS *celebrated Venice's hybrid singularity in his* Cities of Italy *(1904).*

'There is no such magnificent absurdity as Venice' – photograph, 1927.

EZRA POUND
*wrote 'Alma Sol Veneziae
(Baritone)' (a paean to the
'nourishing' sun of Venice) in
the notebook he kept while
living in the San Trovaso
district of Venice in 1908.*

Thou that hast given me back
   Strength for the journey,
Thou that hast given me back
    Heart for the Tourney,

O Sun venezian,
    Thou that thru all my veins
Hast bid the life-blood run,
Thou that hast called my soul
    From out the far crevices.
Yea, the far dark crevices
    And caves of ill-fearing,

      Alma tu sole!
Cold, ah a-cold
    Was my soul in the caves
    Of ill-fearing.

LIST OF CONTRIBUTORS

ADDISON, Joseph (1672–1719)
English essayist, poet, and politician.

ANDERSEN, Hans Christian (1805–75)
Danish writer of fairy tales and novels.

ARETINO, Pietro (1492–1556)
Italian scholar, wit, poet, self-styled 'scourge of princes', and 'secretary of the world', lived in Venice from 1527.

ASCHAM, Roger (1515–68)
English teacher and humanist scholar.

BECKFORD, William (1759–1844)
Millionaire eccentric, author of *Vathek*, a Gothic romance.

BEMBO, Pietro (1470–1547)
Venetian Cardinal, scholar, and poet.

BERENSON, Bernard (1865–1959)
Lithuanian-born, American-educated art critic, collector.

BOCCACCIO, Giovanni (*c*.1313–75)
Poet, scholar, author of *Decameron*.

BROWN, Horatio (1854–1926)
Historian and writer, resident in Venice from 1879.

BROWNING, Elizabeth Barrett (1806–61)
English poet resident in Italy from 1845.

BROWNING, Robert (1812–89)
English poet, died in Venice.

BURNEY, Charles (1726–1814)
Musician and historian of music.

BYRON, George Gordon, Lord (1788–1824)
English poet, lived in Vehice from 1816–18.

CALIARI, Paolo (Veronese) (1528–88)
Verona-born painter.

CALVINO, Italo (1923–86)
Italian fabulist and novelist.

CASANOVA DE SEINGALT, Giovanni Giacomo (1725–98) Venetian-born writer, adventurer, memoirist.

CASOLA, Canon Pietro (b. late 16th century)
Milanese cleric, visited Venice on his way to Palestine, 1594.

CASSIODORUS, Flavius Magnus Aurelius (*c*.485–*c*.580)
Monk, scholar, servant of King Theodoric the Ostrogoth.

CHEKHOV, Anton (1860–1904)
Russian playwright and short-story writer.

CLOUGH, Arthur Hugh (1819–61)
English poet, visited Italy in 1849–1850, where he wrote *Dipsychus*, published posthumously.

COMMYNES, Philippe de (1445–1511)
French diplomat, chronicler, Ambassador to Venice 1494–5.

CORYAT, Thomas (d.1612)
English traveller, visited Venice in 1608, died in India.

DANTE Alighieri (1265–1321)
Italian poet, author of the *Divine Comedy*, expelled from Florence in 1301, died in Ravenna.

DICKENS, Charles (1812–70)
English novelist, visited Venice in 1845.

DISRAELI, Benjamin (1804–81)
English novelist. Prime Minister in 1868 and 1874–80.

DÜRER, Albrecht (1471–1528)
German artist, visited Venice in 1494–5 and 1505–7.

DU MAURIER, Daphne (1907–   )
English novelist, short-story writer.

ELIOT, George (1819–80)
Pseudonym of Mary Ann Evans, English novelist, visited Venice in 1860 and again in 1880.

EMERSON, Ralph Waldo (1803–82)
American essayist, poet, critic.

EVELYN, John (1620–1706)
Diarist, founder member of the Royal Society.

GIBBON, Edward (1734–94)
English historian.

GIUSTINIANI, Bernardo (b. late 15th century)
Venetian historian, scholar, and diplomat.

GIUSTINIANI, Sebastiano (b. late 15th century)
Venetian Ambassador to the Court of Henry VIII.

GOETHE, Johann Wolfgang von (1749–1832)
German poet, dramatist, novelist, scholar, visited Venice in 1786.

GOLDONI, Carlo (1707–93)
Leading Venetian dramatist, comic master of the vernacular.

GOZZI, Carlo (1720–1806)
Venetian dramatist and critic.

GRAY, Euphemia Chalmers (18xx–xx)
In Venice from 1849–1852 with her husband John Ruskin, whom she later divorced to marry painter John E. Millais.

HAZLITT, William (1778–1830)
English critic, essayist, radical.

HEMANS, Felicia (1793–1835)
English poet.

HERZEN, Alexander (1812–70)
Russian writer and radical.

HOWELL, James (1594–1666)
English historian.

HOWELLS, William Dean (1837–1920)
American novelist and social critic. Appointed United States Consul in Venice by Abraham Lincoln.

JAMES, Henry (1843–1916)
American novelist, short-story writer, perpetual traveller.
LAWRENCE, David Herbert (1885–1930)
English novelist and poet.
LEE, Vernon (1856–1935)
Pseudonym of Violet Paget, English essayist, novelist, travel writer, in Italy from 1871.
LITHGOW, William (1582–1645)
Scottish traveller.
LONGFELLOW, Henry Wadsworth (1807–1882)
American poet.
McCARTHY, Mary (1912–)
American novelist, critic.
MACHIAVELLI, Niccolo (1469–1527)
Florentine diplomat and political historian and theorist.
MANDELSTAM, Osip (1891–1938)
Russian poet.
MANIN, Daniele (1804–57)
Leader of the Venetian revolution of 1848.
MANN, Thomas (1875–1955)
German novelist, short-story writer, essayist.
MANUTIUS, Aldus (Aldo Manuzio) (1449–1515)
Venetian printer and publisher.
MENDELSSOHN, Felix (1809–47)
German composer and pianist.
MONTAGU, Mary Worley, Lady (1689–1762)
English poet, critic, travel writer, lived in Italy after 1739.
MONTAIGNE, Michel de (1533–92)
French essayist, visited Venice in 1581.
MORRIS, James (Jan) (1926–)
English writer.
MORYSON, Fynes (1566–1617)
English traveller, visited Venice in 1594.
NASHE, Thomas (1567–1601)
English pamphleteer, poet, dramatist, novelist.
NORWICH, John Julius (1929–)
English historian.
O'FAOLAIN, Sean (1900–)
Irish novelist, short-story writer, biographer.
PASTERNAK, Boris (1890–1960)
Russian poet and novelist.
PATER, Walter (1839–94)
English essayist and critic.
PETRARCH, Francesco Petrarca (1304–74)
Italian poet and Latin scholar, a guest of the Venetian Republic from 1361–68.
PIOZZI, Hester Lynch Thrale (1741–1821)
English writer, friend of Dr Johnson.
POUND, Ezra (1885–1972)
American poet, published his first book in Venice in 1908.
PROUST, Marcel (1871–1922)
French novelist.
ROGERS, Samuel (1763–1855)
English poet.

ROLFE, Frederick (Baron Corvo) (1860–1913)
English novelist, died penniless in Venice.
ROUSSEAU, Jean-Jacques (1712–78)
Swiss-born writer and philosopher.
RUSKIN, John (1819–1900)
English critic of art, architecture, and society. His three-volume *The Stones of Venice* was written 1849–52.
SAND, George (1804–76)
Pseudonym of Armandine Dupin. French novelist, visited Venice with the poet Alfred de Musset in 1834.
SANUTO, Marino (1446–1536)
Venetian diarist.
SARPI, Paolo (1572–1623)
Venetian monk, historian, and adviser to the *Serenissima*.
SHAKESPEARE, William (1564–1616)
Shakespeare wrote two plays set in Venice (*Othello* and *The Merchant of Venice*) but never crossed the English Channel.
SHELLEY, Percy Bysshe (1792–1822)
English poet and radical.
SITWELL, Osbert (1892–1969)
English essayist, poet, novelist.
STOKES, Adrian (1902–72)
English art critic.
SYMONS, John Addington (1840–93)
English essayist, art historian, literary critic, and translator.
SYMONS, Arthur (1865–1945)
English poet and critic.
TAFUR, Pero (c.1410–c.1484)
Catalan traveller, writer.
TORKINGTON, Sir Richard (14xx–15xx)
English priest and traveller.
TOURNIER, Michel
French novelist.
TREVELYAN, George Macaulay (1876–1962)
English historian.
TROLLOPE, Frances (1780–1863)
English travel writer, mother of the novelist Anthony.
TWAIN, Mark (1835–1910)
Pseudonym for Samuel L. Clemens, American novelist.
VASARI, Giorigio (1511–74)
Born in Arezzo, painter, architect, pioneer art historian.
VERDI, Giuseppe (1813–1901)
Leading 19th-century opera composer.
VIDAL, Gore (1925–)
American novelist and essayist.
VILLEHARDOUIN, Geoffroi de (1152– c.1212)
French chronicler, Marshal of Champagne, commander in the Fourth Crusade.
WAGNER, Richard (1813–83)
German composer, died in Venice.
WORDSWORTH, William (1770–1850)
English poet.
WOTTON, Sir Henry (1568–1639)
English poet and diplomat, Ambassador to Venice.

BIBLIOGRAPHY

ADDISON, Joseph, *Remarks on Several Parts of Italy* (London, 1703).

ALIGHIERI, Dante, *The Divine Comedy,* translated by John D. Sinclair (London, 1971).

ANDERSEN, Hans Christian, *The Improvisatore,* translated by M. Howitt (London, 1845).

ASCHAM, Roger, *The Scholemaster* (London, 1570).

BECKFORD, William, *Dreams, Waking Thoughts and Incidents* (London, 1783).

BERENSON, Bernard, *Venetian Painters of the Renaissance* (London, 1897).

BOCCACCIO, Giovanni, *Decameron.*

BROWN, Horatio, *Life on the Lagoons* (London, 1884).

BROWNING, Elizabeth Barrett, *EBB's Letters to Mrs David Ogilvy, 1849–1861*, edited by Peter N. Heydon and Philip Kelley (New York, 1973).

BROWNING, Elizabeth Barrett, *Letters*, edited by Frederick Kenyon (London, 1897).

BROWNING, Robert, *Poetical Works* (Oxford, 1970).

BURNEY, Charles, *The State of Music in France and Italy* (London, 1771).

BYRON, George Gordon, Lord, *Byron's Letters and Journals*, edited by Leslie A. Marchand (London, 1970–1981).

BYRON, George Gordon, Lord, *Poetical Works* (Oxford, 1970).

CALVINO, Italo, *Invisible Cities,* translated by W. Weaver (London, 1974).

CARTWRIGHT, Julia, *Isabella D'Este, Marchioness of Mantua 1474–1539, a Study of the Renaissance* (London, 1903).

CASANOVA, Giacomo Girolamo, *The Memoirs,* translated by Arthur Machen (London, 1930).

CASOLA, Pietro, *Canon Pietro Casola's Pilgrimage,* translated and edited by M. M. Newett (Manchester, 1907).

CHEKHOV, Anton, *Letters of Anton Chekhov,* selected and edited by Avrahm Yarmolinsky (London, 1974).

CLEUGH, James, *The Divine Aretino: Pietro of Arezzo, 1492–1556, a biography* (London, 1965).

CLOUGH, Arthur Hugh, *The Poems* (Oxford, 1951).

COMMYNES, Philippe de, *The Memoirs,* edited and translated by Andrew R. Scobie (London, 1855).

CONSTABLE, W. G., *Canaletto, Giovanni Antonio Canal, 1697–1768* (Oxford, 1962).

CORYAT, Thomas, *Coryat's Crudities Hastily Gobled Up in Five Moneths Travels* (London, 1611).

DICKENS, Charles, *Pictures from Italy* (London, 1846).

DISRAELI, Benjamin, *Contarini Fleming: a Psychological Romance* (London, 1832).

DU MAURIER, Daphne, *Not After Midnight* (London, 1971).

DÜRER, Albrecht, *Literary Remains,* translated by Will Conway (London, 1889).

ELIOT, George, *George Eliot's Life as Related in her Letters and Journals,* edited by J. W. Cross (London, 1885).

EMERSON, Ralph Waldo, *The Journals and Miscellaneous Notebooks* (Cambridge, Massachusetts, 1960).

EVELYN, John, *The Diary* (London, 1905).

GIUSTINIANI, Sebastiano, *Four Years at the Court of Henry VIII: Selection of Despatches, 1515–1519,* translated by Rawdon Brown (London, 1854).

GOETHE, Johann Wolfgang von, *Italian Journey,* translated by W. H. Auden and E. Mayer (London, 1963).

GOLDONI, Carlo, *Memoirs of Goldoni Written by Himself,* translated by John Black (London, 1814).

GOZZI, Carlo, *The Memoirs of Count Carlo Gozzi,* translated by J. A. Symonds (London, 1890).

GRAY, Euphemia Chalmers, *Effie in Venice, Unpublished Letters of Mrs. John Ruskin Written from Venice between 1849–1852,* edited by Mary Lutyens (London, 1972).

HAZLITT, William, *Notes of a Journey through France and Italy* (London, 1826).

HEMANS, Felicia, *The Works of Mrs. Hemans* (London, 1839).

HERZEN, Alexander, *My Past and Thoughts, Vol. Three,* translated by Constance Garnett, revised by Humphrey Higgins (London, 1968).

HOWELL, James, Epistolae Ho-Elianae, *The Familiar Letters of James Howell,* edited by Joseph Jacobs (London, 1892).

HOWELLS, William Dean, *Venetian Life* (Boston, 1867).

JAMES, Henry, *Italian Hours* (London, 1909).

LABALME, Patricia, *Bernardo Giustiniani, A Venetian of the Quattrocento* (Rome, 1969).

LAWRENCE, D. H., *Lady Chatterley's Lover* (London, 1960).

LEE, Vernon, *The Enchanted Wood* (London, 1903).

LITHGOW, William, *Totall Discourses of the Rare Adventures and Painefull Peregrinations* (London, 1632).

LONGFELLOW, Henry Wadsworth, *The Poetical Works* (Oxford, 1916).

McCARTHY, Mary, *Venice Observed* (London, 1961).

MACHIAVELLI, Niccolo, *Discourses,* translated by L. J. Walker (London, 1950).

MANDELSTAM, Osip, *Selected Poems,* translated by Clarence Brown and W. S. Merwin (Oxford, 1973).

MANN, Thomas, *Death in Venice,* translated by H. T. Lowe-Porter (London, 1928).

MENDELSSOHN, Felix, *Letters* (London, 1877).

MONTAGU, Mary Wortley, *The Letters and Works of Lady Mary Wortley Montagu* (London, 1887).

MONTAIGNE, Michel de, *Journal of Montaigne's Travels in Italy by way of Switzerland and Germany, 1580–81,* translated by W. G. Waters (London, 1903).

MORRIS, James, *Venice* (London, 1960).

MORYSON, Fynes, *An Itinerary* (reprinted Glasgow, 1907).

NASHE, Thomas, *The Unfortunate Traveller* (London, 1594).

NORWICH, John Julius, *Venice, The Rise to Empire* (London, 1977).

O'FAOLAIN, Sean, *A Summer in Italy* (London, 1949).

PASTERNAK, Boris, *Safe Conduct,* translated by A. Brown and L. Pasternak-Slater (London, 1959).

PATER, Walter, *Renaissance Studies* (London, 1877).

PETRARCH, Francesco, *Letters from Petrarch,* selected and translated by Morris Bishop (Indiana, 1966).

PIOZZI, Hester Lynch Thrale, *Autobiography, Letters, and Literary Remains* (London, 1861).

PULLAN, Brian, *Rich and Poor in Renaissance Venice, The Social Institutions of a Catholic State* (Oxford, 1971).

POUND, Ezra, *The Cantos* (London, 1954).

PROUST, Marcel, *The Sweet Cheat Gone* [*Albertine Disparue*], translated by C. K. Scott Moncrieff (London, 1941).

ROGERS, Samuel, *Italy, a poem* (London, 1830).

ROLFE, Frederick, *The Desire and Pursuit of the Whole, a Romance of Modern Venice* (London, 1934).

ROUSSEAU, Jean-Jacques, *The Confessions* (New York).

RUSKIN, John, *The Works of John Ruskin* (London, 1903).

SAND, George, *My Life,* translated by Dan Hofstadter (London, 1979).

SAND, George, *Letters,* translated by Raphael Ledos de Beaufort (London, 1886).

SARPI, Paolo, *Maxims.*

SHAKESPEARE, William, *The Complete Works.*

SHELLEY, Percy Bysshe, *The Letters*, edited by Frederick L. Jones (Oxford, 1964).

SHELLEY, Percy Bysshe, *Poetical Works* (Oxford, 1904).

SITWELL, Osbert, *Winters of Content* (London, 1932).

STOKES, Adrian, *Venice, As Aspect of Art* (London, 1945).

SYMONDS, John Addington, *Sketches and Studies in Italy* (London, 1898).

SYMONDS, John Addington, *A Biography*, compiled from his papers and correspondence by Horatio F. Brown (London, 1903).

SYMONS, Arthur, *Cities of Italy* (London, 1904).

TAFUR, Pero, *Travels and Adventures, 1435–1439,* translated and edited by Malcolm Letts (London, 1926).

TORKINGTON, Sir Richard, *The Oldest Diary of English Travel* (London, 1883).

TOURNIER, Michel, *Gemini,* translated by Anne Carter (London, 1981).

TREVELYAN, George Macaulay, *Manin and the Venetian Revolution of 1848* (London, 1923).

TROLLOPE, Frances, *A Visit to Italy* (London, 1842).

TWAIN, Mark, *The Innocents Abroad* (New York, 1869).

TWAIN, Mark, *A Tramp Abroad* (New York, 1880).

VASARI, Giorigio, *Lives of the Artists,* translated by George Bull (London, 1965).

VENTURI, Adolfo, *Paolo Veronese* (Milan, 1928).

VIDAL, Gore, *Vidal in Venice* (London, 1985).

VILLEHARDOUIN, Geoffroi de, *Memoirs of the Crusades,* translated by Frank Marzials (London, 1908).

WAGNER, Richard, *My Life* (London, 1911).

WORDSWORTH, William, *Poems* (London, 1977).

WOTTON, Sir Henry, *The Life and Letters of Sir Henry Wotton,* by Logan Pearsall Smith (Oxford, 1907).

ACKNOWLEDGMENTS

The publisher thanks the following photographers and organizations for their permission to reproduce the photographs in this book:

2 Provincial Security Council, San Francisco/The Bridgeman Art Library; **4** reproduced by Courtesy of the Trustees of the British Museum; **9** Mary Evans Picture Library; **10** Biblioteca Nationale Marciana (photograph by Toso); **11** (left) Mary Evans Picture Library; **11** (right) The Ancient Art & Architecture Collection; **12** Christies, London/Bridgeman Art Library; **13** National Portrait Gallery, London; **14** Mary Evans Picture Library; **17** The Mansell Collection; **19** BBC Hulton Picture Library; **21** The Bridgeman Art Library; **22** The Mansell Collection; **23** Museo Storico Navale; **24** BBC Hulton Picture Library; **26** Topham Picture Library; **28** The Keystone Collection; **29** Museo Storico Navale; **31** Associated American Artists; **33–5** Mary Evans Picture Library; **36** Camera Press; **37** Topham Picture Library; **38** The Ashmolean Museum, Oxford; **41** BBC Hulton Picture Library; **43** reproduced by Courtesy of the Trustees of the British Museum; **44** The Ancient Art & Architecture Collection; **47** Mary Evans Picture Library; **48** Fabbri/The Bridgeman Art Library; **50** The Keystone Collection; **51** The Mansell Collection; **52** BBC Hulton Picture Library; **53–4** Mary Evans Picture Library; **55** Rijksmuseum, Amsterdam; **56** (left) BBC Hulton Picture Library; **56** (right) Mary Evans Picture Library; **58** Service Photographique des Musées Nationaux; **59** BBC Hulton Picture Library; **60** Fiorepress Photo & Press Agency (photograph by A. Sandi); **62** Christies, London/The Bridgeman Art Library; **64** The Mansell Collection; **66–8** Mary Evans Picture Library; **70** Christies, London/The Bridgeman Art Library; **72** Museo Storico Navale; **74** The Ancient Art & Architecture Collection; **76** Explorer Archives; **77** reproduced by Courtesy of the Trustees of the British Museum; **80–3** Mary Evans Picture Library; **84** BBC Hulton Picture Library; **88** BBC Hulton Picture Library; **89** Mary Evans Picture Library; **91** Ann Ronan Picture Library; **94** BBC Hulton Picture Library; **95** (above) BBC Hulton Picture Library; **95** (below) Topham Picture Library; **99** Museo Correr/The Bridgeman Art Library; **100–1** Mary Evans Picture Library; **102** Explorer Archives; **103** Trustees of the Victoria & Albert Museum; **106** Musée de Strasbourg; **108** Fiorepress Photo & Press Agency (photograph by A. Sandi); **109–13** Mary Evans Picture Library; **115** Royal College of Music; **117** The Bridgeman Art Library; **119** The City of Birmingham Museum and Art Gallery; **121** The Illustrated London News Picture Library; **122** Trustees of the Victoria & Albert Museum; **124** The British Architectural Library, RIBA, London; **126** Ann Ronan Picture Library; **129** Scala; **133** The Mansell Collection; **136–8** reproduced by Courtesy of the Trustees of the British Museum; **141** Courtauld Institute Galleries, London (Princes Gate Collection); **142** Ancient Art & Architecture Collection; **147** Rijksmuseum, Amsterdam; **149** (left) The Mansell Collection; **149** (right) British Architectural Library, RIBA, London; **153** Trustees of the Victoria & Albert Museum; **155** Christies, London/The Bridgeman Art Library; **157** Mary Evans Picture Library; **158** The Keystone Collection; **160** The Illustrated London News Picture Library; **163** The Mansell Collection; **165** Mary Evans Picture Library; **168–70** Camera Press; **171** Topham Picture Library; **173** The Ashmolean Museum, Oxford; **174** Explorer Archives; **175** The Mansell Collection; **179** Roy Miles Fine Paintings/The Bridgeman Art Library; **181–2** Mary Evans Picture Library; **184** The Mansell Collection.

The publisher thanks the following for their permission to publish the extracts listed. While we have made every effort to contact all the relevant people and organizations, we regret that at the time of going to press we are unable to publish all their names. We apologize to those concerned.

15, 23, 83, 112, 128, 177 *Italian Journey* by Johann von Goethe, trans by W H Auden and Mrs E Mayer, published by William Collins; **20** *Venice: The Rise to Empire* by John Julius Norwich (Viking Books, 1977) © John Julius Norwich, 1977, reproduced by permission of Penguin Books Ltd; **20, 94** *Gemini* by Michel Tournier, trans by Anne Carter, published by William Collins; **24, 31, 55, 135, 176** *The Divine Aretino: Pietro of Arezzo* by James Cleugh, published by Anthony Blond; **29** *The Divine Comedy* by Dante Alighieri, trans by John D Sinclair, published by The Bodley Head; **37, 120** *Winters of Content* by Osbert Sitwell, published by Duckworth & Co; **42** *Invisible Cities* by Italo Calvino, trans by William Weaver, reprinted by permission of Martin Secker & Warburg Ltd; **59, 79** *Memoirs* by Giacomo Casanova, trans by Arthur Machen, reprinted by permission of the Estate of Arthur Machen; **69, 180** *My Past and Thoughts* by Alexander Herzen, trans by C Garnett, published by Chatto & Windus Ltd; **88** *My Life* by George Sand, trans by Dan Hofstadter, © Daniel L Hofstadter; **96** *Vidal in Venice* by Gore Vidal, published by Weidenfeld & Nicholson Ltd; **103** *The Confessions* by Jean-Jacques Rousseau, in a trans by permission of Random House Inc; **134, 137** *Lives of the Artists* by Giorgio Vasari, trans by George Bull (Penguin Classics, 1965, 1971) © George Bull 1965, 1971, reproduced by permission of Penguin Books Ltd; **151** *Rich and Poor in Renaissance Venice* by Brian Pullan, published by Basil Blackwell; **159** *Lady Chatterley's Lover* by D H Lawrence, reproduced by permission of Laurence Pollinger Ltd and the Estate of Mrs Frida Lawrence Ravagli; **170** © Clarence Brown and W S Merwin 1973. Reprinted from Osip Mandelstam: *Selected Poems* trans by Clarence Brown and W S Merwin (1973) by permission of Oxford University Press; **182** *The Letters of Anton Chekhov* trans by Avrahm Yarmolinsky, published by Jonathan Cape Ltd.

171 by permission of Curtis Brown Ltd on Behalf of Daphne DuMaurier © Daphne DuMaurier 1970.

INDEX

Page numbers in *italic* refer to the illustrations